Retiring to

Australia &
New Zealand

Retiring to

Australia & New Zealand

Deborah Penrith

Alison Ripley

Published by Vacation Work,
9 Park End Street, Oxford
www.vacationwork.co.uk

RETIRING TO AUSTRALIA & NEW ZEALAND
by Deborah Penrith and Alison Ripley

First edition 2006

Copyright © Vacation Work 2006

ISBN 13: 978-1-85458-357-4
ISBN 10: 1-85458-357-3

Publicity by Charles Cutting

Cover design by mccdesign

Typeset by Guy Hobbs

Cover photograph; the Great Barrier Reef

Printed and bound in Italy by Legoprint SpA, Trento

Contents

AUSTRALIA

PART I – BEFORE YOU GO

Setting the Scene

Basics

PART II – A NEW HOME IN AUSTRALIA

Where to Retire

Your New Home in Australia

Housing Finance

PART III – A NEW LIFE IN AUSTRALIA

Adapting to Your New Life

Quality of Life

Personal Finance

Healthcare

Crime, Security and the Police

NEW ZEALAND

PART I – BEFORE YOU GO

Setting the Scene

Basics

PART II – A NEW HOME IN NEW ZEALAND

Where to Retire

Your New Home in New Zealand

Housing Finance

PART III – A NEW LIFE IN NEW ZEALAND

Adapting to Your New Life

Quality of Life

Personal Finance

Healthcare

Crime, Security and the Police

APPENDICES

Appendix 1: Returning Home

Appendix 2: Case Histories

MAPS

PREFACE

To leave your home country is an enormous decision, but a recent BBC report disclosed how popular living abroad has become, particularly with UK residents.

Over the next 40 years, Australia's population will go through a major shift and its ageing population would also be shrinking if it were not for migrants entering the country. Australia is a favoured choice among retirees. If not for family reasons, then for the climate and quality of life: Australia is noted for many things, but most of all it is noted for its outstanding quality of life. It has a relatively unpolluted environment and a low population density: being one of the largest countries in the world, it has one of the smallest population per square kilometre ratios. It is expected, however, that all who go there make an overriding commitment to Australia, its laws and its democratic values.

The number of retirees in Australia is set to rocket over the next 50 years – the Australian Bureau of Statistics project that one in two Australians (around 30 million) will be over the age of 50 by 2051. However, this book concentrates on the here and now and provides information on all aspects of your new life, either as a capital-endowed retiree or as a parent.

Meanwhile across the Tasman Sea, New Zealand continues to attract migrants of all ages who are inspired to move to this wild and beautiful country where house prices are low and the living is easy. Auckland is ranked the fifth best city in the world for quality of life and the climate is varied but more temperate than Britain.

We hope *Retiring to Australia and New Zealand* will prove both an inspiration and a practical guide for people considering or planning to retire Down Under.

Deborah Penrith
Alison Ripley
May 2006

ACKNOWLEDGEMENTS

Deborah Penrith would like to thank all those individuals and organisations who generously helped with this book, especially Anthony Davison, Westpac, London; Richard Hoffman, Commonwealth Bank, London; Denise Blackburn; Raymond Binns, Medicare; Ruth Wilson, Department of Immigration and Multicultural Affairs; Ben Southall, Australian Quarantine and Inspection Services; Liz Young, Australian Funeral Directors Association; Matthew Carpenter, Carpenter Mortgage Services; Leigh McAdam, Centrelink; Lucy Clynes, Foreign Investment Review Board; Clive Herrald, Global Pension Transfers; David Lye, Private Fleet; Alison Verhoeven, Real Estate Institute of Australia; Bob Bunney, Retirement Village Association; and Helen Cameron, Department of Health and Ageing.

Special thanks also to the British retirees who provided case histories, quotes and cost of living indicators: Brian Havard, Mike Osborne, Stuart Robertson-Fox, Barbara Lassiter, Ian Lewthwaite, Jane Knight, Joan Riddle, and Kathleen Calver.

Alison Ripley would like to thank Patricia Heinecke for her skill with the red pen as well as her help with finding contributors, Jan and Teri Sawers for their research skills in sourcing interviewees and everybody else who assisted.

Special thanks also to: Sheila Gavin, Gaby Heinrich, Douglas Jarvis, and Sue Seddon. I hope their stories inspire you as much as they inspired me.

FOREWORD: THE NEW 'OLD' – CHANGING ATTITUDES TO RETIREMENT

At the start of the twenty-first century we are in the midst of a major social transformation. The post-war notion of retirement as a time to put your slippers on and settle in front of the telly with a nice cup of tea is fast becoming obsolete. The very word 'retirement', not to mention the images of encroaching decrepitude that it conjures, no longer fits the reality of how people are living their lives post full-time employment. Today's retirees are often younger, fitter and wealthier than their forebears and together they are reshaping the very meaning of 'old age' and 'retirement'.

Many social commentators suggest that these changes are being wrought by the baby boomer generation. Born between 1945 and 1965, they are a force to be reckoned with, making up almost a third of the UK population and responsible for nearly 80% of all financial wealth. The baby boomers grew up in an era of postwar optimism and new social freedoms, and as such, have always represented a force for social change. Indeed, they have spent a lifetime reconstructing social norms. In 2006 the first wave of this generation is approaching retirement age, and with such political and financial clout their approach to growing old is profoundly different. As *The Times* recently put it: *'the pioneers of the consumer society are unlikely to settle for an electric fire and a can of soup'.*

One of the main reasons that the concept of retirement is changing is that people are living far longer. Life expectancy in the twentieth century rose by 20 years due to better healthcare and greater health awareness. Around 18 million people in the UK are over 60. This is creating something of a crisis in the British economy and if the government had its way, then we would all work until we dropped, easing the pressure on the already over-burdened state pension fund. The new generation of retirees however, are not prepared to do this. Not only are people living longer, they are also leaving the workforce younger. Many are giving up work in their early fifties when they are still fit and active, in order to enjoy a new stage in life – not their 'retirement', according to the American website www.2young2retire. com, but their 'renaissance'.

A recent report by *Demos*, a democracy think tank, claims that the baby boomers are intent on having their time again; of creating a new life phase in which they can revisit their own desire for personal fulfilment, free from the pressures of overwork and childrearing. The report identifies a new 'experience economy' of travel, food, learning and lifestyle. The baby boomers do not want to retreat from the world as the word 'retirement' suggests, but to head out into it with renewed vigour.

The new retirement is all about finding a better life balance. This may not necessarily include giving up work – around half of the people who leave permanent 'career' jobs before state pension age move initially into part-time, temporary or self-employed work, be it in the UK or abroad. It would seem that people are no longer happy to compartmentalise their lives into linear stages – school, work, parenthood – with retirement at the end of the line. Retirees these days are demanding greater flexibility; preferring to see life as a never-ending cycle, in which they can choose to dip in and out of periods of work, education and leisure. Others have the funds behind them to pursue a hobby or interest full-time. And an increasing number of people have realised that they can do either of these things in a climate far removed from the dreary British winter.

Almost a million Britons already draw their state pensions abroad, and this figure does not include the many more who have retired early. According to a report from Alliance and Leicester, one in five older people (an extra four million) will be living outside the UK by the year 2020, lured by the warmer climate, a slower pace of life, health advantages and a lower cost of living.

It would appear that the prevailing gloom that people once felt about the ageing process is slowly being replaced by a sunny optimism. People no longer dread reaching retirement age, but eagerly anticipate a new life stage, in which, released from the shackles of full-time work, they can seek out new cultural experiences.

TELEPHONE NUMBERS

Please note that the telephone numbers in this book are written as needed to call that number from inside the same country. To call these numbers from outside the country you will need to add the relevant international access code; currently 00 from the UK.

To call Australia from the UK: Dial 00 61 and the number given in this book minus the first 0.

To call New Zealand from the UK: Dial 00 64 and the number given in this book minus the first 0.

To call the UK from Australia or New Zealand: Dial 00 44 and the number given in this book minus the first 0.

Australia

Part one

Before
You Go

Setting the Scene
Basics

Setting the Scene

CHAPTER SUMMARY

○ At least 200,000 British pensioners live in Australia, enjoying the climate, outdoor activities and lifestyle.

○ Australia is mostly a harmonious, united and egalitarian nation of 20 million people and has one of the most stable liberal democracies in the world.

○ The country has had year on year growth in its economy and is ranked in the top ten most competitive economies in the world.

○ It is the sixth largest country in the world with a range of climatic zones.

○ Generally, it is an informal, friendly, multicultural society whose people accept and respect all its citizens.

REASONS TO RETIRE TO AUSTRALIA

It has been reported that at least 200,000 British pensioners live in Australia and it has been said to offer 'more dream retirement locations than any other country in the southern hemisphere.' Retirees are attracted by the climate, outdoor activities and laid-back lifestyle. The recurrent theme we found with most of the people we spoke to was climate and quality of life. Says Mike Osborne: *'Australia has widely varied climates, some of which will not appeal to the UK retiree, but I think you gradually become accustomed to a temperature range of around 68 deg F (20 deg C).'*

Bear in mind, though, that the climate across Australia is not all sunshine and heat. Cyclone Larry in northern Queensland, near Innisfail, brought widespread damage to homes, buildings and crops in March 2006; and Cyclone Monica, in April 2006, was the strongest cyclone ever to affect the Northern Territory. Tropical north Queensland can also be intolerably hot and humid and some of Australia's coastal areas experience storms and high rainfall.

Quality of life is both objective and subjective, so it is really up to you how you feel about your life. There has always been a sense of personal optimism and belief in Australia and an improvement in the national mood, due mainly to the robust economy. However, according to the Australian National University, polls suggest a growing tension between values and lifestyle, a tension being heightened by the promotion of a fast-paced, high pressure, hyper-consumer lifestyle on which current economic performance depends. Says expat Stuart Robertson-Fox:

In most respects the quality of life is far better than the UK, no crowds or pollution, more available money, yet plenty of entertainment when required and very little youth violence to worry about.

PROS & CONS

Pros

- Better lifestyle, clean air.
- Stable political system and strong economy.
- Cheaper property, especially in rural areas.
- Tax breaks for financially independent retirees.
- A variety of cuisine and wine; shopping well catered for, particularly in urban areas.
- Starting a new small business is encouraged by most local councils.

Cons

- Investor Visa requirements mean you need a minimum of $1 million or $1.5 million, depending on where you choose to live, and a net annual income of $50,000 or $75,000.
- Pensions are frozen at the rate payable when you leave the UK.
- Private medical insurance cover is essential; lack of GPs, dentists and specialists in remote locations.
- No passenger rail service in some states and non-existent in Tasmania.
- No broadband or mobile phone connections in some of the more remote areas.
- Isolation from family and friends back in the UK.

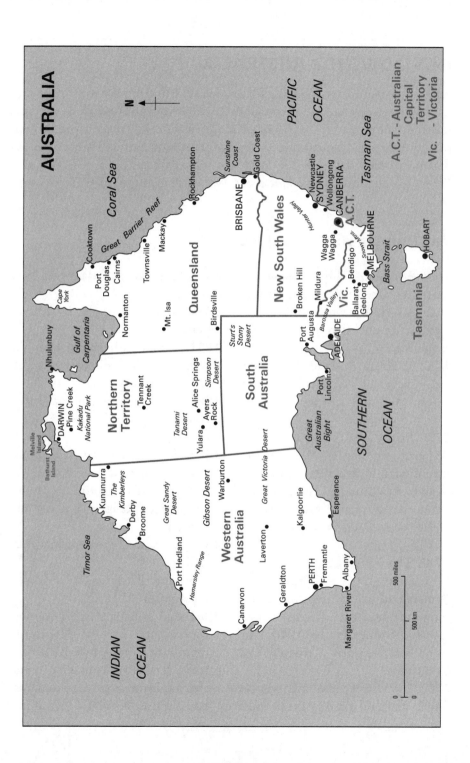

INTRODUCING AUSTRALIA

Aboriginal and Torres Strait Islander peoples inhabited most areas of Australia before the first European contact in 1606. Although Australia is seen as a relatively young country, archaeological and historical evidence suggests it was first settled many thousands of years ago. Scientists have discovered skeletal remains in New South Wales that could possibly be as old as 60,000 years. Below is a chronology of major events, which shaped the Australia we know today.

Key Dates in Australian History

1606 The Dutch ship *Duyfken*, under Captain Willem Jansz lands at Cape York, Queensland, but fails to realise the significance of his discovery.

1642 Abel Tasman, a Dutch explorer, discovers Van Diemen's Land (now Tasmania) and annexes the territory for Holland.

1770 British naval lieutenant James Cook, searching for the southern continent in his ship *Endeavour*, lands at Botany Bay, south of Sydney Harbour, and proclaims the east coast of Australia 'New South Wales'.

1788 The First Fleet, a convoy of 11 ships of mainly British prisoners and led by Captain Arthur Phillip, lands at Sydney Cove, within Sydney Harbour, marking the first European settlement of Australia.

1793 The first free immigrants arrive from England lured by the promise of cheap land.

1829 Australia is proclaimed a British territory.

1850 Western Australia becomes a penal colony.

1851 A gold rush begins after the precious metal is discovered at Ballarat in Victoria.

1868 The last shipment of British convicts lands in Fremantle, Western Australia.

1873 Uluru is first sighted by Europeans and named Ayers Rock.

1880 Australia's notorious bushranger, Ned Kelly, is captured and hanged.

1891 A severe depression hits Australia.

1895 Banjo Patterson writes *Waltzing Matilda*.

1901 On 1 January, the governor-general, the Earl of Hopetoun, founds the Commonwealth of Australia. In this year, the first federal election is held with Edmond Barton elected Australia's first prime minister.

1908 Canberra, in the Australian Capital Territory, is proclaimed the nation's capital.

1911 The first national census is conducted.

1914 Australia becomes involved in World War I.

1915 Australian soldiers land on the shores of Galipoli, Turkey, but are defeated.

1917 The first transcontinental railway is completed.

1927 The federal parliament moves to Canberra.

1932 Sydney Harbour Bridge opens.

1939 Australian soldiers begin fighting in World War II.

1942 Japanese warplanes bomb Darwin and Katherine in the Northern Territory.

1945 Australia becomes a founding member of the United Nations.

1950 Australian troops are sent to battle in the Korean War.

1952 Uranium is discovered at Rum Jungle in the Northern Territory.

1954 Elizabeth II and prince Philip make a royal visit.

1956 Melbourne hosts the Olympic Games and Australia's first television broadcast airs in Sydney.

1960 Aboriginal people are granted Australian citizenship.

1965 The first Australian troops enter the Vietnam War.

1966 Decimal currency is introduced. Australian dollars and cents replace pounds and shillings.

1967 Prime Minister Harold Holt disappears swimming at Portsea, Victoria, and is never found. Aboriginal people are counted in the census for the first time.

1971 Neville Bonner is elected to the Senate, becoming the first Aboriginal to enter the Australian parliament.

1974 Cyclone Tracy devastates Darwin on Christmas Day.

1975 After a constitutional crisis, governor-general Sir John Kerr dismisses prime minister Gough Whitlam, dissolves both houses of parliament and installs a caretaker government headed by Malcolm Fraser.

1977 *Advance Australia Fair* becomes Australia's official national anthem.

1983 Ash Wednesday bushfires tear across Victoria.

1991 The federal government bans uranium mining at Coronation Hill in the Kakadu National Park.

1992 A High Court decision recognises native title, the traditional ownership of Australian land by Aboriginal people.

1996 Liberal John Howard becomes Prime Minister, defeating Paul Keating after 13 years of Labor government.

1999 Failed vote to change Australia into a republic relinquishing links to the British monarchy.

2004 John Howard wins his fourth term in office.

AUSTRALIA TODAY

The Commonwealth of Australia was formed in 1901 through the federation of six states under a single constitution. There are three levels of government: Federal, State and Local. Both the State and Federal systems stem from the British Westminster system, although there are features of the Commonwealth Constitution based on the United States Constitution. The Federal (or Commonwealth) Government is Australia's national government. Legislative power is vested in the Commonwealth Parliament consisting of the Queen, the Senate, and the House of Representatives. Everyday life is governed mainly by the laws of the states and territories.

The founders of this new nation wanted Australia to be harmonious, united and egalitarian and in many respects this has been achieved. The government system is based on liberal democratic tradition and guarantees religious tolerance and freedom of association. It is one of the oldest and most stable liberal democracies in the world and the majority of Australians share a sense that there is a great deal more that unites them than divides them.

Political Parties

The five mainstream political parties in Australia, judging by the results of the 2004 election, are: the Liberal Party (Liberal), the present government; the Australian Labor Party (ALP); The Nationals; Australian Greens (The Greens); and the Australian Democrats (The Democrats). There are at least another 21 parties including, the Hope Party, Liberals for Forests, and The Fishing Party.

There is a degree of racism in policies being espoused by the likes of Australia First, commonly described as a neo-Nazi party, One Nation and the more extreme White Crusaders of the RaHoWa, or racial Holy War, a religious movement. Many parties turned the 2005 Cronulla race riots in Sydney into a political campaign.

Economy

Australia is now in its sixteenth consecutive year of economic growth and recently declared itself debt-free after paying off the last of the $96 billion the Government owed. Traditional agricultural and resource sectors continue to flourish but Australia now has a predominantly services-based economy. These services account for 80% of economic activity. It is ranked in the top ten most competitive economies in the world and is expected to have a growth of 3.5% in 2006. It continues to expand more rapidly than most other Organisation of Economic Co-operation and Development (OECD) countries. A recent report found that Australians are much more confident in the economy than they were a decade ago; 80% are proud of the country's economic achievements.

Geography

Australia is an island continent covering an area of 2,929,892 square miles (7,692,030sq km) and is the sixth largest country after Russia, Canada, China, the USA and Brazil. It is made up of three major landform masses: the western plateau, the central lowlands, and the eastern highlands and its coastline stretches 22,826 miles (36,735 km). The Pacific Ocean lies to the east, the Indian Ocean to the west, the Arafura Sea to the north and the Southern Ocean to the south.

Mount Kosciuszko, in New South Wales is the highest mountain, at 7,309 ft (2,228 m), and the Murray River its longest. The Great Dividing Range, the backbone of eastern Australia, runs from Victoria through New South Wales to north Queensland. The inland region of the Outback includes the MacDonnell Ranges near Alice Springs and the Kimberley ranges in Western Australia. Deserts such as the Great Sandy Desert, the Gibson Desert and the Great Victoria Desert are barren and unpopulated.

Australia administers seven external territories: Christmas and the Cocos (Keeling) islands; the self-governing Norfolk Island; Ashmore and Cartier Islands, Australian Antarctic Territory; and Heard and MacDonald Islands.

The six states, two territories and cities of Australia:
New South Wales (NSW): Sydney
Queensland (QLD): Brisbane
South Australia (SA): Adelaide
Tasmania (TAS): Hobart
Victoria (VIC): Melbourne
Western Australia (WA): Perth
Australian Capital Territory (ACT): Canberra
Northern Territory (NT): Darwin

Climate

Climatic zones range from deserts to snow-capped mountains; from tropical rainforests to cool climate forests. The summer months are December to February, autumn months March to May, winter months June to August and spring from September to November. Australians enjoy a warm, sunny climate where 3,000 hours of sunshine a year can be expected. More than two-thirds of the country, in the west and centre, receive less than 10 inches (250 mm) of rain a year and one-third is desert. Bush fires are prevalent in Tasmania and south-eastern Australia; floods can occur; and tropical cyclones are a threat in the north and north-west. Says Brian Havard who has lived in Australia for 16 years: *'Life here is pleasant enough but it is not as people popularly suppose – unbroken weeks on golden beaches in glorious sunshine. It can be cold and wet and one soon learns to regard the fierce summer sun as an enemy.'*

Population

Australia has a population of more than 20 million people with Europeans making up the majority. The largest populated state is New South Wales with 8.76 million people, followed by Victoria (5 million), Queensland (3.9 million), Western Australia (1.99 million), South Australia (1.54 million), Tasmania (484,000), Australian Capital Territory (324,300) and the Northern Territory (200,800). The largest conurbations are Sydney (4.23 million), Melbourne (3.6 million), Perth (1.8 million) and Brisbane (1.77 million). Every square kilometre in the UK accommodates 243 people; in Australia each square kilometre has just two.

According to the Australian Bureau of Statistics, from 1901 until the end of World War 1, 4% of people in Australia were aged 65 years and over. This proportion had doubled to 8% by the 1947 census, reflecting the slow growth of the younger population during the Great Depression of the 1930s and World War II. As a result of the post-World War II baby boom, the proportion of older persons remained relatively stable at around 8% of the total population until the early 1970s. The proportion of persons aged 65 and over increased from 8% in 1971 to 13% in 2001, mainly due to the continual decline in fertility and reduction in the death rate.

Since 1911, there has been an increase in the proportion of overseas born residents across all age groups. Over the same time period, there has been a large decrease in the proportion of older overseas born residents. In 2001,

WEATHER CHART

Average temperature (Celcius), rainfall (mm)

	Jan	Feb	Mar	Apr	May	Jun	Jul	Aug	Sep	Oct	Nov	Dec
Adelaide												
Max	29	29	26	22	19	16	15	16	19	22	25	27
Min	17	17	15	12	10	8	7	8	9	11	14	15
Rainfall	21	11	25	38	58	79	82	69	62	43	29	29
Brisbane												
Max	29	29	28	26	23	21	21	22	24	26	27	29
Min	21	21	20	17	14	11	9	10	12	16	18	20
Rainfall	160	173	140	89	98	70	62	41	33	93	96	126
Canberra												
Max	28	27	24	20	15	12	11	13	16	29	22	26
Min	13	13	11	7	3	1	0	1	3	6	9	11
Rainfall	62	55	53	50	49	39	42	46	51	66	64	53
Darwin												
Max	32	31	32	33	32	31	30	31	32	33	33	33
Min	25	25	24	24	20	19	21	23	25	25	25	25
Rainfall	431	344	316	98	22	1	1	6	16	72	141	234
Hobart												
Max	22	22	21	18	15	13	12	13	15	17	19	20
Min	12	12	11	9	6	4	4	5	6	7	9	11
Rainfall	42	36	37	46	37	29	47	49	41	49	45	58
Melbourne												
Max	26	26	24	20	17	14	13	15	17	19	22	24
Min	14	14	13	11	9	7	6	7	8	9	11	13
Rainfall	49	47	52	58	57	50	48	51	59	68	60	60
Perth												
Max	32	32	29	25	21	19	18	18	20	22	25	29
Min	17	17	16	13	10	9	8	8	9	10	13	15
Rainfall	7	16	15	42	106	174	163	118	70	47	27	12
Sydney												
Max	26	26	25	22	19	17	16	18	20	22	24	25
Min	19	19	17	15	11	9	8	9	11	13	16	17
Rainfall	7	16	15	42	106	174	163	118	70	47	27	12

the majority (62%) of older persons were born in Australia, with the United-Kingdom and Ireland the next major birthplace (11%).

The composition of Australia's present population of older persons born overseas reflects immigration policy over the last 50 years. There was a significant immigration intake of young adults from Europe immediately after World War II and following the abolition of the White Australia Policy in the mid-1970s, immigrants were attracted to Australia from non-European origins, especially Asia.

Time

There are three times zones in Australia: Eastern Standard Time (EST) operates in New South Wales, Australian Capital Territory, Victoria, Tasmania and Queensland; Central Standard Time (CST) in South Australia and Northern Territory; and Western Standard Time (WST) in Western Australia. CST is half an hour behind EST and WST is two hours behind EST. Daylight saving times are operational in the Australian Capital Territory, New South Wales, South Australia and Victoria from the end of October to the end of March; and in Tasmania from the beginning of October to the end of March.

Metrication

Australia uses the metric system of weights and measures. Speed and distances are measured in kilometres, goods in kilograms and litres, and temperatures in Celsius (Centigrade).

CULTURE SHOCK

Australia is a vast country where the majority of the population lives in cities and coastal areas. Many of the regions in the interior are barren, isolated desert wastelands and have been rejected by locals who prefer a beach culture – an integral part of Australian life. Australians see their retirement in terms of a retreat to some quiet beach with lots of sunshine.

Some restaurants and clubs have dress codes but this is usually to ensure people don't arrive in shorts and vests in the evening. While sport plays an important part in the Australian lifestyle, the nation also has a rich and diverse contemporary arts scene. It reflects the cultural traditions, ancient landscapes, society and varied mix of migrant cultures.

Mike Osborne has been in Australia since February 2000 and lives in Ardrossan on the Yorke Peninsula in South Australia. He notes:

We find a far more tolerant attitude here. Generally folk take you for what you are. The golf course here will have the retired, the doctor and the labourer who will play together and have a drink together afterwards. Folk are easy going on race and while there are problems elsewhere in the country, we only see good humour.

Australians do not like outlandish displays of wealth, pretentiousness and snobbery. They dislike elitism and seem committed to egalitarianism. The 'tall poppy syndrome' means that Australians often avoid standing out or being a 'tall poppy' and love to discredit those who appear to take excessive pride in their own achievements.

English is the spoken language although it is punctuated with Australian, or 'Strine,' words and phrases. When in conversation with an Australian, keep your distance. Maintaining personal space is important in this culture and hugging, patting, or touching other men is socially unacceptable. However, they are enthusiastic conversationalists and discussions are entertaining. Kathleen Calver, who has lived in Australia for 56 years, since migrating at the age of 25 says:

Australia has much to offer. Visiting the wide open spaces on the mainland is a tremendous experience and on the whole I would still say Australians are welcoming, generous hearted people. We felt many of our UK counterparts were more insular. There is, however, a drawback for many people here: the distance from Europe. A great deal depends on a person's close attachment to family in either sphere.

Generally speaking, Australia is an informal, friendly, multicultural society. Its people accept and respect the right of all its citizens to express and share their cultural heritage. You are expected to make an overriding commitment to the country, its laws and its democratic values. While it takes time to acclimatise to the social behaviour in any new country, once you've done this in Australia you will be accepted by the locals. You can then begin to enjoy your new way of life but it would be wise to keep a few of these Aussie *rules* in mind.

Basics

CHAPTER SUMMARY

○ Retiring to Australia means that your state pension is frozen at the level that it stood at when you left.

○ Only two types of visas allow you to enter Australia as a retiree; the Investor Retirement Visa means you need substantial capital.

○ The best way to avoid a costly abortive move to Australia is to have a trial period.

○ Almost 30 airlines fly to Australia from the UK; the best and most cost-effective time to travel is during the Low Season.

○ Opening an Australian account in the UK before you depart has been made easy by two of Australia's main banks with offices in London.

○ Before you depart the UK permanently you should arrange to have your UK pension paid into your bank account in Australia.

○ If you are taking cats and dogs into the country, they face a 30-day quarantine period over there.

THINGS TO CONSIDER

Is it Affordable?

According to the Department of Immigration and Multicultural Affairs (DIMA), the cost of living in Australia is high compared to many other countries and it is essential that you consider how you will provide for yourself and your spouse. You must remember that retiring to Australia means that your UK state pension is frozen at the level it stands when you leave. This is an important consideration as it is not possible to rely solely on this income. Although the exchange rate fluctuates on a daily basis, it would have no effect on your pension. Says Brian Havard:

Life is cheaper than in the UK, which is fine if you are not on a frozen pension. However, some foodstuffs, such as fruit and vegetables, are increasingly expensive. Buying a home is tolerable in towns and cities other than Sydney and Melbourne.

Sydney is ranked 20th, a climb of 47 places, on the list of world's most expensive cities to live (London is third and New York is 13th). Melbourne follows in 68th place, then Brisbane (84th), Adelaide (89th) and Perth (93rd). This survey, conducted by Mercer Human Resource Consulting, measured expenses such as clothing, entertainment, food, housing and transportation.

UK Retirement Pension Forecast

Those who have not yet reached retirement age, but plan to start receiving their UK state pension in Australia should continue to pay national insurance contributions in the UK in order to qualify for a state pension once they reach 65. You should also request a Retirement Pension Forecast. This tells you the amount of state pension you have already earned and the amount you can expect to receive on reaching pension age. This will help you to plan your finances for the future. To receive a forecast, obtain form BR19 from your local social security office or contact the Retirement Pension Forecasting and Advice Unit, ☎ 0845-3000 168.

Cost of Living in Australia Compared to the UK

The figures below were obtained from retirees living in Victoria, South Australia and Tasmania but may change within each state and territory. The UK prices are taken mainly from the *EIU Worldwide Cost of Living*.

Alcohol. A few products are cheaper than in the UK. Local wines, beers and spirits are of extremely good value and quality.

Product	Australia price ($)	UK price (£)	Australia price in £ sterling equivalent
Table wine (750 ml)	10.00	4.99	4.10
Beer – known brand (330 ml)	2.50	0.92	1.02
Scotch (6 year old – 700 ml)	28.00	12.34	11.48

Books and Newspapers. Generally about the same price, although books are more expensive.

Product	Australia price ($)	UK price (£)	Australia price in £ sterling equivalent
Daily local newspaper	1.20	0.60	0.49
Imported daily newspaper	4.50	1.20	1.84
International weekly news magazine (*Time*)	5.00	2.60	2.05
Paperback novel	25.00	6.99	10.25

Cars. New cars are slightly cheaper depending in which state or territory you buy one. A 1300cc is a particularly small car; the norm is 1.8 litre or 2.0 litre. Petrol prices are cheaper but vary (Queensland has an 8 cents/litre concession).

Product	Australia price ($)	UK price (£)	Australia price in £ sterling equivalent
New low priced car (1300 cc)	18,600	8,995	7,626
Unleaded petrol (1 litre)	1.34	0.94	0.55
Annual road tax plus compulsory third party injury insurance	650	160	266.50
Fully comprehensive, no claims insurance premium	600	685.65	246
Cost of a tune up	100	150	41.00

Clothing and Footwear. Australia has national chains offering reasonably priced clothes and international chains are also well represented (no Marks and Spencer). There are scores of boutique stores and smaller chains.

Electronics. Generally electronic goods are less expensive in Australia. If you bring them from the UK they should work adequately.

Product	Australia price ($)	UK price (£)	Australia price in £ sterling equivalent
Personal computer (80 Gb)	999	941	410
Colour Television (66 cm)	1300	500	533

Food. Supermarket products cost slightly more than in the UK but there are many indoor and open-air markets that offer very good value for fresh produce. Most supermarkets carry their own 'home brands' which are always cheaper.

Product	Australia price ($)	UK price (£)	Australia price in £ sterling equivalent
Pasteurised milk (1 litre)	1.38	0.49	0.56
Eggs (12)	3.88	1.02	1.59
Orange juice (1 litre)	3.29	1.22	1.34
Butter (500g)	5.00	1.96	2.05
White bread (1 kg)	1.78	0.55	0.72
Ground coffee (500 g)	17.29	3.30	7.08
Tea bags (25 bags)	1.00	0.30	0.41
Fresh chicken (1 kg)	7.00	1.78	2.87
Potatoes (2 kg)	4.98	1.50	2.04
Onions (1kg)	2.28	0.64	0.93

Healthcare. Pensioners who are temporary residents in Australia need to take out private medical insurance. Visits to the doctor, hospital treatment and prescriptions are not free although you may receive a concession. All dentists are private in Australia. These extra costs should be factored in.

Product	Australia price ($)	UK price (£)	Australia price in £ sterling equivalent
Routine checkup at family doctor	50	85	20.50
X-ray at doctor's office or hospital	110	45	45
Visit to dentist (scale and a filling)	200	60	82
Aspirins (100 tablets)	11.36	7.13	4.65

Leisure. Australians enjoy their leisure time to the full and most activities are affordable. Many of the hundreds of golf courses have special offers. Pensioners receive concessions on services, such as public transport, and entrance to theatres, cinemas and public swimming pools (depending on state and territory).

Product	Australia price ($)	UK price (£)	Australia price in £ sterling equivalent
Four best seats at the theatre	200	214	82
Four best seats at the cinema	100	34	41
3-course dinner at a top city restaurant for 4 people	400	288	164
Compact Disc Album	30	11.99	12.30
Green fees on a public golf course	30	15.00	12.30

Personal Care. Generally about the same price for products and slightly cheaper for services.

Product	Australia price ($)	UK price (£)	Australia price in £ sterling equivalent
Fluoride tooth paste (120g)	3.00	2.27	1.23
Shampoo	4.00	1.78	1.64
Hair cut and blow dry	36.00	40.00	14.76
Toilet tissue (2 rolls)	4.99	0.84	2.04
Dry cleaning (man's suit)	15.00	7.20	6.15

Rents. Generally, about 50% cheaper than in the UK. The figures below compare London with average prices in Adelaide. Rents are cheaper outside the cities.

Product	Australia price ($)	UK price (£)	Australia price in £ sterling equivalent
Furnished moderate 1-bedroom apartment (pcm)	880	700	360
Furnished moderate 3-bedroom house	2400	2137.50	984

Tobacco. Slightly cheaper in Australia.

Product	Australia price ($)	UK price (£)	Australia price in £ sterling equivalent
Cigarettes – Marlboro (20)	10.30	5.03	4.22
Cigarettes – local brand (20)	10.30	4.77	4.22
Pipe tobacco (50 g)	15	9.21	6.15

Utilities. Electricity is considerably more expensive in Australia. Gas is not available in all areas. However, you can use bottled gas for central heating and gas cookers, which costs about $40 (£16) a month (delivered).

Product	Australia price ($)	UK price (£)	Australia price in £ sterling equivalent
Phone line – average monthly rental	35	10.66	14.35
Phone – average charge per local call from home (3 mins)	0.19	0.14	0.07
Electricity, monthly bill (includes air conditioning)	1,666	45	683
Rates	91.60	90	37.55
Water and Sewerage	100	25.83	41

Leaving Family and Friends

As well as sufficient funds, you will also need to possess copious amounts of energy and enthusiasm to deal with the move practically and emotionally. Many people cite moving house as one of the most stressful times in their life, but for most the move may be just down the road, or to another town. It does not involve moving to another country, isolating yourself from family and friends and having to assimilate into an alien culture. Problems often arise when children and grandchildren are left behind. Women often feel this wrench much more than men and for some the homesickness can have a very negative effect on the new life in Australia. You will need contingency plans to stay in touch with and assist close friends, children, grandchildren elderly parents and relatives, to deal with any emergencies that may arise in the UK when you are living in Australia, and to have somewhere for any of the above to stay with you when they want or need to. Warm weather and fantastic views may not be sufficient compensation for the life you have left behind. A trial period (see below) may not be financially feasible but should be considered nevertheless.

Looking Ahead

It is also imperative to consider whether you will be able to cope with your new life in Australia further down the line. While the Australian climate and quality of life may be beneficial to your general life, it is important to consider the future and what will happen if you become seriously ill or are no longer able to care for yourself. Although there is a good network of care services in Australia, it is a long way from home, your family and friends. The UK government is also considering ways of enforcing the rule that people who have lived abroad for more than six months can no longer return to the UK for healthcare, unless they are moving back permanently. If you are a couple, you should also take into account the ramifications if one of you dies or becomes seriously ill. If you have wholly left the British system and then want to return to it, you may find it financially demanding to do so, unless you have made plans for this contingency.

A TRIAL PERIOD

The temptation just to up-sticks and go is huge, especially when confronted by the grey drizzle and dark evenings of British winter. However, such a life-changing decision should never be taken lightly and many people who rush into retirement abroad find that the grass is not necessarily greener. As mentioned above many people miss their family and friends, feel isolated by the cultural differences or simply find economic inactivity interminably boring. Even if you know the area well, your romanticised notion of retirement in Australia may not quite meet the reality.

The simple way to avoid an abortive move, which could end up quite costly and certainly create an enormous headache in terms of paperwork, is to have a trial period. A trial period can take the form of reconnaissance trips staying in different regions for more than the usual holiday length. It also gives you the chance of becoming acquainted with the facilities and attractions of the region you may be interested in.

House-sitting

A way of doing this is to consider house-sitting. There are a number of organisations that assist in helping homeowners and house-sitters and you could register in advance of your arrival in Australia.

Aussie House Sitters (www.aussiehousesitters.com.au) is an Australian owned house-sitting database. To register as a sitter costs $48 for a 12-month membership. Happy House Sitters, (www.happyhousesitters.com.au) manages a list of house sitters and if you wish to register it costs from $150 for one year. Right at Home (www. rightathome.com.au) provides a personal service to homeowners and sitters. They manage short and ongoing stays in Melbourne and around Victoria. The annual cost to sitters is $50 for short-term and $195 for ongoing stays.

RESIDENCE REGULATIONS

New legislation, which came into effect on 1 July 2005, means that the Investor Retirement Visa is the only pathway for retired people, without family in Australia, to live in the country. If your visa application is approved, it will allow multiple travel in and out of Australia initially for four years.

Applications to remain for a further stay of four years can be made but the applicant must satisfy particular criteria. Currently, there is no maximum period for which you can remain in Australia as the holder of a consecutive Investor Retirement Visa. It does not lead to permanent residence in Australia or to Australian citizenship. This visa does have incentives to entice would-be migrant retirees to settle in regional and/or low population growth areas (see *Choosing the Right Location*).

If you apply for the Investor Retirement Visa, you must be 55 years or older, have no dependents (other than a spouse), and be able to be self-supporting in Australia without cost to Australia's social and welfare services systems.

This visa does not provide any entitlement to coverage by Medicare (Australia's national health cover) or to Australian social security benefits. Applicants will be required to hold private medical coverage for the duration of their visa.

A state or territory government agency *must* sponsor a person for the Investor Retirement Visa, and an investment must be made with the sponsoring state or territory government treasury corporation. The Australian Capital Territory (ACT) does not provide sponsorship, as its treasury is currently unable to arrange the required Designated Investments, nor does New South Wales.

Information provided by applicants regarding their intended place of residence in Australia will determine the amount required by them for settlement, annual income and designated investment to meet the financial requirement for the grant of an Investor Retirement Visa.

Investor Retirement Visa holders are subject to 'limited work rights' conditions, allowing you to work for up to 20 hours a week. There are no concessions if you have any family or children in Australia.

Initial Investor Retirement Visa applicants should not undergo medicals until advised by the Department of Immigration and Multicultural Affairs' (DIMA) Perth Business Centre. This is to ensure that the appropriate medical checks are completed.

Application forms for the Investor Retirement Visa are available at www.immi.gov.au, at your nearest Australian diplomatic office, or by calling the DIMA's general enquiry number in Australia at ☎ 13 18 81. The same criteria apply if you wish to renew your Investor Retirement Visa after the initial four years.

To apply for an Investor Retirement Visa you need to:

O Contact a state or territory agency and provide them with form 1249 (State or Territory Government Sponsorship Investor Retirement Visa). They will complete the form and return it to you.

O Contact the Treasury Corporation in the state or territory that will sponsor you (other than ACT and NSW). They will forward current information on the terms and conditions and an investment application form. They will also send detailed instructions on how to lodge the Designated Investment. At the initial inquiry stage, the Treasury Corporation can only indicate the likely rate of return on a proposed investment. The actual rate of return on your investment will be set when you deposit your funds in the Designated Investment. Interest rates change regularly and may differ between state and territory Treasury Corporations. Do not lodge your designated investment form or your designated investment at this time.

O Lodge your application for the Investor Retirement Visa along with the sponsorship and pay the visa application charge. With your application you should submit all appropriate supporting documentation, as outlined in the document checklist, including evidence of your assets, your access to an income stream, and private health insurance.

O Once your application has been processed and all requirements have

been met, the Perth Business Centre will ask you, and your spouse, to complete relevant health and character checks.

○ Once your health and character checks have been finalised, the Perth Business Centre will advise you in writing to lodge the Designated Investment with the Treasury Corporation in the state or territory that has sponsored you. Funds must be in Australian dollars and must be deposited in your name or your name and the name of your spouse. Once the designated investment has been made, funds cannot be withdrawn before the four-year term has expired, unless under exceptional circumstances approved by the Minister.

○ Once you have submitted evidence that the designated investment has been made, the Perth Business Centre will advise you in writing to pay the second application charge.

Charges and Assets

You will need to pay a visa application charge of $180 when you lodge your application. A second visa application charge (VAC) of $8,000 per person is payable once your application has been processed. This charge is made to offset any possible future aged care access costs and will apply regardless of whether aged care or nursing home services are utilised during the period of the visa or not.

Assets of $500,000 (if settling in a regional area) are needed to establish yourself independently in Australia and $750,000 (if settling in a non-regional area); plus an annual income stream of $50,000 (regional area) based on capital for investment, pension rights or both pension rights and capital for investment or $65,000 (non-regional area); plus a set amount for investment in a state or territory government treasury bond with the sponsoring state or territory government, usually of $500,000 (regional area) or $750,000 (non-regional area).

As of 1 July 2005 the previous Retirement Visa (410–Temporary) is closed to new visa applicants and only open to people who currently hold this visa who will be able to continue to apply to rollover their visa.

For more information, contact DIMA Perth Business Centre, ☎13 18 81; e-mail retirement.visas@immi.gov.au.

For information on state and territory sponsorships contact:

NT: Department of Industries and Business, www.nt.gov.au.

QLD: State Development and Innovation, www.sdi.qld.gov.au.

SA: Immigration SA, www.immigration.sa.gov.au.

TAS: Department of Economic Development, www.development.tas.gov.au.

VIC: Business Migration, www.liveinvictoria.vic.gov.au.

WA: Small Business Development Corporation, www.sbdc.com.au.

Government Treasury Corporations

NT: Northern Territory Treasury Corporation, ☎08-8999 7975; www.territorybonds. nt.gov.au.

QLD: Queensland Treasury Corporation, ☎07-3842 4600; www.qtc.qld.gov.au.

SA: South Australian Government Financing Authority, ☎08-8226 9444; e-mail SAFA. mail@saugov.sa.gov.au; www.safa.sa.gov.au.

TAS: Tasmanian Public Finance Corporation, ☎03-6233 7880; e-mail Tascorp@ tascorp.com.au; www.tascorp.com.au.

VIC: Treasury Corporation of Victoria, ☎03-9651 4800; e-mail tcv@tcv.vic.gov.au; www.tcv.gov.au.

WA: Western Australia Treasury Corporation, ☎08-9235 9100; e-mail TreasCorp@ watc.wa.gov.au; www.watc.wa.gov.au.

Parent Visas

The only other way you can retire to Australia is if you have children living and working in Australia. You can then apply for a Parent Visa, which falls into two groups: the Non-Contributory Parent category and the Contributory Parent category. Furthermore, the Non-Contributory Parent category comprises: the Parent (Migrant) visa if applying from outside Australia, or the Aged Parent (Residence) visa if applying from within Australia.

You must be old enough to be granted an Australian age pension: 65 years for men and for women it is gradually being increased from 60 to 65 years. Aged Parent visa applicants must be in Australia when the visa is granted. You will have to meet the 'balance of family' (BOF) test. This means you must have at least half of your children living lawfully and permanently in Australia, or more children living lawfully and permanently in Australia than in any other single country overseas.

Applicants must be sponsored by either an Australian citizen or an Australian permanent resident. You will also have to meet the strict health standards and demonstrate that you are of good character. Due to high demand, this visa category is subject to capping: in the 2005-06 Migration Program year, 1,000 visa places are available worldwide for the Non-Contributory Parent category and 3,500 places for the Contributory Parent category. When the cap has been reached, applicants are placed in a queue and when further places become available, visas are granted in order.

A first instalment fee of $1,935 is payable on lodging an application and a second instalment of $1,135 payable just before the visa is granted. Applicants for a permanent visa in the contributory parent category are required to pay a second visa application charge (VAC), currently $27,850 per adult, at the time of visa grant. Alternatively, applicants can choose to spread the payments by initially applying for a temporary visa in the contributory parent category and pay a lower second VAC at the time of grant. This temporary visa is valid for a period of two years and provides access to Medicare (Australia's national health cover) and full work rights. At anytime during the two-year period, applicants can apply for a permanent visa in the contributory parent visa category. Immediately prior to the grant of the permanent visa, applicants will have to pay the appropriate second VAC and also lodge a $10,000 Assurance of Support bond ($14,000 per couple) to help cover any social security costs in the first 10 years of residence.

If you are granted a Parent visa you become a permanent resident of Australia on arrival or on grant. The Parent visa categories do not provide for a roll-over and you are eligible for Australian citizenship after you have lived in Australia for the prescribed period.

Emigration Consultants

Professional assistance can ease the process of settling in Australia. The Migration Bureau (Argyll House, All Saints Passage, London SW18 1EP; ☎020-8875 5442; fax 020-8875 5443; e-mail london@migrationbureau. com; www.migrationbureau.com) is one of Australia's largest and longest-established, private immigration consulting groups. They are officially recognised specialists in obtaining permanent residence visas for Australia and offer a complete personalised service including professional assistance with residence visa processing and re-settlement services.

Embassies and Consulates

It's advisable to register with your embassy or consulate when you arrive in Australia. This enables the authorities to keep you up to date with any information you need as a citizen resident overseas. Also, in the event of an emergency, it helps them to trace individuals, advise you of any diplomatic problems, and inform you of a death of a relative overseas.

British High Commissions and Consulates in Australia

British High Commission, Yarralumla: ☎02-6270 6666; and Canberra, ☎1300 367 066.

British Consulate-General, Sydney: ☎02-9247 7521; Melbourne, ☎03-9652 1600; Brisbane, ☎07-3223 3200; and Perth, ☎08-9224 4700.

British Consulate, Adelaide: ☎08-8212 7280.

Honorary Consul, Hobart: ☎03-6213 3310.

Australian High Commission and Consulate in the UK

Australian High Commission: ☎020-7379 4334; www.australia.org.uk.

Australian Consulate: ☎0161-237 9440; www.australia.org.uk.

GETTING THERE AND AWAY

These days nearly 30 airlines fly to Australia from the UK and destinations around the world. Qantas is Australia's national carrier and currently operates 27 London to Australia services. Sydney and Melbourne are the most popular gateways but Brisbane, Adelaide, Perth, Darwin, Cairns and Hobart have international terminals.

- Sydney is 10,560 miles (17,000 km) from the UK and takes 22 hours 30 minutes.
- Melbourne 10,510 miles (16,910 km); 21 hours 40 minutes.
- Brisbane 10,270 miles (16,530 km); 22 hours 30 minutes.
- Adelaide 10,090 miles (16,240 km); 24 hours 40 minutes.
- Perth 9,000 miles (14,480 km); 19 hours 20 minutes.
- Darwin 8,830 miles (14,210 km); 18 hours 10 minutes.
- Cairns 11,140 miles (17,920 km); 24 hours 30 minutes.
- Hobart 10,844 miles (17,451 km); 22 hours 40 minutes.

Fares vary enormously according to the seasons, Christmas and special events. The cheapest time to fly to Australia is during the Low Season, from March to June. The Mid Season (or Shoulder), from July to November, and during February is more expensive and Peak Season, from December to January, is quite pricey.

Charter flights operated by tour operators are usually the cheapest way to travel to Australia. You can check www.travelbag.co.uk, www.airlinenetwork. co.uk, or www.travelmood.com for the latest deals. Currently you can expect to pay about £599 to Sydney and £662 to Darwin.

WEBSITES SELLING FLIGHTS

www.austravel.co.uk
www.lastminute.com
www.ebookers.com
www.expedia.co.uk
www.cheapflights.com
www.opodo.co.uk

THE AIRLINES

Scheduled flights will usually offer the possibility of a stopover in their home country, which can be a welcome break. The following airlines depart from Heathrow, London (with stopovers):

Air New Zealand: ☎0800-028 4149; www.airnewzealand.com, to Brisbane, Cairns, Melbourne and Sydney.

Air Mauritius: ☎020-8897 3545; www.airmauritius.com, to Perth, Melbourne and Sydney.

Austrian Airlines: ☎020-7766 0300; www.aua.com, to Melbourne and Sydney.

Cathay Pacific: ☎020-8834 8888; www.cathaypacific.com, to Perth, Adelaide, Brisbane, Cairns, Melbourne and Sydney.

Emirates: ☎0870-243 2222; www.emirates.com, to Perth, Brisbane, Melbourne and Sydney (also departs from Gatwick, Birmingham, Glasgow and Manchester).

Gulf Air: www.gulfairco.com, to Sydney (also departs from Dublin).

JAL: ☎0845-774 7700; www.jal.com, to Adelaide, Brisbane, Cairns and Sydney. Korean Air to Brisbane and Sydney.

Malaysia Airlines: ☎0870-607 9090; www.malaysiaairlines.com, to Adelaide, Brisbane, Melbourne, Perth and Sydney (also departs from Manchester).

Qantas: ☎0845-774 7767; www.qantas.co.uk, to 32 destinations in Australia.

Royal Brunei: ☎020-7584 6660; www.bruneiair.com, to Brisbane, Darwin, Perth and Sydney.

Singapore Airlines: ☎0844-800 2380; www.singaporeair.co.uk, to Adelaide, Brisbane, Melbourne, Perth, Sydney (also departs from Manchester).

Thai Airways: ☎020-7491 7953; www.thaiair.com, to Perth, Brisbane, Melbourne and Sydney.

United Airlines: ☎0845-844 4777; www.united.com, to Sydney and Melbourne.

Virgin Atlantic: ☎0870-380 2007; www.virgin-atlantic.com, to Sydney.

By Sea

If you have the time and money and want to relax in luxury, travelling by sea to Australia is always a possibility. You can book a segment of a world cruise that includes Australia. These are offered by Cunard on *Queen Elizabeth II* (☎0845-071 0300; www.cunard.co.uk); P&O Cruises: *Oriana* (☎023-8065 5058; www.pocruises.com); and Saga Holidays: *Saga Rose* (☎01303-711111; www.saga.co.uk). P&O Cruises offer sailings from

Southampton to Sydney where a twin cabin would cost between £7,529 and £8,649. They do offer amazing discounts on the brochure fare, so check with the company.

PREPARATIONS FOR DEPARTURE

It is a good idea to begin the essential preparations many months in advance. Every aspect of daily life will need to be considered as you decide what should be cancelled in the UK, what should be transferred to Australia and how it should be done. Checklists can be helpful but how you manage these depends on your personal circumstances and requirements. Although not definitive, the items below are essential:

Finance

The difference between UK and Australian financial systems means that up to half the value of some of your UK assets and pensions can be lost on emigrating This can be avoided through pre-departure financial planning from a UK based crossborder specialist who understands both countries' systems. You should seek advice six months prior to departing to optimise your position. For specialist advice on whether or not to transfer your pension to Australia – and whether you are eligible, please contact an organisation such as Prism Xpat on ☎0845 450 4004 (☎+44 207 554 8548).

Banking

You will need to convert your money into Australian dollars and transfer the funds into an Australian bank account. You may decide to transfer funds before leaving home or wait until you have arrived in Australia.

Until quite recently, you had to be in Australia before opening an Australian bank account but now the major banks are offering specialist migrant banking services. Westpac has a Migrant Banking section to enable migrants to bank from their home country before moving to Australia. You can open an Everyday account and a Savings account for transfer of funds to Australia, apply for a credit and ATM card for collection when you arrive in Australia, retain some of your funds in a selected foreign currency in a Westpac Foreign Currency Account, and apply for Internet and telephone banking to access your accounts from anywhere in the world.

All you have to do is complete an application form and send it to Westpac in London. Within four working days two accounts are opened: A standard transactional account (cheque book, debit/eftpos (switch) card, Internet and telephone banking); and a high interest savings account. These accounts are linked so that you can transfer funds between the two. Both are opened in Australia but are available for deposits only and are not activated until they have been properly identified for anti-money laundering purposes. Generally accounts are only activated when you arrive in Australia and visit any Westpac branch with identification. If you need your account activated before leaving the UK, you will have to go into Westpac's London office for an identity verification check, or your banker or solicitor must complete an Acceptable Referee form confirming they have known you for 12 months or more and confirm your identity.

The Commonwealth Bank's office in London offers a similar facility where you can open an account and deposit funds before you leave the UK. All funds are converted on receipt at the commercial exchange rate applicable at the time of receipt, unless instructed to the contrary. Funds are then held in sterling currency but the bank requires holding instructions to this effect prior to receipt.

Until you are committed to staying in Australia, you may delay selling up all your assets. This may take a year or so but could be risky with fluctuating exchange rates. At the time of writing, the rate has been fairly stable at £0.41 pence to the dollar.

You may wish to deal directly with a bank to transfer your money or choose a broker. Organisations dealing in foreign exchange have their own spreads, so it's a good idea to obtain a couple of quotes to compare the rates, service and other costs (see *Personal Finance*). It also makes sense to maintain your account in the UK. If you decide to return to the UK in the future this will eliminate the red tape in opening an account.

> **Main Australian Banks**
> Australia and New Zealand Bank (ANZ): www.anz.com.
> Commonwealth Bank of Australia: www.commbank.com.au.
> National Australia Bank Limited: www.national.com.au.
> Westpac Banking Corporation: www.westpac.com.au.
>
> **Australian Banks in the UK**
> Australia and New Zealand Bank (ANZ): ☎020-7378 2121.
> Commonwealth Bank of Australia: ☎020-7710 3990.
> National Australia Bank Limited: ☎020-7710 2100.
> Westpac Banking Corporation: ☎020-7621 7000.

Medical Matters

It's probably a good idea to visit your GP to tell him or her of your decision to retire to Australia and to have a final check-up. It's not possible to take your medical records away with you, but once you've found a doctor in Australia these can be forwarded. Depending on your visa, the Department of Immigration and Multicultural Affairs (DIMA) in Australia may require you to have a medical examination. More information is available from the Australian High Commission in London (☎020-7379 4334; www.australia. org.uk). It also maintains a list of panel doctors in England, Scotland, Wales, Isle of Man, Channel Islands, and Northern Ireland.

Mail Forwarding

Whether you have sold your UK property, are letting it out, or are simply leaving it vacant, you will need your post to be forwarded on to your new address in Australia. If you are keeping your UK home and therefore address, this is likely to generate more post than if you have sold up your UK assets and left the UK entirely. If you have a trusted neighbour, or your tenants are friends you can ask them to check your post, throw away obvious junk and readdress any important looking mail to you in Australia. Alternatively, you can arrange to have your post redirected by the Royal Mail. You can arrange this at any post office by completing form *P944 Soc.* The time limit for redirecting mail is two years and it costs £69.80 per surname, per year. Special Delivery, Parcelforce and signed for mail cannot be forwarded. There are also commercial Accommodation Address mail forwarding services, which can be found with a simple Google search. These services allow you to use their address and forward your mail on once a week, for a fee of around £15 per month.

Pensions

You should arrange for your occupational and state pension payments to be paid into your bank account in Australia. To do this you need to contact the pensions service in the UK (www.thepensionservice.gov.uk; ☎0845-606 060) and search/ask for details of Overseas Direct Payment in local currency. For occupational and private pensions contact your provider. If you open an Australian bank account before leaving the UK, you will receive your account number and can therefore arrange for your pension provider to have your pension transferred into the account on a regular basis.

Those who move to Australia before reaching retirement age, but do not intend to work, should arrange to continue paying national insurance contributions in the UK in order to qualify for a British state pension when they reach 65. Before you go, seek advice on this issue from the Inland Revenue National Insurance Contributions Office (☎0845-302 1479; www.hmrc.gov. uk/nic/). For more details, see Pensions and Exportable UK Benefits in the *Personal Finance* chapter.

Pets

Generally, dogs, cats and horses may be moved to Australia but are subject to very strict quarantine controls. Other household pets, such as caged birds, are prohibited. Rules and fees are set by Australian Quarantine and Inspection Services (AQIS). Your animals will be quarantined for at least 30 days on arrival and you are responsible for all fees and accommodation.

The quarantine entry fee for each animal is $10; the veterinary inspection fee is $71 per half hour; document clearance $27; transport from the airport to quarantine station $95 to $120; accommodation for a cat $13.55 a day and for a dog $17.55 a day. Fees are calculated after your pet arrives in Australia. You will be invoiced for these services, which is payable prior to collection of your animals.

An import permit is required and your application must include your pet's microchip number. The permit contains Veterinary Certificate A and B and must be completed and endorsed by an official veterinarian in the country of export before you arrive in Australia. Further advice can be obtained at AQIS

(☎02-6272 4454; e-mail animalimp@aqis.gov.au; www.aqis.gov.au).

According to Airpets Oceanic, Perth, Melbourne and Sydney are the three ports of entry for pets into Australia. To transport a cat costs about £850 (plus the quarantine fees above) and for dogs, such as a Labrador, £2,200. The demand for space means that Melbourne and Perth quarantine stations are fully booked months in advance so notice is required at least two to three months in advance (Sydney, one month).

Dogs and cats are required to be up to date with their normal yearly vaccinations (rabies vaccination is not required by Australian authorities) and dogs need to pass three blood tests. Only certain airlines and routes are used (BA and Qantas carry pets on most flights) but many only take bookings from recognised agents. Therefore, it is best to contact a reputable pet travel agent.

Information on exporting pets from the UK is dealt with by local Animal Health Divisional Offices. A full list of these offices and contact details is available at http://www.defra.gov.uk/corporate/contacts/ahdo.htm or the Department for the Environment, Food and Rural Affairs (DEFRA) Helpline, ☎0845-933 5577.

Useful Contacts	
Airpets Oceanic:	☎01753-685571; www.airpets.com. Pet exports, pet travel schemes, boarding, transportation by road/air to and from all UK destinations.
Pet Plan:	☎0800-107 0204; www.petplan.co.uk. Offers travel insurance for pets.
IRT:	☎01638-508080; www.flyirt.com. Horse, dogs and cats transporter.

Removals

When deciding what to take with you to Australia, you'll have to be quite ruthless. Removal costs are high and you may be better off replacing some items when you arrive in Australia rather than shipping them.

Remember that all Australian homes, whether purchased or rented, come with a cooker installed so do not ship your own. It's also advisable to buy a new refrigerator on arrival, as Australian fridges are much bigger (500 litre capacity) and have built-in fans to deal with the climate. A separate freezer is often a necessity.

The majority of homes have built-in cupboards, so you may wish to leave your wardrobes behind. In Australia, washing machines are top loaders (front loaders are more expensive) so if yours is in good condition you may be better off shipping it. The electrical system is the same as in the UK (240V) so your appliances should be suitable.

Car boot sales or charity shops are a good way of getting rid of some of the unnecessary items you have collected over the years. You should definitely take belongings of sentimental value as these can sometimes make resettling in another country a little easier.

The most viable option is by sea freight; your goods will be packed (or you can pack yourself) and placed in a container, shipped to Australia, checked through customs and delivered to your new home. Packing yourself may incur a higher insurance premium. If you decide to ship only a small quantity of goods, a shared container will be much cheaper. If you have enough for a 20-foot container, you will get sole use of it.

A standard carton is 4.5 cubic feet (24x20x16); book cartons generally range from two cubic feet to nine cubic feet. Shipping is charged by volume, not weight. It's a good idea to get a few quotes and then choose the one that best suits your pocket but ensure they demonstrate a level of expertise and service.

There are a plethora of international shipping companies and it's a good idea to look for those who are members of the British Association of Removers (☎01923-699480; www.removers.org.uk) as these are likely to be more reputable companies. BAR has set up International Movers Mutual Insurance so that clients of any of its member companies will be compensated for loss or damage, or in the case of bankruptcy, the removal will be completed by another BAR member.

Before you start phoning around for quotes, there is a useful website which does the bulk of the work for you: www.reallymoving.com. Simply type in the pick-up and drop-off points and a rough estimate of how many cubic feet you'll be moving (their estimator will work this out for you) and the site will email your request to several companies. Over the following few days personalised quotes will trickle into your inbox.

Customs

As a first-time migrant, you are entitled to bring all your household effects that you have owned and used for the whole of a 12-month period immediately before leaving for Australia. Certain items are excluded and are subject to other requirements, such as motor vehicles or parts; caravans, boats and trailers; fur apparel; and yachts.

You may bring in the following in your accompanied baggage:

o $900 worth of goods (gifts, souvenirs, cameras, perfume, electronic equipment, leather goods, jewellery, watches, sporting equipment);
o 2.25 litres of alcoholic beverages; and
o 250 cigarettes, or 250 grams of cigars or tobacco products.

Firearms, weapons and ammunition may be prohibited or require a permit and safety testing to import them. All medicinal products must be declared, as well as all animal and plants materials and food products. Garden equipment, lawnmowers and outdoor furniture will be specially inspected, fumigated and cleaned (at your expense). Currency of $10,000 or more must be reported on arrival. If you fail to declare or dispose of quarantine items you could be fined $220 on the spot or prosecuted and fined more than $60,000 and risk 10 years' jail sentence.

A full explanation on all prohibited products is available from Australian Customs Services, ☎02-6275 6666; e-mail information@customs.gov.au; www.customs.gov.au.

Odds and Ends Checklist

o Cancel any regular subscriptions to newspapers, magazines, book and wine clubs, or arrange to have them redirected if this possible and appropriate.
o Dispose of anything you don't want to take with you via eBay, a car boot sale, or charity shops.
o Book disconnection of mains services.
o Notify bank, credit card company, car registration, passport office and so on of change of address.
o Cancel gym or other UK club memberships.
o Cancel the milk/newspapers.
o Return library books.
o Cancel contracts with gas, electricity and telephone companies and settle accounts.
o If you are renting out your UK home take meter readings for gas and electricity and settle bills before tenants move in and make an inventory of items left in the house to be attached to the tenancy agreement.
o Notify dentist, doctor, optician, vet.

Part two

A New Home

in Australia

Where to Retire
Your New Home in Australia
Housing Finance

Where to Retire

CHAPTER SUMMARY

O When seeking the location for your retirement it is a good idea to list your priorities and realise that you may have to compromise on some of them.

O There are popular retirement destinations all over Australia. Properties with sea views are considerably more expensive.

O While the Australian Capital Territory is not currently offering state sponsorship, an Investor Retirement Visa requirement, it is a pleasant place to live.

O New South Wales, again, not currently open to state sponsorship, is a popular destination for other visa migrants.

O The Northern Territory is one of the fastest growing economies in the country and has the smallest population.

O The 'Sunshine State' of Queensland attracts retiree migrants to Toowoomba, Yeppoon and Hervey Bay.

O South Australia is the headquarters of the Australian wine industry and has many cultural, music and food festivals held across the state.

O Migration to Tasmania has escalated in recent years but property has remained affordable.

O Melbourne in Victoria is Australia's cosmopolitan capital.

O Western Australia is the country's largest state and attracts many retirees to its capital city, Perth.

CHOOSING THE RIGHT LOCATION FOR RETIREMENT

Selecting the right retirement location is one of the most important factors when you are planning your move to Australia. Lifestyle and climate tend to be the major considerations but cost of housing, crime, security, transport infrastructure, medical and other facilities all play an important part. Regular reconnaissance trips may not be an option as they can become financially prohibitive.

Cities and towns in Australia's interior or northern regions, such as Darwin and Alice Springs, often experience incredibly hot weather in summer which you may find intolerable. The weather in Perth, Adelaide and Sydney is often compared to the Mediterranean while Tasmania has a much cooler climate. Recent floods and cyclones in Queensland, the Northern Territory and Western Australia, biting winds throughout the southern states and weather warnings in Victoria may not be your idea of 'sunny Oz'.

Australia offers retirement destinations all over the country. However, under current visa restrictions, you should take into consideration the areas that the Department of Immigration and Multicultural Affairs (DIMA) has nominated as possible stopping places. These areas are currently all of South Australia, the Northern Territory and Tasmania; New South Wales, except Sydney, Newcastle, the Central Coast and Wollongong; Queensland, except the greater Brisbane area and the Gold Coast; Victoria, except Melbourne metropolitan area; and Western Australia, except Perth and surrounding areas. Eligible postcodes for these areas are available at www.immi.gov.au/migration/skilled/regional.

Other areas attracting retirees include the seaside towns of Port Macquarie, Nelson Bay and Merimbula in New South Wales; Hervey Bay in Queensland; Victor Harbour in South Australia; Echuca and Yarrawonga in Victoria. According to a survey compiled by Deakin University, Wide Bay in Queensland emerged as place where people are the most content. Wide Bay, which takes in the coast of Hervey Bay and the World Heritage-listed Fraser Island, has topped a recent poll for well-being and sense of community.

The top nine electorates for well-being were Wide Bay, Richmond (NSW), Eden-Monaro (NSW), Ryan (Queensland), Higgins, Bendigo (Victoria), Murray (Victoria), Riverina (NSW), and Mayo (South Australia).

The bottom nine were Sydney, Parramatta (NSW), Perth (WA), Gorton (Victoria), Hasluck (WA), Werriwa (NSW), Reid (NSW), Rankin (Qld) and Grayndler (NSW).

Victoria was the happiest state and WA was the saddest, scoring lowest in terms of sense of community and the most insecure future.

Other Considerations

Leisure Facilities. Depending on what your leisure interests are – golf, sailing, skiing, equestrianism, water sports or bridge, how close are the nearest facilities? Many of the town councils can provide a new residents' kit for clubs, community services and other interest groups.

Planning for the Future. The British Consulate advises people to look ahead when considering where to buy their retirement home. While it may be ideal to live in a beautiful but remote spot in your fifties and early sixties, as you get older the long trek to the nearest shops and amenities may become a real burden. You should also consider the provision of medical facilities in the area where you are hoping to buy.

Security. Talk to the local police about high crime areas and neighbourhood watch schemes.

Part-time work. You may wish to find part-time or voluntary work so make sure it's viable in your area. If you want to start a small business most local real estate agents know of local businesses for sale.

Noise. Check that neighbours are not incompatible as this can cause major unrest.

REGIONAL GUIDE

AUSTRALIAN CAPITAL TERRITORY (ACT)

Area: 900 square miles (2,330 sq km)
British-born residents who have chosen this region: 17,210 (2001 census)
Capital: Canberra
Median house price: $361,000
Airport: Canberra International Airport, 6 miles (10 km) east of the city
Tourist office website: www.canberratourism.com.au

The Australian Capital Territory (ACT) is the smallest of Australia's regions and 53% of it is nature park or reserve. The ACT is completely surrounded by New South Wales and has a population of 322,900.

Canberra, designed by Chicago-born architect Walter Burley Griffin, is the seat of the Australian government with Capital Hill (the site of Parliament House) its centrepiece. Situated on the ancient lands of the indigenous Ngunnawal people, Canberra's name means 'meeting place' from the Aboriginal word Kamberra. It has wide streets and a mixture of museums, galleries, shopping, restaurant, wineries, and entertainment.

The Canberra Hospital (☎02-6244 2222) and Calvary Public Hospital (☎02-6201 6111) deliver acute and speciality care; while Community Health (☎02-6207 9977) provides community-based health services. At Health First (☎02-6207 7777) you can speak to a registered nurse 24 hours a day, seven days a week.

The city is home to the National Library of Australia (www.nla.gov.au) and the Public Library (☎02-6205 9000), which also operates a Mobile and Home Library. Action (☎02-6207 7611; www.action.act.gov.au) provides public transport and CountryLink (☎13 22 32; www.countrylink.info) offers train and coach services. Other regular coach services can be found at www.visitcanberra.com.au.

The city is also home to some great sporting venues: Bruce Stadium (rugby), Manuka Oval (cricket), Tuggeranong Southern Cross Stadium (five-aside indoor soccer) and the Hockey Centre.

Typical Properties for Sale in the Australian Capital Territory			
Location	Type	Description	Price
Spence	Duplex	3 bedrooms. Built-in cupboards. Landscaped back garden. Adjoining reserve.	$305,000
Narrabunda	Unit	2 bedrooms. Slate flooring, living room opens on to balcony. Located just above golf course.	$295,000
Yarralumla	House	3 bedrooms, two bathrooms, open plan kitchen, wine cellar. Private and secure, close to village centre. Close to the lake.	$785,000

NEW SOUTH WALES (NSW)

Area: 309,130 square miles (800,643sq km)

British-born residents who have chosen this region: 275,740 (2001)

Capital: Sydney

Other main cities/towns: Gosford, Newcastle, Parramatta, Wollongong

Median house price: $520,000

Airport: Sydney Airport, 6 miles (10 km) south of the city.

Tourist office website: www.visitnsw.com.au

New South Wales (NSW) is seven times the size of the UK, makes up 10% of Australia's land mass and has a population of 8.7 million. It is the economic powerhouse of the country and is a popular destination for migrants.

Sydney is Australia's largest and most expensive city with a population of 4.23 million. However, recent reports state that its population growth is lagging behind that of Brisbane and Melbourne because some people are leaving to escape inflated property prices. It is a multicultural city and boasts the Sydney Opera House, Harbour, Bridge and golden beaches. It is also well known for some of the best wines Australia has to offer, great restaurants and a lively arts scene.

Healthcare is readily available in the state with a total of 84 private hospitals, 229 public hospitals and 280 community health centres. Two of the top ten busiest hospitals in Australia are in NSW: Westwood Hospital (3rd) and Liverpool Hospital (10th). You can find your area health service at www.health.nsw.gov.au.

CityRail trains provide an extensive service throughout Sydney and the suburbs, as well as further afield. CountryLink has a comprehensive rail and coach service throughout the region as well as direct trains to Melbourne and Brisbane. Information on regional transport services can be obtained from the Transport Infoline (☎13 15 00; www.131500.com.au).

RETIREMENT HOTSPOTS

Bowral: In the southern highlands, south-west of Sydney. It has a range of medical professionals and dentists, a public and private hospital. Rail connections to Sydney, Melbourne and Queanbeyan. There are many golf courses in and around Bowral, including the Bowral Country Club Golf Course and Bowral Golf Course. If you have an interest in the history of cricket, visit the Bradman Oval and Museum

Nelson Bay: On the heads of Port Stephens, north of Sydney, close to the Hunter Valley. Limited healthcare services. There is a golf and bowling club and the town hosts an annual food and wine festival. Other activities in the area include snorkelling, parasailing and dolphin watching.

Port Macquarie: Discovered in 1818, it is situated on the north coast. Good medical facilities at the Port Macquarie Base Hospital and Port Macquarie Private. Daily flights to Sydney from its commercial airport and regular bus services. There are two golf courses and two bowling clubs.

Merimbula: Situated on the south coast, Merimbula offers boating, fishing, surfing, swimming, walking and whale-watching. It has a commercial airport, a number of doctors and dentists, a golf course and a bowling club.

Typical Properties for Sale in New South Wales			
Location	Type	Description	Price
Beecroft	Split level home	3 bedrooms, en suite, lounge and dining area. Within walking distance of shops and transport.	$585,000
Bowral	Townhouse	3 bedrooms, 2 bathrooms, lounge with bay window. Easy walk to town. Distant views to golf course and Oxley Hill.	$455,000
Manly	Modern studio	One bathroom, large sunny balcony. Security parking. Located in the heart of cosmopolitan Manly.	$329,000

NORTHERN TERRITORY (NT)

Area: 519,768 square miles (1,346,200 sq km)

British-born residents who have chosen this region: 6,770 (2001 census)

Capital: Darwin

Other main cities/towns: Alice Springs, Katherine, Tennant Creek

Median house price: $279,000

Airport: Darwin Airport, 7 miles (12 km) from the city

Tourist office website: www.nt.gov.au

Extending from the tropical waters of the Arafura Sea in the north to the Simpson Desert in central Australia, the Northern Territory focuses on indigenous Australia. It is home to the real Outback and has the iconic monolith Uluru (Ayers Rock) in its Red Centre. The Kakadu National Park has prolific wildlife and awe-inspiring Aboriginal art sites.

It is one of the fastest growing economies in Australia with the smallest population of only 200,800 people. Tourism is one of its highest income generators with Aboriginal art and culture, geographical features, flora and fauna being key attractions for visitors. Darwin is both modern and sophisticated and often referred to as the 'multicultural capital of Australia.'

The Royal Darwin Hospital and Darwin Private Hospital have a range of general practitioners and local visiting specialists, health clinics and dentists. Private medical specialists, GPs, allied health practitioners and other agencies provide healthcare and family support services. The Royal Flying Doctor Service and the Aerial Medical Service provide emergency and routine care to people in remote areas.

Darwin Bus and Abbus provide a public transport network to Darwin and

Alice Springs respectively. More information on routes, fares and concessions is available at www.dpi.nt.gov.au. The Ghan, www.gsr.com.au, operates weekly rail return services from Adelaide to Darwin and twice weekly to Alice Springs.

RETIREMENT HOTSPOT

Palmerston: A thriving, satellite town 12 miles (20 km) from Darwin. There is a public bus service operating around Palmerston and into Darwin. Boating is available on the Elizabeth River and there is a gym and Olympic size swimming pool.

Typical Properties for Sale in the Northern Territory

Location	Type	Description	Price
Roseberry	New home	4 bedrooms, 2 bathrooms, well-appointed kitchen, walk-in wardrobe. Double garage.	$445,000
Driver	Unit in small complex of four	2 bedrooms, gallery-style kitchen. Short stroll to golf course, parks and local shopping center.	$189,000
Darwin	Off-plan apartment	2 bedrooms, 2 bathrooms, en suite. Secure complex. Close to CBD.	$299,000

QUEENSLAND (QLD)

Area: 665,611 square miles (1,723,936 sq km)
British-born residents who have chosen this region: 177,760 (2001 census)
Capital: Brisbane
Other main cities/towns: Cairns, Mt Isa, Mackay, Rockhampton, Maryborough
Median house price: $350,000
Airport: Brisbane Airport, 9 miles (15 km) north-east of the city centre
Tourist office website: www.tq.com.au

The 'Sunshine State' of Queensland has a population of 3.9 million and is attracting migrants at unprecedented rates. It is renowned for its laid-back lifestyle and sub-tropical to tropical climate. It includes one of the wonders of the world, the 1,242-mile (2,000-km) Great Barrier Reef. Figures show that southeast Queensland continues to boom, growing by 53,300 people, or more than a 1,000 a week.

Brisbane remains the fastest-growing city, with a growth rate of 1.9%, while coastal regions continued to lure those in search of the much-touted 'sea change.' Caloundra, north of Brisbane, grew by 2,800 and Cairns by 3,000 people. Cosmopolitan Brisbane is the heart of the state's cuisine, arts, cultural, sports and tourism scene.

The state has a high quality and cost efficient public and private health system. The public transport system combines train, bus and ferries underpinning an excellent road, rail and river infrastructure.

RETIREMENT HOTSPOTS

Toowoomba: Inland from Brisbane and known as the 'Garden City' of Queensland. It has many practising doctors living in the area and is served by four private and public hospitals. Travel is mainly by car and bus; no rail links as yet. The *Toowoomba Chronicle* is published daily. It has many sports clubs, three golf courses, 11 bowling clubs and bushwalking and fishing opportunities.

Yeppoon: On the coast, north of Brisbane, it sits on the same latitude climate belt as Rio de Janeiro and Acapulco. The golf courses have grazing kangaroos and low-flying pelicans. The champion golfer Wayne Grady has his golf course as the centrepiece of the Great Barrier Reef Resort Village. The area also offers bowls, tennis and sailing clubs; private and public hospitals, doctors and dentists.

Hervey Bay: Discovered by Captain James Cook in 1770, Hervey Bay has 8 miles (14 km) of golden beaches. Public facilities are constantly being upgraded. There is also good fishing, as well as golf, bowls, tennis, horse riding and sea kayaking.

Typical Properties for Sale in Queensland

Location	Type	Description	Price
Hervey Bay	House	3 bedrooms, 1 bathroom, ceramic tiles throughout open plan living area. Close to marina.	$290,000
Gaythorne	Villa	2 bedrooms, 1 bathroom, open plan living. Boutique development of only three. Landscaped gardens. Close walking distance to bowling club and shopping centre.	$282,000
Maleny	Country house	3 bedrooms, 2 bathrooms. Single garage and single carport. Located in the Sunshine Coast Hinterland.	$410,000

SOUTH AUSTRALIA (SA)

Area: 380,068 square miles (984,377 sq km)
British-born residents who have chosen this region: 126,080 (2001)
Capital: Adelaide
Other main cities/towns: Mt Gambier, Whyalla, Port Augusta
Median house price: $252,500
Airport: Adelaide Airport, 4 miles (7 km) from the city.
Tourist office website: www.southaustralia.com

South Australia is Australia's third largest state and has a stunning coastline of 2,371 miles (3,816 km), unspoilt beaches and, although barely the height of Ben Nevis in Scotland, the rugged Flinders Ranges. It is the headquarters of the Australian wine industry, producing a great range of wines from its 17 wine regions, such as the Barossa Valley, and more than 270 cellar doors. Many cultural, music and food festival are held across the state.

Adelaide is a city of more than one million people (of the total 1.5 million population), a city which cherishes its relaxed, cosmopolitan way of life as much as its backdrop of hills and parkland settings. Says expat Mike Osborne:

We live near Adelaide because my wife found the city so sympathetic. Where else in the world can one live in semi-rural surroundings, yet be a 25-minute drive from the centre of the city of one million inhabitants: theatres, museums, art galleries, very good restaurants, and an airport with some international connections.

A comprehensive range of medical and paramedical services are available through the network of public, private, community, religious and other general hospitals. Adelaide Metro (☎08-8210 1000; www.adelaidemetro.com.au) provides metropolitan bus, train and tram services. Bus SA (www.bussa.com.au) can give you details of the regional bus network operators. Mike Osborne describes his local area:

We live in Ardrossan on the Yorke Peninsula, 150 km by road from Adelaide. It has a population of about 1,100 people. A coastal town with lots of facilities – hospitals, schools and all the shops you usually need. It's a working town with lots of farming and some light industrial work. Climate is good, rates cheap and the area is safe: little in the way of crime. Folk are wholesome and the majority hard working, taking you for what you are, not just for what you've got.

RETIREMENT HOTSPOTS

Victor Harbour: On the southern side of the Fleurieu Peninsula. Once a key centre for whaling, Victor Harbour now offers golf, bowls, croquet, tennis and diving. It has two local wineries: Scott's Victor Harbour Winery and Duredons, both open for tasting and sales. There is a daily train service from Adelaide, a public library, and a couple of Lions and Rotary clubs.

Typical Properties for Sale in South Australia

Location	Type	Description	Price
Victor Harbour	Apartment	2 bedrooms, 1 bathroom, on the ground floor. Minutes to main street, shopping center and beach.	$136,000
Onkaparinga Hills	House	3 bedrooms, master bedroom en suite, built in wardrobe and opens onto a rear garden. Open plan living.	$320,000
Woodville North	Unit	2 bedrooms, gas kitchen. Carport and shed. Close to shopping and easy transport.	$175,000

TASMANIA (TAS)

Area: 26,382 miles (68,331 sq km)
British-born residents who have chosen this region: 21,800 (2001)
Capital: Hobart
Other main cities/towns: Burnie, Devonport, Launceston
Median house price: $252,000
Airport: Hobart International Airport, 13 miles (22 km) from the city
Tourist office website: www.discovertasmania.com.au

'If I was obliged to emigrate I certainly should prefer this place," Charles Darwin, 1836.

Tasmania is Australia's smallest but most mountainous state and is separated from the mainland by the 149-mile (240-km) stretch of Bass Strait. It is an archipelago of more than 300 islands and about 40% is set aside in the Tasmanian Wilderness World Heritage Area of national parks and state and coastal reserves. The area alone encompasses 1,976,840 acres (800,000 ha).

Hobart is the country's second oldest city and its population of 220,000 (484,000 total population) enjoy its culture, lifestyle, heritage and wealth of cafés, bars and, restaurants.

Migration into the state has escalated because property has remained so affordable. This is particularly evident in Launceston where the median price jumped by about $20,000 in 2005.

A range of hospital-based treatment and care is provided at the Royal Hobart Hospital, Launceston General Hospital and the North West Hospital in Burnie. The state has an excellent public infrastructure, a well-developed internal transport system and reliable air and sea links. The *Spirit of Tasmania* ferries carry passengers and vehicles on daily services across the Bass Strait. Passenger bus services are offered by Mersey Link Bus Service (☎03-6423 3231; www.merseylink.com.au); Redline Coaches (☎1300 360 000; www. redlinecoaches.com.au); and Tassielink Regional Coaches (☎03-6231 6090; www.tigerline.com.au).

RETIREMENT HOTSPOTS

Hotspots include the traditional inner-suburban areas of Battery Point, West Hobart and South Hobart and other suburbs such as Moonah, Lutana and Geilston Bay, East Launceston, and some areas in Ivermay, Devonport, Burnie and Sandy Bay. According to the Real Estate Institute Tasmania (REIT), places such as Mountain River, Latrobe, Mount Nelson and Smithton are likely to continue being Tasmania's areas of growth.

Typical Properties for Sale in Tasmania

Location	Type	Description	Price
Launceston	House	Built in 1919. 4 bedrooms, en suite. Private courtyard garden. 5-minute walk to CBD, parks and shopping centre.	$495,000
Battery Point	Townhouse	Georgian-style. 3 bedrooms, 2 bathrooms. Double carport. Cottage garden.	$730,000
Burnie	House	3 bedrooms, 1 bathroom, sun-filled lounge, smart kitchen. Built on elevated block with outstanding urban and sea views. Convenient to city; quite, private location.	$189,000

VICTORIA (VIC)

Area: 87,876 square miles (227,600 sq km)
British-born residents who have chosen this region: 209,080 (2001)
Capital: Melbourne
Other main cities/towns: Ballarat, Bendigo, Geelong, Hamilton, Horsham
Median house price: $357,000
Airport: Melbourne Airport, 15 miles (25 km) from the city
Tourist office website: www.visitvictoria.com

Victoria is roughly the size of the UK but Australia's second smallest state, covering only 3% of the continent's land mass with a population of 5 million. It has a wealth of attractions, national parks and forests, lakes and mountains and 14 wine regions making up more than 350 wineries.

Melbourne is Australia's second largest city and is situated on the Yarra River. It is known as Australia's cosmopolitan capital and has a sense of style, elegance and colonial heritage. The city hosts glamorous festivals and events, shopping, arts, eating and drinking. According to expat Jane Knight:

Melbourne is an exciting and vibrant place to live in as there is always something going on.

Melbourne's Hotspots

Cape Schanck, Lovely Banks, Waurn Ponds, San Remo, Sunderland Bay and Point Lonsdale are all being driven by the sea change trend. In its hill change locations, Cockatoo and Emerald, both close to Dandenong Ranges and Wright Forest, have seen significant growth. Other high performers included Doreen and Mickleham. In terms of units, Point Lonsdale and San Remo ranked in the top 20, joined by other seaside suburbs Dromana, Safety Beach, Newtown and Whittington.
Source: API Magazine

Regular health services are available in regional Victoria and Melbourne. The city also has a tram network, stretching 155 miles (250 km) across this elegant, colonial conurbation. It boasts glamorous festival and events, shopping, the arts, eating and drinking.

RETIREMENT HOTSPOTS

Echuca: Meaning 'meeting of the waters', Echuca is a thriving port. It has a hospital in the town and a rail and bus service to and from Melbourne. The Back Nine Golf Course is situated on the Campaspe River and there is a bowling club in the town.

Typical Properties for Sale in Victoria

Location	Type	Description	Price
Ehuca	Unit	2 bedrooms, 1 bathroom, lounge, kitchen/dining. Garage and private courtyard. Close to shops, sporting grounds, swimming pool and transport.	$239,000
Carlton	Apartment	2 bedrooms, lounge on north-facing balcony. Within walking distance of fashionable Carlton city.	$420,000
Newport	House	3 bedrooms, 2 toilets, modern kitchen. Within minutes of city. Quiet location, opposite Newport Lakes reserve and close to golf course.	$360,000

WESTERN AUSTRALIA (WA)

Area: 975,592 square miles (2,526,786 sq km)

British-born residents who have chosen this region: 201,950 (2001)

Capital: Perth

Other main cities/towns: Albany, Broome, Bunbury, Carnarvon, Coolgardie, Geraldton, Mandurah, Northam, Port Hedland

Median house price: $250,000

Airport: Perth Airport, 12 miles (20 km) east of the city

Tourist office website: www.westernaustralia.com

Western Australia is the largest of Australia's six states, covering about one third of the continent from north to south. Hundreds of people relocate to Western Australia, especially its capital city Perth, on a permanent basis. Over the past year, it has recorded the second highest level of population growth, after Queensland. The population is two million with Perth itself exceeding 1.8 million. Brits are Perth's largest migrant group making up 12.4% of the population.

Much of Perth has been built in very recent times but it is the world's most isolated city. It also ranks as one of the best locations in the world for quality of life. It has 900 acres (364 ha) of bushland in the centre of the city, excellent restaurants and a smattering of galleries and museums.

Perth has recorded the highest overall house price growth rate of Australia's capital cities while the suburbs of Mandurah and Rockingham are also booming, along with Singleton, Bunbury, Busselton and Broome.

The state has 93 public hospitals; more information is available from the Department of Health (www.health.wa.gov.au). There are many transport services operating in the various regions, towns and cities. Transperth (☎13 62 13; www.transperth.wa.gov.au), provides public transport in the Perth metro area. Great Southern Railways (www.gsr.com.au) operates the Indian Pacific rail journey from Sydney to Adelaide to Perth, twice a week in both directions. For more information on all public transport services contact the Public Transport Authority (☎08-9326 2000; www.pta.wa.gov.au).

RETIREMENT HOTSPOT

Mandurah: Located in the Peel Region, it is one of the fastest growing regional cities in WA. There are many medical and dental clinics in the region and there are bus services between Perth and Mandurah's main towns. Fishing and sailing plays an important part in recreational activities, as does golf. The area is known as the 'golf coast of Australia.'

Typical Properties for Sale in Western Australia

Location	Type	Description	Price
Perth	Apartment	2 bedrooms, 1 bathroom, on ground floor. Real timber floors throughout. Security parking.	$369,000
Kiara	House	4 bedrooms, 2 bathrooms, games room. Quiet street.	$460,000
Mandurah	Two-storey house	4 bedrooms, 2 bathrooms, walk in wardrobe. Stunning water views. Peace and quite, located in Mandurah Quay.	$769,000

Your New Home in Australia

CHAPTER SUMMARY

○ The property market in Australia is in a period of transition after a boom cycle.

○ Any foreign person wishing to buy residential property in the country must first seek approval from the Foreign Investment Review Board (FIRB).

○ The best way of finding a property is through local newspapers, real estate agents, auctions, housing journals or the internet.

○ Due consideration should be given to the type of property, whether it be a unit, villa, townhouse or self-build.

○ Everyone's talking about the 'new' retirement and many retirement villages in Australia have embraced this shift into active and independent lifestyles.

○ Typical fees in purchasing a property include valuation, survey reports, conveyancing, stamp duty, inspection and insurance.

○ The concept of 'chains' does not exist in the property market in Australia.

○ Swimming pools are a delight but maintenance can take up a lot of time.

○ Figures show that 29% of Australians rent their homes and 13% of older people live in rented accommodation.

OVERVIEW OF THE AUSTRALIAN PROPERTY MARKET

The Paris-based Organisation for Economic Cooperation and Development (OECD), recently claimed that Australia's house prices are seriously overvalued (by as much as 52%). This angered many property commentators and homebuyers, who believe that the Australian property market is influenced by three factors: demographic trends, supply and demand trends and land-to-asset ratio, which the OECD did not take into account. According to the Real Estate Institute of Australia (REIA), house prices rose at unprecedented rates from about mid-2002 through to about mid-2004 and then moderated.

During 2005, the property market was in a period of transition with some markets booming, others steady and some flat or declining. Demand for residential property was strong in Darwin and Perth reflecting the stable economies in the Northern Territory and Western Australia. Buoyed by its resources boom and an increase in migration, Western Australia was by far the best performing state in terms of median house price growth. The current Australian median house price is $394,531.

After years of little growth in property values, the Northern Territory was second off the block and entered into a boom cycle, spurred on by an increase in mining activity and some major infrastructure improvements. Queensland, on the whole, held up reasonably well, with regional centres in particular riding high and helping to keep median prices up.

Overall the New South Wales property market declined even though the state government axed the controversial vendor tax. Victoria remained stable with a few areas performing above the norm. More investment is expected in Victoria as people realise how affordable it is.

Tasmania is in a period of stabilisation after a property boom of proportions never experienced before. Some regional areas of South Australia and parts of Adelaide performed well while the state on the whole was fairly flat. The Australian Capital Territory and Canberra showed a decline in prices.

According to REIA, following a slowdown in house prices in Sydney, Melbourne, Canberra and Brisbane, prices began to ease off in Adelaide, Darwin, Hobart and regional areas. Prices in Perth have continued to climb, demand remains high, and the Australia New Zealand Bank (ANZ) predicts that an estimated 163,000 dwellings a year are required to satisfy this demand for housing.

The sea change phenomenon is far from being old news in Australia as droves of people continue to move closer to the coast. One million Australians are expected to move to coastal locations in the next 15 years. One of the problems with the sea change phenomenon is that in some cases the pace for growth and population change is outpacing the development of new infrastructure. Sixty forward-thinking councils have joined forces to deal with what they've dubbed the 'sea change challenge' in a direct response to the crowding of the country's coastline. New South Wales, Queensland, South Australia, Tasmania, Victoria and Western Australia have formed the national Sea Change Task Force to develop policies to protect the coastal environment and establish sustainable limits to growth.

Almost 20% of the nation now lives on the provincial coast in cities such as New South Wales's Tweed Heads, Queensland's Hervey Bay, South Australia's Victor Harbor, Tasmania's Latrobe, Victoria's Bass Coast and Western Australia's Mandurah.

Remember: there are always more properties on the market during winter and early spring. However, there is the same number of buyers about and demand for property is greater, which in turn generates higher prices. Properties with water frontage are worth two to three times more and anything that's on a golf course will have a price $50,000 above a non-golf course lot.

The Housing Industry Association's figures showed the sale of new homes and units increased by 1.2% in December 2005 to 8,053 dwellings. Sales of new houses rose by 2.6%, while the sale of multi-unit dwellings fell by 7.8%.

Since Sydney's property peak in 2002, it is now experiencing its longest decline yet with a four-year 20% to 25% fall in its dwelling prices. The fall began because Sydney dwellings had risen too high too fast and nervous banks began squeezing prospective buyers. Sydney has not encouraged migrants and the recent Cronulla riots may underline the trend. This decline has meant a rising demand for rental accommodation and Sydney rents are increasing.

House prices in Perth are now more expensive than those in both Melbourne and Brisbane following West Australia's five-year resources-led property boom. The median price of a house in Perth is now $363,000, behind only Sydney ($518,000) and Canberra ($409,500).

Australia Property Monitors estimates that the price of a house in Sydney has fallen by 5.1% over the past year, while prices in Perth have soared by 18.7%. House prices in other capitals have risen between 2% and 2.6%.

The price falls that have occurred in Sydney, together with stable or increasing prices in other capitals, have brought price relativities between Sydney and the other capitals back to the pre-boom levels of the early to mid-1990s, says the Reserve Bank of Australia.

Interest rates have been relatively stable at low rates, increasing by only 1.25% since December 2001. The REIA has called for 'ineffective and inequitable state property taxes to be abolished': some state governments rely on property taxes to collect up to 30% of total state taxes.

Median house prices (March 2006)

Canberra $368,000	Adelaide $277,000
Darwin $328,000	Hobart $276,500
Sydney $518,000	Melbourne $375,000
Brisbane $320,000	Perth $325,000

Other dwellings (flats/units/townhouses) median prices

Canberra $289,000	Adelaide $210,000
Darwin $242,000	Hobart $185,000
Sydney $358,000	Melbourne $307,000
Brisbane $266,000	Perth $258,000

BUYING A PROPERTY: RULES FOR FOREIGNERS

Any foreign person wanting to buy residential property in Australia must first seek approval from the Foreign Investment Review Board (FIRB), ☎02-6263 9795; www.firb.gov.au. Residential real estate in Australia means all urban land other than commercial properties. Acquisitions of 'hobby farms' and 'rural residential' blocks by foreign interests are included in the residential real estate category.

Foreign persons can buy second-hand property but they must live in it as their principal place of residence, they must not rent it out and they must sell it when they leave the country. You have to be in possession of a temporary visa valid for more than 12 months to purchase second-hand real estate.

You can also purchase a newly built dwelling (house and land package) provided no one's ever lived in the house. An off-the-plan purchase is also possible provided no more than 50% of the dwellings have been sold to foreign people. For all of the above FIRB approval is still required. You can live in a newly built house and an off-the-plan purchase, or leave it empty, and you won't have to sell it when you leave. You can also buy vacant land but must make an undertaking to commence continuous construction of something on the land within 12 months and you must spend more than 50% of the cost of the real estate on construction.

FIRB is required to make an approval decision within 30 days of receiving an application and have up to another 20 days to advise the parties of its decision. It is therefore usual to make the contract subject to obtaining the board's approval, where necessary, within 45 days from the date of the contract. A full outline on Australia's investment policy and an application form for straightforward residential real estate proposals can be obtained from the FIRB.

For properties to be purchased at auction, prior foreign investment approval must still be obtained and advice provided whether the parties were successful or not. If the auction is successful, a copy of the signed contract must be forwarded to the FIRB afterwards.

The reason you need approval is that the Australian Government believes that foreign investment in the housing sector should increase the supply of homes and should not be speculative in nature. Foreigners cannot normally get approval to buy houses, flats or units, which have been occupied. This is because Australia's foreign investment policy is designed to increase the supply of new housing.

You should not sign contracts before you receive foreign investment approval, unless the contract is conditional on such approval. The Australian Government cannot give approval after you have signed the contract.

If you don't get the necessary approval beforehand, you may have to cancel the contract or sell your new property. You may also be fined or imprisoned if you:

o Provide false or misleading information;
o Don't comply with a development condition;
o Buy a property after your application has been rejected; and
o Didn't apply for approval and your purchase was inconsistent with Australia's foreign investment policy.

If you are a foreigner and your Australian grandmother or uncle left you a unit or a house in their will, then the title to that property can be transferred to you without notifying FIRB nor do you have to seek its approval.

Australia's legal system is based on the English system, so the process of buying property is quite easy. In addition, the exchange rates between the two countries means buying in Australia can seem very cheap indeed.

FINDING A PROPERTY

The most common way of finding a suitable property whether in a rural, regional or metropolitan area is through newspapers. Local and metropolitan newspapers list properties for sale, inspection and auction times, estate agents, contacts and auction results. Apart from this, the easiest way to look for a home is through a real estate agency.

Register your name and requirements with an estate agent and ask them to let you know when a suitable property comes up. Give them precise details otherwise they may show you properties they are finding difficult to sell. These agencies do not charge for their services because the seller pays the agent's commission. However, they are only paid when a sale is made so usually the level of service often depends on whether they think you are a serious buyer or not.

You can also do your own research and buy privately. Find out what houses are 'open for inspection' in your local paper. Visiting these will give you a good idea of the sort of properties available and travelling around in the area you've chosen will give you a feel for what it's like.

Other sources are real estate industry magazines, and lifestyle programmes. Also, talk to builders who are putting up houses in the areas you have short-listed, as they may know of new properties for sale or the value of properties in the areas. Consider attending real estate seminars and auctions or popping into an 'open house.'

Real estate groups advertise through journals such as *Homes Pictorial* and *The Realtor*, which are published regularly. They are available from real estate agents and contain photographs and illustrations of properties available. Landcom (☎02-9629 2999; www.landcom.com.au) and other developers also publish brochures about their estates and land and housing packages.

Real Estate Institutes

Real Estate Institute of Australia (REIA): ☎02-6282 4277; www.reia.com.au.

Real Estate Institute of ACT (REIACT): ☎02-6282 4544; e-mail reiact@reiact.com.au; www.reiact.com.au.

Real Estate Institute of NSW (REINSW): ☎02-9264 2343; e-mail info@reinsw.com.au; www.reinsw.com.au.

Real Estate Institute of the Northern Territory (REINT): ☎08-8981 8905; e-mail info@reint.com.au; www.reint.com.au.

Real Estate Institute of Queensland (REIQ): ☎07-3249 7347; e-mail publicaffairs@ reiq.com.au; www.reiq.com.au.

Real Estate Institute of South Australia (REISA): ☎09-8366 4301; e-mail executive@ reisa.com.au; www.reisa.com.au.

Real Estate Institute of Tasmania (REIT): ☎03-6223 4769; e-mail admin@reit.com.au; www.reit.com.au.

Real Estate Institute of Victoria (REIV): ☎03-9205 6666; e-mail reiv@reiv.com.au; www.reiv.com.au.

Real Estate Institute of Western Australia (REIWA): ☎08-9380 8222; e-mail admin@reiwa.com.au; www.reiwa.com.au.

Other Sources

An excellent source for property prices, movements and trends is the monthly *Australian PropertyInvestor* magazine, published by Australian Commercial Publishing (Suite 902, Level 9, Toowong Tower, 9 Sherwood Road, Toowong, QLD 4066; ☎07-3720 9422; e-mail admin@apimagazine.com.au; www.apimagazine.com.au). It is available from newsagents or direct from the publishers. Costs $8.95 a copy, or $149 for a 12-month subscription ($189 internationally).

Australian Property Magazine, www.austprop.com.au, lists properties for sale and to rent.

www.realestate.com.au and **www.realestateview.com.au** are good national sites where you can search for properties by suburb and price range.

Australia PropertyWeb list properties for sale, for auction and for lease across Australia.

For more information, check the Home Purchase Assistance Authority (an agency of the New South Wales Department of Housing) at www.hpaa.nsw.gov.au.

Auctions

Auctions are another way of buying a property. It is a well-established and proven practice and represents about 20% of all sales across Australia. At an auction, bidders make an unconditional offer, so the sale is fairly certain. Most properties for sale at auction have a reserve price. If yours is the successful bid, you will be required to pay the deposit (usually 10% of the purchase price) on the spot. If you are nervous about bidding, you can ask someone else to bid on your behalf.

There is no national code of practice as far as auctions are concerned because laws relating to the real estate industry are state-based and therefore vary from one state to another. State real estate institutes have a code of practice to which their members are obliged to adhere and may offer specific guidelines for auctions.

Changes to the Australian auction system were made in July 2005. Vendors can now bid at an auction where previously they were unable to do so. A vendor bid is a counter bid made by the auctioneer to ensure a property reaches a price at which it can be sold. In most states and territories, vendor bids and the identity of the bidder must be declared before the auction commences, or each time such a bid is made.

There is some dummy bidding or false bidding at an auction by non-genuine bidders in the crowd with no real intention to buy the property and without adequate disclosure of their interest. Legislation is being put in place by most states and territories to prohibit misleading and deceptive practices, such as dummy bidding. In NSW, legislation includes the provision to impose fines of up to $55,000 for people who make 'dummy' or 'false' bids.

All bidders at auctions will have to be registered in a bidders record for the auction. Once registered, bidders must be given a number to display when bidding. Auctioneers can only accept a bid from a person who is registered. The advantages of an auction are:

○ Inspections of the property are conducted in a well-organised manner.
○ The process of interested persons bidding for the property may result in a realistic price being set by the community and not by the seller.
○ The successful bid is known at the fall of the hammer.
○ If the reserve price is not reached, the highest bidder has the first option to negotiate with the seller through their agent.
○ If a bid is accepted, the contracts are exchanged on the spot.

WHAT TYPE OF PROPERTY?

Due consideration should be given to the type of home to buy. Running and upkeep of a large property may become a hindrance and, therefore, a unit or townhouse may be less demanding than a house with garden. In many towns and cities, houses are still detached and there is little in the way of two-storey accommodation. Proximity to facilities and the availability of public transport are also important to your decision-making.

Units, Villas or Townhouses

Villas and townhouses are built on smaller individual blocks of land, which can mean substantial savings and make it possible to live in a more convenient location closer to facilities. They can have common walls or be detached and provide a small private outdoor area or garden space. Firstly, you should check the layout of adjoining units and the proximity of neighbours. Car parking space should be registered on the title but this is not always the case, so it's advisable to make enquiries. Also, find out if it is a carport or a lock-up garage. Don't assume that unit numbers correspond to car spaces or garage numbers, or that any free space is available for your visitors.

You can buy units and townhouses off-plan, which means buying a property before it is built. If you opt for buying off-plan, a conveyancer or solicitor should check the terms and conditions of the contract to ensure that what is in the plan is the same as the property you are buying. To ensure that you are getting value for money, find out the cost of similar properties in the area and how much values have gone up in recent years. The following disadvantages may apply when buying off-plan:

○ Sales may take place prior to approval of the development application from the local council;
○ Standard of workmanship is not guaranteed;
○ The builder may change the plans before building begins; and
○ The contract has to be signed and the deposit paid with a waiting period before completion and settlement (which may be two to three years).

Self-Build

You should take into account available amenities when deciding on the location of the land you wish to purchase. Consider the availability, adequacy and cost of connecting and maintaining services such as water, electricity, gas, telephone, sewerage, and fire control. Check if the site is subject to flood restrictions.

A main roads search will show you if any roads that are not council concerns are to be constructed near your new purchase, which could affect the value of your property. Also a contaminated land search will show if there is a mine shaft under your property or if there has been a spill of contaminated waste on your property in the past.

The actual boundaries of your land need to be determined and a registered surveyor should be consulted to check and peg these. If you buy land and then build a home, stamp duty is only payable on the purchase price of the land. You have several choices as to how to build your home and each has its own advantages and disadvantages.

House and land package. Can be purchased through Landcom or from a private owner/developer. When you purchase through Landcom you require a $100 deposit to reserve a block of land. You then approach a builder for a price to build the house design of your choice. Within seven days a tender letter should be received from the builder. You then take the tender letter with plans and specifications to your lender.

If the lender does not approve the loan, Landcom will refund the $100 deposit. If approved, you will need to pay a deposit to the builder for the preparation or working drawings and specifications. This deposit can range from $800 to $2,000. It is usually non-refundable and includes payment of Council charges and fees to other relevant authorities.

After 30 days, customers with loan approval are expected to exchange contracts on the land amounting to the balance of 5% of its value. The land is usually settled 30 days after exchange with the funds coming from your lending body. A deposit (usually 10% of the purchase price) is paid on the house and land package; contracts are signed and exchanged, with the balance of the purchase being paid at settlement.

Project Home. Some companies are volume home builders and build many new homes a year. They range from basic budget to upmarket designs. These houses are often offered at reasonable prices compared with custom builders. You can view samples of these homes at home display villages where you can choose the type that best suits your budget and needs. Find out exactly what is included in the home as any changes required by you after construction may be expensive and will cause delays. Once you've decided, get a quote from three or four builders to build the house on your block of land. This is important because the price tag of display homes does not include any site costs.

Custom-built Home. Most of these builders build a few houses a year and are generally one-offs. Being individual homes they tend to be more expensive to build. Begin by having a suitable design drawn up by an architect or draftsperson. The plans and specifications will be used by the council for approval and by the builder to quote and build. The cost of employing an architect normally amounts to 6% to 8% of the value of the house. You can find a suitable architect through the Royal Australian Institute of Architects (☎02-6273 1548; www.architecture.com.au). Many builders also offer a planning service (designing the house, preparing the plans and building).

Kit Home. The plans and components of your home are delivered to your block of land, ready for you or your builder to construct. This option is seen more in the country than in the cities. The quality of these kits varies considerably, so it is important to deal with a reputable company.

Owner-building. This applies to anyone who takes on the job of managing their own residential building work and includes all the roles usually undertaken by a builder. Apart from the plumbing, electrics and gas fitting, you may perform the work yourself but you will need to obtain an Owner-Builder Permit. You do not need to hold formal trade qualifications.

Generally, you will be required to pay the builder a deposit of 5% to 10% depending on the value of the house. When your home is finished, there is usually a 90-day warranty period for you to tell the builder about any minor building defects you have noticed. States and territories have different rules about warranties; ask a solicitor about warranty periods before you sign a building contract.

Make sure the builder is fully licensed. The name of the authority responsible for builders' registrations varies across the states and territories. The best way to find a good tradesperson or builder is through the local Yellow Pages (www.yellowpages.com.au), by contacting the Master Builders Association (☎02-8586 3555; www.masterbuilders.com.au), the Building Commission (☎1300 360 320; e-mail bpb@buildingcommission.com.au; www.buildingcommission.com.au), or through acquaintances or friends who have had similar work carried out and can recommend someone.

Once your new home is finished, you must have a Certificate of Occupancy before you move in. This confirms that your home is fit to live in and is usually issued by a local building authority or a certified building inspector.

Portable, Mobile, or Relocatable Homes

These homes offer affordable home ownership, often in good locations, but can be transported to another site. They are generally built in a factory and transported in sections to a site. Maintenance costs depend on the condition and size of the dwelling, as well as the site fees charged. They are usually set up in caravan parks or manufactured home estates, with power and water available. While caravan parks generally offer short-term and holiday accommodation, they are also becoming very popular with older people as permanent accommodation.

While people own their portable homes, they generally do not own the land where it is parked and they pay fees to the landowner. This means portable homeowners have less permanency than they would in other sorts of homes. Make sure you understand the leasing arrangements before you sign any contract to take up a parking spot – for instance, ask whether the property can be mortgaged without your knowledge.

Retirement Villages

The retirement village industry in Australia began in the late 1960s. The earlier villages were either developed by the church, charitable and community sectors as a by-product of their aged care or other activities, or by local government as a form of social housing. In the mid 70s, the federal government phased out capital subsidy for the construction of self-care or independent living units operated by churches, charities and other benevolent groups and so the modern retirement village industry in Australia emerged.

The entry of the private sector created a significant shift in the industry - a move from the one bedroom villa or bed-sit to the more complex and significantly larger developments, which included larger units with amenities providing for both social and sporting activities. Since the mid 1990s, there has been a move to two-, three- and even four-bedroom units with two bathrooms or, as a minimum, two toilets.

In Australia, everyone's talking about the 'new' retirement, with a focus on active and independent lifestyles, and many retirement villages have embraced this shift in their approach to services and facilities. Today's retirees are looking for comfort, convenience, security and quality facilities for recreation and social living. Villages have responded by developing new services, designing new facilities and adapting their environments to meet the growing popularity of this kind of lifestyle.

For those looking to make the move to a village, knowing where to start can be daunting. How do you select a village that will meet your particular needs? More importantly, how can you be sure that it will live up to its promises and how can you assess it against others in the market?

The Retirement Village Association (RVA) of Australia has developed a national accreditation system that sets standards for retirement villages and their services. Choosing an accredited village means residents have the confidence of living in an environment that strives to offer all-round quality of life.

This includes upholding high standards for the physical services, surroundings and facilities, as well as ensuring high quality of staff through rigorous and ongoing training and development. To be accredited and to remain so, villages are constantly assessed and judged and service levels, responsibility, accountability and quality are always under review.

RVA Accreditation is not about the status, location, size or wealth of a village, so retirees can seek out an accredited village from more than 400 across the country. Latest information would suggest there are in excess of 800 villages throughout Australia providing accommodation for more than 140,000 residents.

Approximately half of the villages in Australia are private villages. The private sector was the last to enter the industry and, therefore, it represents the newer and more innovative sectors of the industry. Initially the private sector was developing larger 'lifestyle' villages on the outskirts of towns on large tracts of land. The availability of this type of land has significantly reduced however and newer developments are occurring in inner city locations and are being developed as medium- to high-rise apartments. Nevertheless, they are still including many 'lifestyle' features and offer quite substantial units in excess of 1,076 square feet (100 sq m) of living space, many over 2,152 sq ft (200 sq m).

A small percentage of villages had been developed by local governments but these were primarily started in the 1970s and early 80s and are reaching the end of their economic life. While some local governments have encouraged new development, many have lost interest in this type of accommodation and don't see social housing as their responsibility (social housing is a state responsibility in the Australian context) and are leaving the market.

The remainder are operated by church and charitable groups or community organisations and while this group provided the significant proportion of the accommodation in the early years, it was more akin to social housing than an alternative accommodation choice for seniors. However, in the past eight years, due to reductions in the availability of capital from government for aged care and other activities, many organisations within the church, charitable and community sectors have been forced to redevelop older villages and develop up-market villages to generate funds for their charitable activities.

According to the RVA, there is a significant difference in the types of village across Australia and the facilities on offer. Some of the older villages are merely groups of dwellings occupied by the elderly. Others are significant developments, almost the equivalent of suburbs in their own right, with sporting facilities, club houses (some licensed), on-site medical staff and access to the type of services normally expected from local government (swimming pools, libraries, cafés or restaurants). The villages maintain their own streets, street lighting and traffic management. A few of the larger villages are being developed in conjunction with golf courses and attract the younger retiree.

There are a few common terms used by the industry in general, as follows:

Villa. Used to describe your village residence. This can be a one-, two-, three-, or even a four-bedroom dwelling that may form part of a high- or medium-rise complex, a terrace housing arrangement, be it semi-detached or stand-alone depending on the nature of the development. They are also sometimes referred to as Independent Living Units.

Serviced Apartments. Provide supported accommodation for residents who require some assistance with daily living. These are generally one or two bedroom apartments, where services such as cleaning, laundry and assistance with personal care are offered. Meals are usually provided in a dining room setting, although a small kitchenette is usually included within your apartment.

Resident Funded Village. Villages where residents 'purchase' their villa or apartment under one of a number of arrangements and also contribute to the capital infrastructure cost of the village and the cost of ongoing management.

Communal Facilities. Is a term used for a wide range of amenities and services offered to residents. Villages provide a number of recreational, service and social facilities.

States and territories have different legislation to protect the rights of retirement village residents but all address a common range of issues. On the whole, it sets clear standards for managing and owning retirement villages, disclosing details about the village, and supplying clear explanations on how the finances are run. It also ensures that the way a village is set up and operates cannot be changed without the approval of the residents.

The legislation also covers what is included in 'residency agreements,' such as cooling-off periods; residents' financial interests; the relationship between owners, residents and managers (including methods to resolve disputes); and the residents' rights to voice in management. To find out more about the specific provisions in your state and territory, ask a solicitor who understands retirement village law.

The Retirement Villages Act is a protection act that regulates the operation of all retirement villages – private and non-profit – particularly in relation to the rights and obligations of residents and operators, security of tenure and termination of contracts.

Retirement villages usually offer 'self-care' or 'serviced' accommodation. Self-care units are for residents who can live independently. In serviced units, you can have meals, house cleaning, laundry and some personal care provided.

Some retirement villages also offer hostel or nursing home accommodation, or arrange community aged care packages for residents.

In a retirement village, the management looks after things like the supervision of electricity, water supply and cleaning services, maintenance, repairs and the communal facilities. Retirement villages can also have a body corporate or a group of elected residents to help manage the village.

There are as many purchase options as there are operators who can conceive them. The retirement village industry in Australia is heavily regulated in so far as 'consumer protection' legislation is concerned, but there is little regulation as to the types of accommodation and services that can be provided. Both government and the industry recognise that there is a need for consumer choice and there is no shortage of operators willing to provide that choice.

There are generally five different types of contractual arrangements that are offered by village operators:

Loan and Licence. This is the most common arrangement and is the way most churches and charitable organisations operate their villages. You pay a fixed up-front interest-free loan; sometimes a proportion of this loan is non refundable. Recurrent charges, usually on a fortnightly or monthly basis, are also payable. This agreement grants you a right to occupy the premises but you do not own them nor have a legal interest in them.

Leasehold. A common contractual arrangement offered by privately run retirement villages. The lease, usually expressed for 99 years or 199 years, is registered on the title deed which gives you added protection should the village be sold. You pay an up-front deposit and prepaid rent or premium. The amount will vary depending on market forces. Recurrent charges are payable.

Strata Schemes. Also offered by privately run villages, you pay the agreed purchase price to the owner of the premises. This entitles you to occupy the premises and become a member of the owners' corporation. You will also have to pay strata levies, on a quarterly basis, to the owners' corporation and enter into a service contract with the operator before you move in. You usually have the right to sell your premises at any price you like.

Rental. A small number of villages, usually self-contained premises, operate solely on a rental basis. You sign a residential tenancy agreement and pay rent like other tenants.

Company Title Schemes. This means the village is owned by a company in which you purchase shares at market value. The shares give you the right to occupy the premises but you are considered, under the retirement village laws, to own them.

Before you sign a contract, it is important to get a disclosure statement which contains information about the size and location of the village; the proximity to hospitals, shops, and public transport; contact details for the current operator; security measures; type of contracts you may be asked to sign; type and level of services and facilities available; full financial management details including costs to gain entry, reside in and leave the village; details of all available premises in the village; details of village ownership including the year of original construction and name of original developer; residential care facilities; and compliance with the legislation.

Sometimes retirement village units are advertised before they have been built and you are invited to buy off-plan. Beware of the pitfalls in this arrangement.

Fees. The demand for retirement accommodation in Australia is reflective of the general population. One size does not fit all and depends on a retirees preference. Accommodation can be obtained from anywhere within the range of $25,000 to $800,000 and in newer developments, probably more.

Rental retirement accommodation is available, but it is a fairly small but expanding segment of the market. Rental accommodation is usually linked to the provision of other services such as meals and domestic assistance and can cost up to 85% of the aged pension.

- **Waiting List Fee.** A number of retirement villages operate a waiting list. Some of them charge a fee to join the list. The maximum fee that can be charged is $200 and is fully refundable if you no longer wish to be resident of the village.
- **Holding Deposits.** Some operators may allow you to pay a holding deposit on particular premises. This prevents the operator from offering the premises to any other person pending your entry into a residence contract with the operator. It can only be charged on vacant or new premises or if the existing resident has given notice to vacate.
- **Ingoing Contribution/Purchase Price.** If you are not going to own the premises you may be asked to pay an ingoing contribution. If you are to own the premises you will have to pay the agreed purchase price.
- **Contract Preparation Cost.** There are usually costs associated with the preparation of your village contract which are incurred by the operator, such as legal and other expenses. These costs must be split equally between you and the operator.

○ **Recurrent Charges.** At every village you will have to pay recurrent charges to meet the expenses of operating the village. The amount varies from village to village. In a strata scheme you will have to pay levies in addition to any recurrent charges.

○ **Fees and Charges on Termination.** At some villages a set amount of your ingoing contribution may be non-refundable. In addition, the amount you will get back will be further reduced by departure fees. This is a percentage per annum of the relevant ingoing contribution or purchase price (calculated on a daily basis) for a specified maximum number of years of occupancy.

Useful Contacts

The **Retirement Village Association (RVA) of Australia**, www.rva.com.au, can provide you with more general information about retirement villages in Australia and you can locate a range of villages in your state or territory by searching the online Village Directory. The RVA has offices throughout Australia, as follows:

Retirement Village Association of NSW and ACT, ☎02-9747 4732.

Retirement Village Association of South Australia and NT, ☎08-8338 4500.

Retirement Village Association of Queensland, ☎07-3725 5555.

Retirement Village Association of Victoria and Tasmania, ☎03-9629 4520.

Retirement Village Association of Western Australia, ☎08-9322 9909.

Primelife, ☎1800 550 550; www.primelife.com.au, is one of Australia's leading developers and managers of retirement communities with about 60 villages.

Village Life, ☎07-3514 6400; www.villagelife.com.au, is another large provider of accommodation for seniors with about 30 villages where units are available for rent. Each village comprises about 50 villa style one-bedroomed units and a community building. Rent is based on the dollar equivalent of the standard single age pension plus the dollar equivalent of the maximum rent assistance. The latter also applies to self-funded retirees and those receiving a different form of pension.

Another form of independent living for older people is provided by **Abbeyfield House**, ☎03-9419 8222; e-mail admin@abbeyfield.org.au; www.abbeyfield.org.au, a non-profit organisation run by volunteers (the local societies). Each house is for up to 10 people over 55 and capable of independent living, although residents may use Home and Community Care programmes.

Retirement village information is available online from *It's Your Life* at www.itsyourlife.com.au. This useful site will help you with what retirement villages are and how they work, finding suitable accommodation to meet your requirements, and finding legal advice.

The *Retirement Village Handbook* includes legal structures, departure fees, service charges, stamp duty, General Sales tax (GST), refurbishment and capital replacement costs, security of tenure, operator default, termination, vacating the premises, capital losses, credit risk, and parking. It is a comprehensive guide to resident funded retirement villages in Australia. It costs $75 ($49,95 for Seniors Card holders) and can be ordered from ☎02-8230 2424; e-mail info@itsyourlife.com.au, or via the Its Your Life website. This site also includes a *Property Marketplace* where you can browse through a database of individual homes that are available for occupation.

FEES, CONTRACTS AND CONVEYANCING

A quarter of the money you pay for a new house or unit in Australia is consumed by charges imposed by local, state and federal governments. According to a report commissioned by the Property Council of Australia, government charges associated with a typical house and land package have risen an average of $77,000 since 2000. The report found that the buyer of a typical Sydney house and land package would pay more than $1,455 a month over the life of a mortgage to cover the taxes.

Costs associated with buying a residential property depend on where and how the property is bought. This makes government costs the biggest expense that new homebuyers face apart from construction, topping even the price of land. In Western Australia, however, as from 1 July 2005, the government halved the stamp duty on mortgages and will completely abolish it by July 2008.

Costs

Stamp Duty. A state tax imposed on documents that record contracts of sale and some loan applications. In each state, but not the territories (ACT and NT), stamp duty is a one-off fee based on the value of the house, payable on the property purchased and in most cases must be paid prior to settlement.

Conveyancing/Solicitor's Fees are the legal fees charged for the time involved in the conveyancing and the disbursements (cost of searches, inquiries and so on) in respect of the property.

Land Transfer Registration Fee. A small fee payable to the Land Titles Office to register the new title.

Mortgage Registration Fee. It is common practice for lenders to charge administration fees for setting up a mortgage.

Other fees, such as search fees, building and pest inspections and an emergency services levy are also charged. Contact the state or territory in which you decide to live for their costs associated with buying a property:

Australian Capital Territory

Duties: ACT Office of Financial Management, ☎02-6207 0028; www.act.gov.au.
Land titles and fees: Registrar-General's Office, ☎02-6207 0491; www.rgo.
act.gov.au.
Conveyancing fees: Law Society of the ACT, ☎02-6247 5700.

New South Wales

Duties: Office of State Revenue, ☎02-9685 2122; www.osr.nsw.gov.au.
Land titles and fees: Land Titles Office, ☎02-9228 6666; www.lpi.nsw.gov.au.
Conveyancing fees: Law Society of NSW, ☎02-9926 0333; www.lawsoc.nsw.asn.au.

Northern Territory

Duties: Stamp Duties Office, ☎08-8999 7949; www.nt.gov.au/ntt/revenue.
Land titles and fees: Land Titles Office, ☎08-8999 6520.
Conveyancing fees: Law Society of the NT, ☎08-8981 5104.

Queensland

Duties: Office of State Revenue, ☎07-3227 8733; www.osr.qld.gov.au.
Land titles and fees: Department of Natural Resources, ☎07-3405 6900; www.dnr.
qld.gov.au.
Conveyancing fees: Law Society of Queensland, ☎07-3842 5888; www.qls.com.au.

South Australia

Duties: Department of Treasury and Finance, ☎08-8226 3750; www.treasury.
sa.gov.au.
Land titles and fees: Land Titles Office, ☎08-8226 3983.
Conveyancing fees: Law Society of South Australia, ☎08-8229 0222.

Tasmania

Duties: Department of Treasury and Finance, ☎03-6233 3068; www.tres.tas.gov.au.
Land titles and fees: Land Titles Office, ☎03-6233 3574.
Conveyancing fees: Law Society of Tasmania, ☎03-6233 8383; www.taslawsociety.
asn.au.

Victoria
Duties: State Revenue Office of Victoria, ☎03-9628 6777; www.sro.vic.gov.au.
Land titles and fees: Land Victoria, Land Registry, Title Registration Services, ☎03-9603 5444.
Conveyancing fees: Law Institute of Victoria, ☎03-9607 9311; www.liv.asn.au.

Western Australia
Duties: State Revenue Department, ☎08-9262 1100; www.wa.gov.au/srd.
Land titles and fees: Land Titles Office, ☎08-9273 7373; www.dola.wa.gov.au/keeper_titles.
Conveyancing fees: Ministry of Fair Trading, Registrar of Settlement Agents Supervisory Board, ☎08-9282 0839.

The First Home Owners Grant is an Australia-wide scheme brought in to offset the cost of GST when purchasing a home. This applies to purchasers who have not owned property in Australia before but they can have owned property overseas. This grant of $7,000 is not means tested so provided the purchaser is a resident of Australia they would be eligible. A recent case in Perth saw a millionaire migrant who purchased a $10 million mansion qualify for the grant!

Typical Fees

Note: these are approximate costs for New South Wales and may vary in each state and territory.

Home Loan Application. Charged by a lending body when a formal loan application is made. $0-$800. Additional costs may be incurred for the preparation and registration of the mortgage.

Valuation. Your lender will usually require a formal valuation of the property for lending purposes. This fee may be included in the application fee charged by your lender. $0-$300.

Mortgage Insurance. Required when the buyer is borrowing more than a set proportion of the property's valuation as specified by the lender. Premiums vary according to the amount borrowed, property price and the loan-to-value ratio. This is a one-off payment. $300-$12,000.

Survey Report. Shows where the property is in relation to the boundaries of the land. $400-$600.

Conveyancing. No set fees but generally $600-$2,500.

Disbursements. Charged by your solicitor or conveyancer:

o Title search: $20-$60.
o Local council: $40-$100.
o Local Council building certificate: $70.
o Sydney Water: $15.
o Drainage diagram: $15.
o Department of Education and Training: $13.
o Land tax: $15.
o Roads and Traffic Authority: $22.
o Transgrid (electricity/power stations): $21.
o Council rate enquiry: $50.
o State Rail Authority: $24.
o Outstanding Notices for Council: $40-$150.

Stamp Duty. Contract stamp duty is payable on the purchase price of the property. This must be paid within three months of the date of exchanging contracts, unless buying off-plan or a house and land package.

o Up to $14,000: $1.25 per $100 ($10 min)
o $14,001 to $30,000: $175 plus $1.50 per $100
o $30,001 to $80,000: $415 plus $1.75 per $100
o Over $80,000: $1,290 plus $3.50 per $100
o Over $300,000: $8,990 plus $4.50 per $100
o Over $1,000,000: $40,490 plus $5.50 per $100.

Mortgage Stamp Duty. Payable on the mortgage. Up to $16,000 the rate is $5. It then increases by $4 for every $1,000 (or part thereof) borrowed above $16,000. A fee of $75 applies to register the mortgage. A further fee applies to register the transfer document.

Building Inspection. Checks structural soundness, indicating visible quality defects and necessary repairs. $275-$600.

Pest Inspection. Checks for any signs of past or present pest infestation. $160-$300.

Strata Inspection. Examines and reports on the written records of the owners corporation. It is in addition to the certificate supplied to the buyer by the seller providing relevant information about strata levies, insurances and so on. $180-$300.

Insurance. You should arrange home insurance before completing the purchase. The cost will be dependent on the age, size, location and type of construction. Two types of cover are available: Replacement Cover pays to reinstate your property to its former condition. Indemnity Cover pays to repair or reinstate your property taking into account depreciation on the dwelling. $220-$1,000.

Electricity. A reconnection fee of $180-$200 is payable as a security deposit if you are a new customer.

Telephone. A reconnection fee of $59 if connected where there was a phone before; or $209 if there was no phone previously.

Inspection and Surveys

It is advisable that a building inspection be undertaken before the exchange of contracts. A property can be inspected by a builder or architect to assess whether there are any defects that might affect your decision to buy. An inspection should include foundations; the condition of all structural timber (floor joists, rafters); all load bearing walls and members; the outer skin of the building (brick, stone, timber, fibro); plumbing and electrical wiring; kitchen and bathrooms and a building inspection.

 Archicentre (☎1300 13 45 12; www.archicentre.com.au), and the Housing Industry Association (HIA) (☎02-6249 6366, www.hia.asn. au), provide an inspection service. For a fee, they inspect and report on the state of the property, including the structural condition, damp and termites. Other companies are listed in the Yellow Pages under *Building Inspection Services*.

Contracts

The process of exchanging contracts to complete a property transaction in Australia is known as 'settlement.' It is a far easier process than in the UK and the concept of the 'chain' does not exist. Once a vendor agrees to an offer, a contract is signed stipulating a date for settlement, which will usually be 30 days from the date of offer.

Contracts vary between states and territories and are known as *Contract of Sale, Agreement for Sale of Real Estate, Contract for Sale of Land by Offer and Acceptance,* or *Contract Note.*

Most states and territories allow a 'cooling-off' period which varies from two to five days after signing a contract; Queensland does not have a cooling-off period. At any time in the period you can change your mind and the contract is not binding. Check the cooling off period in your state or territory.

Whatever the type of contract, they all include:

O   The name(s) of the person(s) purchasing the house. If there is more than one owner, the property will be held by co-owners as 'joint tenants' or 'tenants in common' (which covers what will happen to the property if one of the owners dies).

O   A description of the property, such as the block and section number.

O   The amount you agree to pay for the property.

O   The deposit (usually 5% of the purchase price).

O   Any conditions you want to impose on the sale of the house and the dates these have to be completed by.

O   Any special items included in the purchase price, such as curtains, dishwasher, light fittings.

Gazumping also happens in Oz and can take two forms:

O   The intending buyer believes that the property has been secured by payment of an initial or part deposit, then proceeds to arrange finance, legal and other matters. When ready to exchange contracts, the intending buyer finds that another buyer has exchanged contracts on the property; or

O   The seller, or the real estate agent, accepts two or more initial deposits and then tells the intending buyers that the price has gone up. The intending purchasers are then left to outbid each other as if it were an auction. This is unfortunate for the buyer, but the seller is entitled to get the best price for the property.

Conveyancing

The legal recording of the ownership of a property when it is sold involves the transferral of the ownership or title and is known as conveyancing. You can do it yourself, use a solicitor or a licensed conveyancing agent. This legal process varies between states and territories and it is important to appoint someone who operates in the same state as the property for sale.

Both solicitors and conveyancers charge a fee and 'disbursement' costs. Disbursements are the charges that come up during the conveyancing process and include search fees, inspection or building reports, phone calls, and so on.

For more information on conveyancers, contact the Australian Institute of Conveyancers (☎08-8212 4088; e-mail assist@aicsa.com.au; www. aicnational.com.au). Divisions of the Institute are present in New South Wales, Northern Territory, South Australia, Victoria and Western Australia.

Do-it-yourself conveyancing kits or self-help systems explain the steps for conveyancing and offer an alternative to the conventional legal process. If you decide to do it yourself, you will need the right kit and forms.

In ACT, NSW, Queensland and Victoria the Australian Property Law Kit is available (☎1800 252 808; e-mail info@diyconveyancingkits.com.au; www. diyconveyancingkits.com.au for more information). Otherwise contact the Law Consumer's Association (☎02-9267 6154). You will be required to join the association to obtain a kit. Obviously, there are potential pitfalls doing it yourself.

Home Ownership Titles

A title deed is a legal document that provides evidence that you own your property. The types of ownership titles and how they legally affect your property vary slightly across the states and territories. For more information you will have to contact the land titles office in your state of territory, or ask a solicitor.

Titles for standard residential housing, include:

Common Law or Old System Title. Consists of a series of title documents called a *chain of title*. Following a sale, Common Law Title will be converted to a qualified Torrens Title.

Torrens Title. This is the most common type of ownership and is the name given to the government system of recording ownership of land. It usually applies to a standard residential suburban house with its own yard. Some townhouse or courtyard blocks also have Torrens Title. As long as any repayments on mortgages are kept up to date and there are no government or council plans to resume the land, Torrens Title ownership offers the most permanency.

As a Torrens Title owner you are responsible for the cost of all rates, services, maintenance and improvement to the property. Subject to regulations, you can also alter the building or property. You might also have to meet the terms of any building 'covenants' you have signed. These are agreements with developers that have terms and conditions about alterations.

Company Title. This is where unit owners are actually shareholders in a private company.

Strata Title. This is the common method of unit ownership. Strata Title properties can be a block of units, flats or apartments; high rise, townhouse, or duplex; residential, commercial or retail; mixed use (retail/residential or commercial/residential); resorts; serviced apartments; and caravan parks. Each state and territory has laws about properties that are part of group housing. Under a Strata Title, the land and buildings are subdivided into 'lots' and 'common' property. The lots are the units (dwellings) and other areas – for example, laundries, car spaces, garages and marinas – that belong to individual owners.

All lots are allocated a 'unit entitlement.' These are shown on the strata plan. The plan is approved by the local council and registered at the land titles office. 'Certificates of Title' are then issued for each lot by the land titles office. The land titles office also issues Certificate of Title for the 'common' property. This is for property that belongs to all the owners, collectively (stairways, foyers, gym, swimming pool, tennis court, meeting room, golf course, and so on).

Before moving into Strata Title group housing, consider whether there are common walls and a noise problem; whether you have enough privacy; and whether pets are allowed. Strata Title properties usually have a body corporate which collects body corporate levies from the unit owners. These levies are on top of council and water rates.

By law, the owners of Strata Title group housing have to form a *body corporate* to control the administration and funding of common property. With a body corporate, all owners have to contribute to the costs of common areas, such as lighting the paths, and maintaining the building exteriors and gardens, the lifts and the swimming pools.

The body corporate committee is usually elected by the unit owners. Sometimes a committee that represents a large number of unit owners appoints a professional managing agent to look after the accounts and administration.

Community Title. A form of subdivision which allows common property areas to be incorporated into a land subdivision.

SWIMMING POOLS

With the severity of the Australian climate, a swimming pool can be an ab-solute joy. It is the centre of a healthy lifestyle and can be the focus of mental relaxation. However, it can be costly to install and maintain. The average size of a pool in Australia is 16 ft x 30 ft (5 m x 9 m) and costs about $28,000.

Planning permission is required from your local council or shire and pool fencing is mandatory. The most popular pools are free form concrete and fibreglass. Domestic pools are normally 5 ft (1.5 m) deep but diving boards are not allowed. Pool cleaners plugged into a skimmer are normal. You can swim all year round and in Brisbane and the southern states pools are heated; while in Cairns and the tropics pools are chilled. Lighting is not necessary (there's loads of sunshine) but for evening entertainment around the pool barbecue, lighting can create a wonderful ambience. In Queensland, 40% of all homes have a pool and the lifestyle is based around being outdoors.

The initial filling of an average suburban pool needs about 50KL (11,000 gallons/50,000 litres). Water is then used in filter backwashing, evaporating and splash out averages 5 gallons (23 litres) a day, totalling 1,847 gallons (8,395 litres) a year. This represents 3.5% of an average household water use.

During the summer it is recommended that the filter should run for eight to 10 hours a day and whenever people are using the pool. You must maintain the right chemical balance (alkaline level, pH and sanitiser) and the correct water level. Covering the pool saves water, helps keep the pool clean, cuts energy costs by reducing heat loss.

All swimming pools that are more than 12 inches (300 mm) deep must be guarded with safety barriers and fitted with self-locking devices. Gates must swing outwards. Failure to meet these building regulations could impose a $500 fine.

Older pools can be renovated to include such modern advances as automatic in-floor cleaning systems, computerised controls for chemical dosing and internal pool finishes. If you buy a house with a pool you can get information about it from your local Planning and Land Authority or council.

Many parts of ACT and surrounding NSW areas have clay or rock just under the surface and during periods of heavy rain can build up a temporary underground water table. If a pool, installed in an area with subterranean water, is emptied the upward pressure of the water under the floor can cause it to lift.

Installing solar pool heating can increase the use of your pool by up to four months. By using the heating energy from the sun, the cost to heat a pool in this way is very economical.

The ideal temperature for leisure swimming is around 68 to 77 deg F (20 to 25 deg C). This temperature is very rarely achieved naturally. For most of the swimming season, the normal water temperature would be around 65 to 68 deg F (18 to 20 deg C). Most of the temperature gained during the day is lost overnight, leaving the pool cold again in the morning.

Gas heating can quickly and efficiently heat your pool to a comfortable temperature for swimming whenever it is required. This means you can extend your swimming season for as long as you like, thus increasing the return on what was probably a fairly large investment in your pool.

A pool blanket can keep evaporation to a minimum, save water and save on the cost of chemicals as you don't have to rebalance your pool after topping up. They also keep the pool cleaner by about 80% to 90%.

Useful Contacts
Swimming Pool and Spa Association of Queensland: www.spasa.com.au
Fluid Concept Pools: www.fcpools.com.au.

THE RENTAL SCENE

Latest figures show that 29% of Australians rent their homes. This will increase to a 40% market share by 2015 as residents are increasingly forced to rent. According to the Australian Bureau of Statistics, 13% of older persons live in rented accommodation. Almost half of these rent their home from a state or territory housing authority; a further 44% from a private landlord; and most of the remaining 11% from community and church groups, housing cooperatives or caravan parks.

Renting a property may mean a better standard of housing in a good location. At present however, there are not enough properties in the right areas and this has put a lot of pressure on the rental market. According to the *Australian PropertyInvestor*, homebuyers are holding off buying a property and are renting, which means that rents are expected to increase by 7% in 2006 before increasing to about 10%.

In New South Wales, there hasn't been much of an oversupply and the vacancy rate is 2.4%. Queensland has an undersupply of residential rental stock, with only a 2.5% vacancy rate for detached houses and a 3.5% vacancy rate for attached dwellings, which is made up mainly of apartments and townhouses. The demand for rental property, especially detached houses, has increased substantially over the past 12 months. Across most of Tasmania, there's a shortage of rental properties in the lower to middle range sector of housing. In Victoria, the cost of private rental accommodation continues to increase faster than inflation and affordability for those on lower incomes remains tight.

The state and territory real estate institutes all provide information on renting and leasing and provide links through their respective websites to a number of different sources of additional information such as Departments of Fair Trading and Rental Boards.

The laws relating to renting a property vary from state to state. Specific information about renting a property and a list of rental agents may be obtained from the consumer affairs authority in your state or territory. Contact details are:

> **ACT:** Office of Fair Trading, ☎02-6207 0400; www.fairtrading.act.gov.au.
>
> **NT:** Office of Consumer and Business Affairs, ☎08-8999 5184; www.nt.gov.au.
>
> **NSW:** Department of Fair Trading, ☎02-9895 0111; www.fairtrading.nsw.gov.au.
>
> **QLD:** Office of Fair Trading, ☎07-3246 1500; www.fairtrading.qld.gov.au.
>
> **SA:** Office of Consumer and Business Affairs, ☎08-8204 9777; www.ocba.sa.gov.au.
>
> **TAS:** Office of Consumer Affairs & Fair Trading, ☎03-6233 4555; www.consumer.tas.gov.au.
>
> **VIC:** Consumer Affairs Victoria, ☎1300 558 181; www.consumer.vic.gov.au.
>
> **WA:** Department of Consumer & Employment Protection, ☎08-9282 0777; www.docep.wa.gov.au.

If you plan to move into a rental property you should ask the real estate agent about the area you are interested in. Take time to familiarise yourself with the area and check out the shops, public transport routes, restaurants, theatres and post offices. Once you have found a place to rent, you may be required to pay a deposit or reservation fee to secure the property and if you change your mind you may forfeit this deposit.

When moving in to a property you may be required to pay rent in advance and a security deposit of between four to six weeks' rent, known as a rental bond. The real estate agent is also required to complete a condition report indicating the condition of the property when you take possession. The real estate agent will regularly inspect the property to ensure it is being cared for.

When you sign the tenancy agreement you are entering into a legally binding agreement and the rent must be paid on time. Increases in rent are common and the appropriate notification of this will be given in writing. You should discuss notice requirements with the real estate agent.

The landlord is responsible for council and water rates, building insurance (except for personal belongings) and repairs and maintenance to the building. The amount of rent you pay depends on the market. Over the past 12 months, rent increases have ranged from 3.3% in Canberra to 21% in Perth for three-bedroom accommodation. Rents for two-bedroom units, apartments and town houses also increased significantly over the year, ranging from a 3.4% increase in Sydney to 29% in Perth.

Median Weekly Rents (three-bedroom houses) (March 2006)

Canberra $310	Adelaide $230
Darwin $300	Hobart $250
Sydney $260	Melbourne $230
Brisbane $250	Perth $230

Vacancy Rates

Canberra 2.8%	Adelaide 1.7%
Darwin 4.4%	Hobart 2.2%
Sydney 2.6%	Melbourne 2.1%
Brisbane 2.1%	Perth 1.6%

Contracts

Although the Residential Tenancies Act does not require tenancy agreements to be in writing it is preferable that they are. There are two types of tenancy agreements:

Fixed-term. You agree to rent a property for a fixed amount of time. If you remain in the property after the expiry date has passed and a new tenancy agreement is not entered into and you are not asked to leave, the tenancy agreement becomes periodic.

Periodic. This is usually on a weekly, fortnightly, or monthly basis for an indefinite period.

When a tenant wishes to end a tenancy, the period of notice depends on the type of agreement. You should give your notice in writing. A fixed-term tenancy ends on the expiration of the term but you must give at least 14 days notice. To end a periodic tenancy the landlord must give the tenant 42 days notice and a tenant must give 14 days notice.

Following the termination of a tenancy, the tenant is entitled to the recovery of the security deposit.

A copy of the Retail Tenancies Act can be obtained from the Department of Fair Trading in your state or territory.

UTILITIES

Electricity, gas and water supplies are controlled throughout Australia by the authorities in each state and territory. Costs vary between the states and territories and between urban and rural areas. Remote outback areas may attract particularly high charges, especially for water.

Water

The average Australian household uses 240KL (52,792 gallons/240,000 litres) of water each year and it is a valuable and scarce commodity in Australia. Water restrictions and saving measures are often in place in extreme summer conditions. Water is supplied to homes by state authorities and water and sewerage service charges apply to every connected residential property, along with a metered water usage charge. Says Mike Osborne: *'You get so many litres* *at a fixed lower price and then consumption above that at a higher level. We get about 125,000 litres for 45 cents a kilolitre and after that it is about $1.10.'*

Outside the cities, households have 5,000-gallon (22,730-litre) rainwater tanks, which are mandatory planning items for many homes. Septic tanks are also connected to the common effluent systems. The common effluent system collects solids but the liquids are taken into local treatment plants and used to water open spaces, such as golf courses. The tanks are emptied by the local council at regular intervals. Some homeowners have a borehole sunk in their garden to tap into the water table but it is an expensive alternative.

To find a water utility company in your area, contact the Water Services Association of Australia, ☎03-9606 0678; e-mail info@wsaa.asn.au; www. wsaa.asn.au.

Electricity and Gas

Most new homes in Australia are connected to both gas and electricity supplies. Gas is relatively cheap but some of the older homes are not connected to the gas supply. Some remote areas do not have a natural gas supply and LPG (liquid petroleum gas) is used, obtained in bottle form. Electricity is the most important source of domestic energy but is considerably more expensive than gas. Australian households are being encouraged to use smart electricity meters to cut power bills and reduce pressure on the government to build massive new power stations around the country.

Smart meters, otherwise known as interval meters, allow consumers to calculate the cost of their electricity consumption hour by hour, giving them the option of using low-cost off-peak power for dishwashers, pool filters or washing machines rather than high-cost electricity at times of peak demand.

Some states, including Victoria, Queensland and Western Australia, are already trialling time-of-use charging systems that work in a similar way to the pricing of long-distance telephone rates. The price consumers pay for electricity depends on the time of day the electricity is used.

Customers take advantage of off-peak electricity charges by using power in the cheaper times, which can save as much as 30% on electricity bills. Depending on their level of sophistication, the electronic meters can cost from about $200 to more than $700 each.

Heating accounts for 50% of a home's energy use. It's important that your home is able to retain the heat you put into it for as long as possible. A fully insulated home can save you up to $300 a year in heating and cooling costs. Australian homes are very seldom centrally heated. Many people heat their homes by reverse cycle air conditioning, which is a warm air blower in the same unit as the air conditioner cooler. Others heat their homes with slow combustion wood burning stoves. Generally, you can expect to pay about $800 to $1,000 a year.

The voltage in Australia is 240/250V, 50Hz and power takes three-pin plugs, which have two diagonally slanting pins above one straight pin. Wild storms, lightning strikes, strong winds and driving rain can all play havoc with the power supply. Darwin and surrounding areas are the most lightning prone in the world, due not only to the location in the tropics but also because ironstone in the ground attracts lightning. In Central Australia too, wild storms can cause upheaval and damage and there are frequent power shortages.

Energy Suppliers

AGL: New South Wales, South Australia, Victoria, www.agl.com.au.

TRUenergy: New South Wales, South Australia, Victoria, www.truenergy.com.au.

Power and Water: Northern Territory, www.powerwater.com.au.

Advance Energy: New South Wales, www.countryenergy.com.au.

EnergyAustralia: New South Wales, www.energy.com.au.

Ergon Energy: New South Wales, Queensland, Victoria, www.ergon.com.au.

Energex: Queensland, www.energex.com.au.

Tarong Energy: Queensland, www.tarongenergy.com.au.

Aurora Energy: Tasmania, www.auroraenergy.com.au.

Citipower: Victoria, www.citipower.com.au.

Origin Energy: Victoria, www.originenergy.com.au.

United Energy: Victoria, www.unitedenergy.com.au.

Western Power: Western Australia, www.westernpower.com.au.

Residential Rates

Council rates are levied annually and include a refuse charge for the collection of domestic rubbish and charges for amenities provided by the council. Council rates are determined by the location and size of the property and are calculated by the Valuer-General on its gross value. For instance in ACT, annual rates are made up of a valuation-based charge and the fixed charge. The fixed charge for 2005-06 is set at $392. Rate notices are usually issued on a quarterly and charges are payable to the local or shire council on or before the discount expiry and due date. You can pay in advance or by instalment. There is a scheme for retirees to claim a discount but contact your local council to check if this is available in your state or territory. Expat Mike Osborne explains the rates:

The highest rates for classy homes in good suburbs of Adelaide are rarely more than $2,500 a year. In the country, it is well under 40% of those levels. We have a newly-built single storey home, three big bedrooms, en suite, two lounges, veranda and a built-in double garage, totalling 250 square metres on a 1,100 square metre block, and we pay $800 a year.

Foreign Exchange… How to get the most from your money

When you start to plan your retirement down under there are lots of things that you need to consider to make sure that your new life is a happy one. Currencies Direct explain how one of the most important things that you need to consider, and often one of the most overlooked, is foreign exchange.

If you're retiring to Australia or New Zealand you will no doubt have to change your hard earned money from sterling into Australian or New Zealand dollars. Whether it's to buy a new house or simply to transfer your savings to live off, foreign exchange can't be avoided. Unfortunately, no one can predict the exchange rate as many economic and political factors constantly affect the strength of the pound. Exchange rates are constantly moving and there is no guarantee that they will be in your favour when you need your money, so it is vital that you protect yourself against these movements. A lack of proper forward planning could potentially cost you thousands of pounds and reduce your spending power abroad.

For example, the affect the exchange rate can have on the cost of a new house can be seen if you look at what happened to the New Zealand dollar during 2005. Sterling against the dollar was as high as 2.7040 and as low as 2.4245. This means that if you were buying a property worth $300,000 it could have cost you as little as £110,946 or as much as £123,736, a difference of almost £13,000.

However, it is possible to avoid this pitfall by buying and fixing a rate for your currency ahead of time through a **forward transaction**. This is the *Buy now, Pay later* option and is ideal if you still have some time to wait before your money is due down under or if you are waiting for the proceeds from the sale of your UK property. Usually a small deposit will secure you a rate for anywhere up to 2 years in advance and by doing so you will have the security of having the currency you need at a guaranteed cost and knowing exactly how much your new home will cost.

Another option available to you if you have time on your side is a **limit** order. This is used when you want to achieve a rate that is currently not available. You set the rate that you want and the market is then monitored. As soon as that rate is achieved the currency is purchased for you. You can also set a 'lower' level or 'stop' to protect yourself should the rate drastically fall. This is ideal for when you don't have to make an immediate payment and you have a specific budget available.

If however you need to act swiftly and your capital is readily available then it is most likely that you will use a **spot transaction**. This is the *Buy now, Pay now* option where you get the most competitive rate on the day.

It is however fair to admit that many of us do not have the time or sufficient knowledge of these options to be in a position to confidently gauge when the foreign currency rates are at their most favourable, and this is where a foreign exchange specialist can help. As an alternative to your bank, foreign exchange specialists are able to offer you extremely competitive exchange rates, no commission charges and lower transfer fees. This can mean considerable savings on your transfer when compared to using a bank.

It is also very easy to use a foreign exchange specialist. The first thing you will need to do is register with them as a client. This is usually very straightforward and requires you to complete a registration form and provide two forms of identification, usually a copy of your passport and a recent utility bill. Once you are registered you are then able to trade. Your dealer will talk you through the different options that are available to you and help you to decide which one is right for you depending on your timing, circumstances and foreign currency needs. Once you have decided which option is best for you and agreed a rate you will then need to send your money. With clearance times at each end some companies can complete the transfer for you in as little as a week.

Even once you have retired and left the UK you may find yourself in the position where you need to regularly transfer funds from your UK bank account to your Australian/New Zealand account. This may be because you are still receiving a pension in the UK or perhaps you have decided to rent out your house until you settle and so are receiving rental income. If this is the case using a reputable foreign exchange specialist to do the transfers for you can make sure that you get more of your money each time, even on small amounts. This is because unlike your bank they will offer you competitive exchange rates on these smaller amounts plus they won't charge you commission and transfers are often free.

Currencies Direct is a leading commercial foreign exchange company; offering superior rates of exchange and a personalised service they meet the needs of thousands of private and corporate clients every year.

With offices in the UK, Spain, Australia, South Africa and India Currencies Direct is always on hand to help you. For more information about their services, please contact one of their dealers who will be happy to discuss your currency requirements with you.

UK Head Office: 0845 389 0906
Email: info@currenciesdirect.com
Web: www.currenciesdirect.com

Housing Finance

CHAPTER SUMMARY

- One of the most important considerations is whether or not to sell your UK residence in order to fund the move abroad.
- In Australia, a non-resident can borrow up to 80% of the purchase price of the property.
- The major cost when buying a property is the stamp duty.
- It's advisable to transfer your money through a foreign exchange specialist.
- Insurance is a complex business but there are many organisations in Australia to advise you.

AFFORDING THE MOVE

Deciding What To Do With Your UK Property

About 257,000 Britons own overseas real estate. A recent report by the Office for National Statistics puts the total investment at more than £23 billion. Outside Europe, Australia was one of the more exotic destinations. However, before departing for Australia, deciding what to do with your home in the UK is a crucial consideration.

Most people sell their UK home and use the funds to buy a home in Australia. Others who can afford it hang on to their UK property in case things go wrong in Australia. However, this can be financially prohibitive because of the vast distances one has to travel between the UK and the Antipodes. Also, it can be an issue when trying to settle in a new country as the thought of returning to your home of many years is always going to be a major pull.

The Commonwealth Bank's free online Property Value Guide (www.equity.

webcentral.com.au), gives you an insight into property values in Australia. It is compiled monthly from information gathered by the bank and includes comprehensive information on properties.

AUSTRALIAN MORTGAGES

A non-resident can borrow up to 80% of the purchase price of the property (permanent residents up to 100%) but borrowing at this level in Australia requires strict criteria to be met. The borrower will also need to show proof of ongoing income to support the debt repayments. However, firstly you will need to obtain approval from the Foreign Investment Review Board (FIRB) before purchasing a property (see *Your New Home in Australia*).

In Australia, there are anti-discrimination laws preventing banks from turning down a borrower based on age. Basic no-frills home loans are around 6.60% to 6.80%. These allow additional repayments without penalty or redraw but don't have offset or line of-credit facilities. Variable or fixed rates are the most popular mortgage types. Variable can be 'principal and interest' or 'interest only' for up to 10 years. Fixed rates are available for between one and 10 years from most lenders. Three-year rates are attractive at the moment at around the same level (6.55% to 6.80%) so a lot of people are applying for fixed rates. A 20% deposit is advisable.

Average upfront costs for a standard residential loan is around $600 to $800. This normally includes the banks legal costs and a valuation. Some lenders often do special nil application fee offers. Mortgage insurance is also payable if borrowing more than 80% of the property value. This is a one-off upfront payment, but can be added to the loan in most instances, and can vary between 0.5% and up to 3% of the loan value. This insurance covers the bank in case they don't recover enough to cover the debt in the event of a forced sale, but the borrower pays the premium and is still sued by the insurance company for the loss.

Australia has only recently introduced reverse mortgages. This is where a person with an unencumbered property can borrow up to 25% of its value (depending on age) and not make any repayments until they either move out, sell the property, or pass away. They are principally aimed at the asset rich or cash poor retirees with fully owned homes who need some cash for renovations, living and so on but don't have an income to support repayments. The interest compounds over time but so does the value of the property so your net equity stays about the same.

Types of Loans

Standard variable interest rate loan. This is the usual loan and therefore the most popular type of home loan. Fluctuating interest rates can cause repayment levels to rise and fall.

Basic variable interest rate loan. Offers a lower interest rate and repayment.

Fixed interest loan. Offers fixed interest for a specific period. After this period the loan is renegotiated for another fixed term or reverts to the variable interest rate current at the time.

Part-variable/part-fixed rate loan. Often referred to as split or combination loans. You pay a fixed interest rate on a portion of the loan and interest on the remaining portion at the standard variable rate.

Capped or introductory interest rate loan. Interest rate is fixed for the capped period (6 to 12 months). This rate cannot go higher but may go lower if the lender's standard variable interest rate falls below the capped rate.

All-in-one loan. A variable interest rate loan allowing the borrower to place all their income into one account thereby reducing the loan balance and the interest paid. It operates like a transaction account where you can access the account to meet day-to-day expenses.

Home equity loan. Allows you to use your equity in the home to gain access to an immediate source of funds.

Consolidated loan. Allows you to combine several loans, such as a home loan, credit card debit and personal loan, into a single variable or fixed-rate loan. This can result in a lower overall repayment and interest rate.

Interest-only loan. Requires the interest to be paid during the loan term with the principal becoming due at the end. These are usually short-term loans (one to five years) and are often utilised for investment property purchases and may suit the retiree.

Bridging loan. Used for the purchase of a new property while awaiting the sale of an existing property. It is a short-term housing loan where repayments meet the interest only. The principal becomes due at the end of the loan term. High interest rates are charged on this type of loan.

Additional loan features include making fortnightly rather than monthly repayments; extra repayments, a mortgage offset account, which is a savings account operated in combination with, but separate to, a home loan; and a redraw facility where you can withdraw additional repayments which have been made previously.

If you apply for a mortgage in Australia when you are over 55 your options may be limited because you may not have enough income to keep making the repayments. Under the 'Consumer Credit Note' it is up to the lender to assess whether a borrower can afford to pay back the loan. If you put down less than 20% of the property's price as a deposit, most lenders will ask you to pay for lender's mortgage insurance. This can cost up to about 2.5% of the loan amount.

Financial information is available from Centrelink Financial Information Service (☎13 10 21; www.centrelink.gov.au); and the National Information Centre on Retirement (☎1800 020 110; www.nicri.org.au).

Banks are the biggest lenders in Australia's owner-occupied home loan market. They lend funds with up to 30-year terms and the deposit required can vary from 5% to 25%. At Westpac's London office you can apply for mortgage pre-approval before you leave the UK and then start house hunting as soon as you arrive in Australia.

Other lenders include:

○ *Building societies.* Building societies operate in much the same way as banks.

○ *Credit unions.* Most credit unions lend housing funds to members and can be good sources of finance when additional funds are required.

○ *Mortgage managers.* Organise funding for homebuyers from a variety of sources.

○ *Mortgage brokers.* Act as agents between borrowers and prospective lenders.

○ *Co-operative housing societies.* Provide housing loans predominantly to low and moderate income earners.

○ *Solicitors.* Some solicitors have clients' funds available for housing loans. Usually, these loans are available for two or three years only and at the end of this time finance has to be obtained from another source.

○ *Finance companies.* Have loans available but generally these are not suited to first mortgage housing loans because interest rates can be higher than other sources.

○ *Vendor finance.* Sometimes the vendor is prepared to lend part of the purchase funds to the buyer, usually over a two or three year term.

New South Wales has a Mortgage Assistance Scheme (☎1800 806 653; www.housing.nsw.gov.au) which assists people experiencing difficulties, following unforeseen circumstances, with their existing mortgage.

Current basic variable home loan AAPR (annualised average percentage rate) is between 6.38% and 6.71% depending on the financial institution; and for premium variable home loans 6.32% to 6.59%. A one-year fixed home loan carries a rate of 5.94% to 6.60%; three-year fixed home loan 6.47% to 6.49%; five-year fixed home loan 6.59% to 6.69%.

PROPERTY TAXES

The biggest single cost is the **stamp duty** on the purchase of a property, although concessions do apply in most states for 'First Home Buyers' (permanent residents who have never bought property in Australia before). In NSW, for example, no stamp duty is paid for property purchases up to $500,000 for First Home Buyers.

A typical $400,000 property in NSW would attract stamp duty of $13,500. Stamp duty is also paid on the loan, about $4 per $1,000 of debt; therefore a $200,000 loan would incur about $800 of stamp duty. The mortgage insurance also attracts stamp duty, 9% in NSW. So, if the premium was $1,000, stamp duty would be another $90. There are also a few other small incidental government charges, such as a registration of mortgage fee.

Capital Gains. There is no separate tax on capital gains; it is a component of your income tax. You are taxed on your net capital gain at your marginal tax rate (see *Selling Your Australian Property* in *Returning Home*).

Council Rates. Council rates are charged on an annual basis. Rates differ within each state and territory but, generally, can amount to between $500 to $800 a year (see *Utilities* in *Your New Home in Australia*).

TRANSFERRING MONEY

Foreign currency specialists such as Currencies Direct (☎0845-389 0906; www.currenciesdirect.com) can convert your local currency into Australian Dollars. Banks usually offer foreign exchange services, but these often compare badly to specialist foreign exchange dealers on rates and charges.

Exchange rates change constantly and 10% fluctuations in a relatively short space of time are not uncommon. This could effectively increase, by 10%

or more, the amount that you will have to pay to start your new life. For example, a UK couple wishing to purchase a property in Perth for $200,000 would have paid the Sterling equivalent of £82,857 in September 2005. Three months later they would have paid £86,949 for the same property. By securing an exchange rate in advance, they could have made a saving of over £4,000 on their new home.

How to Buy your Currency

There are several options available to you when purchasing currency, and your personal dealer will be able to find the best option to suit your individual situation. **Forward Contracts** allow you to fix an exchange rate for up to two years. This option allows you to lock into favourable rates, even if you do not have all your local currency available to transfer at the time of purchase. Forward buying removes the risk of adverse currency movements that could lead to the cost of your emigration, increasing between the time of finalising your plans and the actual payment. **Spot Contracts** allow you to make a foreign currency transaction immediately to a nominated bank account (up to five working days ahead). The exchange rate will be the rate for the day that you arrange the contract. You can also take advantage of movements in the foreign exchange markets by placing an order in the market. This allows you to try and attain the best rate possible by setting a rate at which, if the markets reach it, you will then buy your currency. To protect you if the markets go against you, you can also place what is called a 'stop loss order' that will place a minimum exchange rate in the market so that you do not face exchange rate risk. **Making Regular Overseas Payments.** If you need to make regular overseas payments such as pension transfers or mortgage payments, you should speak to a currency specialist about setting up a regular payment plan. This will remove the worry caused by exchange rate fluctuations when making currency payments over a period of time and the transfer fees will only be at a fraction of the cost charged by your bank.

Currencies Direct's Overseas Regular Transfer Plan charges customers no transfer or commission fees and offers substantially better rates of exchange than the banks. Setting up a direct debit also means that payments are automated each month, therefore providing complete peace of mind. On transfer fees alone you could save £300 per year (based on the average bank charge of £25).

Specialist currency dealers can provide a more personalised service and help protect you against adverse currency movements by using their expertise to monitor exchange rates in order to achieve the best possible rate of exchange. Guidance on the currency markets can prove to be very valuable indeed. For example, if the UK couple had purchased the same property for $200,000 on 15ᵗʰ March 2006, it would have cost them £84,871. However, just two weeks later on 29ᵗʰ March 2006, the same property would have cost just £80,499. A dedicated foreign currency dealer can monitor the markets on your behalf and give you guidance on when might be the best time to buy your Aussie Dollars.

Charges. If you ask your bank to send your funds to Australia you should expect them to charge you for doing so. The local bank in Australia is also likely to make a substantial charge for receiving the money into your Australian account. However, a reputable currency broker may be able to reduce those overseas charges substantially or even eradicate them completely in some cases.

INSURANCE

Buying the right home insurance for your needs can be confusing and many Australians use a broker to help them negotiate the surfeit of policies now available. Home insurance premiums vary and are usually payable on an annual or bi-annual basis. Obtain a copy of any contract you are considering and assess it carefully. Make sure that such things as fixtures, bushfires, landslides and floods are covered.

Advice can be obtained from:

o National Insurance Brokers Association (☎02-9964 9400; www.niba. com.au).
o Insurance Council of Australia (☎02-9253 5100; www.ica.com.au).

People aged 50 and over experience half the number of break-ins than under-30s because they are more likely to install security features, such as alarms, window locks and deadlocks. Many insurance companies provide discounts to these 'low risk' customers.

Useful Contacts

GIO (Suncorp in Queensland): ☎13 10 10; www.gio.com.au. The latest company to launch an insurance product aimed specifically at 55-64 year olds.

Australian Pensioners Insurance Agency (APIA): ☎13 25 55; www.apia.com.au. The market leader for the over-55s market segment. Discounts are also offered by the major insurance companies in each state and territory.

National Seniors: ☎07-3211 9611; www.nationalseniors.com.au. Offers all forms of insurance.

Homes@50: ☎13 21 32; www.nrma.com.au/home. Available in most states under the brands NRMA Insurance

SGIC and SGIO: ☎13 32 33; www.sgic.com.au (SA) or www.sgio.com.au (WA).

The Over 50s Insurance Agency: ☎13 31 30; www.over50s.com.au. Also committed to the insurance needs of mature Australians.

A list of insurance brokers is available from the Australian Government Directory, www.agd.com.au, or the Yellow Pages, www.yellowpages.com.au.

Part three

A New Life
in Australia

Adapting to Your New Life
Quality of Life
Personal Finance
Healthcare
Crime, Security & the Police

Adapting to Your New Life

CHAPTER SUMMARY

○ **Shopping.** Fresh food markets, held throughout Australia, are very welcoming and the best place to buy local produce.
○ Australian cuisine has come a long way since its seven-course meal of a 'six-pack and a meat pie.'
○ Fish and chip lovers can find a host of 'chippies' throughout Australia.
○ Melbourne is known as the 'gourmet capital of the southern hemisphere.'
○ Australia has 51 wine regions producing some famous and some lesser-known labels to the rest of the world.
○ **Motoring.** Australians drive on the same side of the road as in the UK and some concessions are offered to retirees on a driver's licence and vehicle registration.

SHOPPING

Australia has an array of quality fresh produce and goods available in modern, well-equipped shopping centres. Items bearing a green and gold kangaroo trademark symbol have been manufactured in Australia and are usually more expensive. The large shopping centres offer speciality shops for clothing and goods as well as supermarkets. Many have cinema complexes and food halls.

Shopping online has become a popular pastime in today's world. According to the Australian Bureau of Standards, the older population is proportionally more likely to spend a higher amount each year on goods and services purchased via the internet than other age groups. Travel and accommodation are the most common type of purchase for older persons, computer software and financial services next, then books and magazines and tickets to entertainment or cinema.

At the ever-popular www.ebay.com.au you can find brand named items and collectables; dstore.com.au sells sports goods, toys, books, health goods and videos; www.wishlist.com.au has gifts for everyone, flowers, wine and books; www.shoptheweb.com.au has anything from travel, art, homewares and hampers; www.hardwareshop.com.au for all your DIY needs; and www.collinsbooks.com.au is a specialist online bookselling site.

Markets

The weekly Old Bus Depot Markets (www.obdm.com.au), a Sunday institution in Canberra, are renowned for handcrafted jewellery, art, clothing, furniture and regional food and wine produce. Every Saturday morning you'll find the Regional Growers Market offering fruit, vegetables, flowers, seafood, meat and cheeses. The Belconnen Fresh Food Markets have exotic locally produced gourmet delights.

Sydney is famous for its multitude of markets. The suburbs of Balmain, Glebe, Rozelle, Bondi and Paddington sell everything from homewares to vintage clothing. The Sydney Fish Market (☎02-9004 1100) has excellent fresh fish. You can find more at www.marketsonline.com.au and www.paddingtonmarkets.com.au.

South Australia has wonderful local produce and the Adelaide Central Market is the state's most visited attraction.

The Victorian Producers' Market is held annually (usually March) at the Plaza of the Melbourne Museum (Nicholson Street, Carlton; ☎03-9823 6100). You can buy everything from new season fruits and vegetables, farmhouse cheeses, nuts, breads, honey, meats and olive oils direct from the farmers and producers. The Queen Victoria Market in Melbourne sells everything from persimmons to pineapples, pasta and organic wine and fresh dairy produce.

The Fremantle Market, Western Australia, has more than 150 stalls selling seafood, gourmet items, clothes, jewellery, fresh fruit and veg, and antiques.

Local Shops

Ugg boots, made from Australian sheepskin, are found in most shoe shops but you can also buy a kangaroo-skin rug at www.uggstore.com.au.

The Canberra Centre is the state's largest mall, with three floors of fashion, department stores, designer labels, home wares, gift shops and boutiques.

Bundle Mall is the shopping nucleus of Adelaide with more than 600 retail stores.

The historic and heritage-listed Melbourne General Post office (GPO) is now a sophisticated precinct for fashion, food and shopping.

Perth's central shopping area is full of gemstone and fashion shops, major department stores and other designer outlets.

Handicrafts. Craft ACT's galleries, in the Civic Square, display contemporary craft and design from Canberra's artists. Craftspeople and farmers converge on the Hall Markets on the first Sunday of every month

Necessities. The corner shop, known as a 'deli' in Australia, stock a wide range of exotic foods in addition to essential items. David Jones and Myer Jones are the leading department stores present in all cities and major shopping centres, while Woolworths, Target and K-Mart carry almost everything. The main food stores are Coles and Woolworths and there are a plethora of smaller chains and boutique chains.

Home Comforts. If you miss your homeland treats, a range of British confectionary is available from The British Lolly Shop (Shop 35, Sorrento Quay, Hillarys Boar Harbour, Hillarys, Perth, WA 6025; ☎08-9448 4388; e-mail info@thebritishlollyshop.com; www.thebritishlollyshop.com). Items include boiled British sweets, Blackpool rock, Walkers crisps and Mars bars, Cadburys, McVities and Rowntree products.

Opening Hours

Shops are generally open from 8.30am to 5.30pm, Monday to Friday; 8.30 to 4.30pm on Saturday; and late night to 9pm one day a week. Shopping centres and shops usually only open on a Sunday (from 10am to 4pm) in the tourist areas and larger cities. In some areas you may be able to find a 24-hour shop.

FOOD AND DRINK

Australian cooking has always been known for its slabs of steak, lamingtons, pavlovas, and pumpkin scones, or its seven-course meal: 'a six-pack and a meat pie.' However, waves of immigrants from China, Greece, Italy, India,

Indonesia, Lebanon, Malaysia, Thailand, Vietnam and Turkey have brought with them their own tastes and styles. The outstanding seafood and sunny climate has made al fresco Mediterranean-style eating a popular choice.

Australia has a mouth-watering range of seafood, including prawns, lobsters, crayfish, octopus, oysters, mussels and mudcrubs, as well as a huge variety of fish. Meat also plays an important part in the Australian diet. Beef, lamb, pork and poultry of all cuts and types are available, as are the 'bushmeat' options, such as kangaroo, emu and crocodile. 'Bush tucker' is popular and a number of restaurants offer these native Aboriginal foods. Many Australians believe that the barbecue is their national dish and they can be sumptuous affairs with tiger prawns, marinated rump streak, chicken fillets or stuffed, whole fish.

Regional Specialities

New South Wales. Pacific oysters are native to Japan and were introduced to Australia in the 50s. Try the Sydney rock oyster. As you travel north in NSW, seafood and tropical fruit become cheaper and more plentiful, with freshly shucked oysters for about $10 a dozen. Bilpin is synonymous with apples; you can stop and buy apples and fresh apple juice.

Victoria. Freshwater fish, including yellow belly perch, red fin, yabbies and the famed Murray Cod are found in Victoria. Good seafood is also available in Geelong; while western Victoria offers western district lamb, berries, specialist cheeses, trout, yabbies, wild and farmed game, olives and their oil; and north-west Victoria is the centre of Australia's citrus and dried fruit industries.

Queensland. Brisbane has the best calamari ever. At Coffs Harbour, you can sample the local speciality: Clarence River prawns.

Tasmania. The island state is renowned for its seafood, which you can buy direct from the fishing boats in the ports. Taste fresh Tasmanian Atlantic salmon, ocean trout, blue-eye, trumpeter, flathead, orange roughy and black mussels. From December to April roadside stalls sell apples, cherries, stone-fruit and berries. Tasmanian leatherwood produces a wonderfully flavoured honey.

Western Australia. The largest beekeeping operation in the country can be found on the Gingin Coast. Here you can also taste locally grown olives, citrus fruits, beef and lobster. The Famous Miami Bakehouse in Mandurah has more than 100 varieties of gourmet pies, speciality breads and fresh cream cakes.

Eating Out

There are 30,000 restaurants and cafes in Australia, as well as 1,490 wineries with cellar door facilities of which nearly two-fifths have an on-site restaurant or facilities to serve light meals. Everywhere you go you'll find a host of fusion and Pacific-rim style cooking.

Canberra has a range of cafés and restaurants serving Spanish, Malaysian, French, Thai, Chinese, Italian and modern Australian at the 1920s shopping centres of Kingston and Manuka. Dickson offers a flourishing Chinatown and Ethiopian, Vietnamese, Korean, Malaysian, Japanese, Turkish, Italian and Thai cuisine.

Fish and chip lovers can tuck in at the following 'chippies':

o Southern Beach in Cronulla, New South Wales, overlooks the beach and surf club. A seafood pack with New Zealand Hoki fish, crumbed prawns, calamari and chips costs about $12.50.

o Tweed River Seafoods, Chinderah, New South Wales, is rated as the best fish and chips in the state.

o Wynyard Wharf Seafoods in Wynyard, Tasmania, has a choice of four fresh fish types and flavoursome oysters at realistic prices.

o At Morrisons Seafoods, Strahan, Tasmania, a seafood basket with white fish, a calamari ring, scallop, crumbed prawn and chips costs about $8.

o Daylesford Seafood Bar, Daylesford, Victoria, serves whiting and chips for about $10.

o Robe Seafoods, Robe, South Australia, doesn't look like much from the outside but once inside it's worth it.

o Peters, Surfers Paradise, Queensland is one of the original fish and chip shops on the Gold Coast. The trawler fleet docks behind the shop, so you can be assured of fresh fish.

Waterside dining is a popular pastime, especially in Sydney. Visit www.bestrestaurants.com.au to find out more on dining in New South Wales and to discover where the locals frequent.

Known as the 'gourmet capital of the southern hemisphere,' many Melbourne suburbs have their own culinary character: from the Greek atmosphere on Lonsdale Street, or Carlton's 'Little Italy' to Chinatown around Little Bourke Street.

In Western Australia, *The Wine and Truffle Company* (www.wineandtruffle.

com.au) is an interesting experience, where you can taste their wine and take part in seasonal truffle hunts. Perth has more restaurants per capita than any other city in the country.

Wine

Wine-grape growing and winemaking are now carried out in every state and territory in Australia. Fundamental to the organisation and development of the Australian wine industry is the geographic division of the country into wine zones, wine regions and sub-regions. The system, referred to as geographic indications (GI), governs the wine making process and the marketing of wine to both the domestic consumer and overseas markets. Australia has 51 wine region and nine sub-regions.

The Kamberra Wine Company (☎02-6262 2333; www.kamberra.com.au) in the Australian Capital Territory, seven minutes from the city's CBD, offers a gateway to the Canberra District's wineries.

South Australia is the heart of the nation's wine industry with 17 wine regions and more than 300 cellar doors, producing some famous labels such as Penfold's Grange and Jacob's Creek. The Barossa, Clare Valley, McLaren Vale, Adelaide Hills and Coonawarra are known internationally and all are no more than a 90-minute drive from Adelaide.

Tasmania produces chardonnay, pinot noir, gewürztraminer and Riesling. The *Tamar Valley Wine Route* and *Wine South Tasmania* brochures are available at Tasmania's Visitor Information Centres. A list of wineries in Tasmania can be found at www.winediva.com.au/wneries/tasmania.

Victoria boasts more than 400 wineries, home of some of the great Australian names of winemaking, such as Great Western, De Bortoli, Brown Brothers and Domaine Chandon. Sauvignon blanc, peppery shiraz, sparkling white wines, pinot noir, chardonnay and fortified tokays and muscats are produced across the state.

In the southwest of Western Australia, you'll find the Pemberton, Manjimup, Geographe, Blackwood Valley, Great Southern and the ever-popular Margaret River wine regions. Together they produce about 26% of Australia's premium wines.

Other Drinks

In the earliest days of the colony, the demand for rum made it at times the principal currency. Drinking was a male group activity that occurred mainly in hotels but this has changed in recent years. The range and sophistication of drinks available has increased enormously and is sold through a wide range of outlets and people drink at home more often.

More than three quarters of Australians drink alcohol, and wine consumption has increased more than threefold since the 1940s. Consumption of spirits peaked during the gold rushes but by the end of the 19th century Australia had become a beer drinking country. Tasmania's Cascade and Boag's beers are highly acclaimed. James Boag's premium was named the best premium beer at the Australian Liquor Industry awards. Both breweries have limited-release beers, including Boag's Honey Porter and Cascade Brewery's Four Seasons range. Otherwise, Lark Distillery produces bush liqueurs flavoured with native pepper berry.

MEDIA

Strong competition exists in Australia's newspaper, radio, and television industries as well as online news media. News Limited and the Fairfax Group are the largest newspaper publishers. There is one national daily, *The Australian*, 35 regional dailies, and 470 other regional and suburban papers. ACP is the largest magazine publisher. On a per capita basis, Australia has one of the highest newspaper and magazine circulations in the world.

The *Australian Women's Weekly* (a monthly) is the most popular Australian women's magazine. Its readership and circulation make it the most widely read magazine in the history of Australian publishing. It is particularly famous for its cooking section. Australian editions of *Women's Day*, *New Idea*, *Vogue*, *Cosmopolitan* and *Marie Claire* are available in all newsagents and most supermarkets. There are also numerous special interest publications, such as *Australian Gourmet Traveller* and *House and Garden*. International magazines, such as *Time* and *National Geographic*, are widely available but are pricey because copies are imported.

Australia has two national public broadcasters, the Australian Broadcasting Corporation (ABC) and the Special Broadcasting Service (SBS). The ABC has a national free-to-air television service, five domesticated radio networks (Local Radio, Radio National, Classic FM, Triple J, and NewsRadio), an international television service (ABC Asia Pacific), an international radio service (Radio Australia), and an online service (ABC Online). SBS is Australia's national multicultural and multilingual broadcaster with SBS Television broadcasting in more than 60 languages and SBS Radio in 68, more than any other network in the world. SBS Online provides text and video services as well as audio-on-demand. The radio stations are available in all Australian capital cities plus Newcastle and Wollongong. Sydney and Melbourne listeners have access to two SBS radio frequencies, while one is available elsewhere. Currently there are 264 operational commercial stations (funded by advertising) and more than 300 community (publicly funded) radio stations.

Newspapers

National: *The Australian*, www.theaustralian.news.com.au.

NSW: *The Daily Telegraph*, www.dailytelegraph.news.com.au; *Sydney Morning Herald*, www.smh.com.au.

SA: *The Advertiser*, www.theadvertiser.news.com.au; *Sunday Mail*.

QLD: *The Courier Mail*, ☎07-3666 8000; www.couriermail.news.com.au; *The Sunday Mail*, www.thesundaymail.news.com.au.

TAS: *The Mercury*, www.themercury.com.au.

VIC: *Herald Sun*, www.heraldsun.news.com.au; *The Age*, www.theage.com.au; *The Weekly Times*, www.theweeklytimes.com.au; *The Border Mail*, www.bordermail.com.au.

WA: *The West Australian*, www.thewest.com.au; *Sunday Times*, www.sundaytimes.news.com.au.

ACT: *The Canberra Times*.

NT: *Northern Territory News*, www.ntnews.news.com.au.

Nowadays, you can listen to a multitude of radio stations from around the world via the internet, as well as many local stations. It is interesting to pick up overseas stations and hear news from other countries. All you need to do is download a media player and have speakers and a sound card to play these stations. However, the sound can be interrupted at times if you are working on other parts of the internet, which can be frustrating. Digital radio is due to come on stream in the six state capitals by 2009.

Of the 52 licensed commercial television services in Australia the three main networks, Seven, Nine, and Ten, broadcast mainly in the major capital cities. The others, such as Prime Network, WIN television, and Southern Cross, focus on regional areas. Digital TV was launched in 2002 and until recently 920,000 free-to-view-digital receivers have been sold.

There are also three major Pay TV operators – Austar, Optus Television, and Foxtel. Austar operates primarily on a digital satellite platform, Optus is currently a cable-only operator, and Foxtel uses cable and satellite. Under current legislation, analogue TV services are due to be switched off in 2008. However, recent reports estimate this to be pushed back to 2012.

Bookshops and Libraries

Books may be slightly more expensive than those in the UK but all major publishers distribute in Australia. Large bookshops are found in all Australian cities, including a number of chains. Angus & Robertson (www.angusrobert-son.com.au) is Australia's leading bookstore chain; and Dymocks Booksellers (www.dymocks.com.au) has stores nationwide. There are also a number of smaller independent and speciality bookshops, such as All Arts Bookshop (www.allarts.com.au) and Boffins Bookshop (www.boffinsbookshop.com.au).

Every state and territory has excellent library services both at the local and state level, and the National Library of Australia provides research facilities and is home to the national archives.

CARS AND MOTORING

Driving a car plays a significant role in our lifestyle and independence as we get older. In Australia, almost everyone concerned with road safety want to keep drivers on the road for as long as possible if they drive safely. With this in mind, the traffic authorities in each state and territory have set out guidelines on evaluating your driving ability along with a medical, physical and driving test.

It is a legal requirement under Australian licensing laws that only one licence can be used for driving in Australia. In most states and territories, you need to apply for a local licence after being resident there for three months.

Driver's Licences and Testing for Persons of Advanced Age

ACT. After the provisional period of three years has been completed, you can obtain a full licence, which is renewable on each birthday divisible by five years. You will need a medical statement from your doctor to say you are fit to drive when you are 75 and over. There is no age-based road testing.

The ACT Transport Roads and Traffic (www.rego.act.gov.au) has an online *Older Drivers Handbook*, which is useful for anywhere in Australia. It includes a form for self-assessment of your driving performance.

NSW. You can use your UK licence for three months and thereafter you must get a

NSW licence. If you hold a current NSW Pensioners Concession Card you may be eligible for a free licence. You may be required to undergo an eyesight test, knowledge test and in some cases a medical examination. A driving test is required when you reach 85 and then annually.

More information is available from Roads and Traffic Authority NSW (☎13 22 13; www.rta.nsw.gov.au).

NT. When you arrive in the NT you can use your current overseas licence with an International Driving Permit for the first three months. After this time you must transfer your licence to the NT. No medical or age based testing. Registration fees for private vehicles are based on the cubic capacity of your car's engine.

The Motor Vehicle Registry (☎1300 654 628; www.mvr.nt.gov.au) collects the registration fee and compulsory third party insurance at the time you register your vehicle.

QLD. After three months in Queensland you must apply for a local licence. You must pass a written test, which will cost you $16.30 and consists of 30 general questions. Once you pass this, you can buy a driver's licence for any period from one to five years. One year costs $24.95; up to $63.95 for five years. Drivers 75 and older are required to obtain a medical certificate, which can be valid up to five years. No age-based road test.

More information from Queensland Transport (☎07-3834 2011; www.transport.qld. gov.au).

SA. If you are an overseas licence holder and a temporary resident you may drive in South Australia for the duration of the visa providing your overseas licence remains current. You must carry your driver's licence and visa with you when driving as evidence of your temporary residence status. If you obtain permanent residency, you must get a SA licence within three months of becoming a resident. All overseas licence holders are required to undertake and pass a theory test but you will not be required to complete a practical test if you come from the UK or USA. A licence costs $24 a year plus $15 administration fee and can be obtained for up to 10 years. Your doctor is required to complete a Certificate of Fitness each year for 70 year olds and older.

Contact Transport SA (☎08-8204 8255; www.transport.sa.gov.au) for more information and a copy of the *South Australian Older Drivers Handbook.*

TAS. After three months as a permanent resident in Tasmania you must obtain a Tasmanian drivers licence. You will need to pass a knowledge and practical driving test. After you turn 65, you still need to renew your driver licence when it is out of date. No renewal fee applies. It is only necessary to pay a small fee for the photo-card. To keep your licence after you turn 75, you need to have an annual medical examination. From age 85 you will need a medical examination and a driving test annually.

The Department of Infrastructure, Energy and Resources – Transport (☎1300 135 513; www.transport.tas.gov.au) has more information. The *Tasmanian Older Drivers Handbook*, available online, has valuable guidance for all older drivers.

VIC. The three-month rule applies in Victoria as well. You do not have to pass the theory, driving and hazard perception test if you hold a UK or USA licence. No medical or age-based testing. Contact VicRoads (☎13 11 71; www.vicroads.vic.gov.au) for more information.

WA. The three-year time frame applies in Western Australia. From 1 January 2006, the owner of a licensed vehicle will be responsible for identifying who was in charge of their vehicle at any given time. A licence for one year costs $33.80; up to $53.60 for five years for pensioners and seniors. Persons aged 85 and over are required to take a driving test each year before their licence is renewed. Medicals are required before the renewal of a licence in the year a person is 75, 78, 80 and then annually.

Further information is available from the Department for Planning and Infrastructure (☎08-9427 6404; www.dpi.wa.gov.au).

Australians drive on the left of the road, as in the UK. Speed limits differ between states and territories but are generally 62 mph (100 kph) to 68 mph (110 kph) on the highways (motorways) and 30 mph (50 kph) to 37 mph (60 kph) in built-up areas. Be careful when driving on country roads at night in cold weather. Cattle and kangaroos lie on the tarred road surface because it holds the warmth of the sun. Car lights blind and mesmerise the animals and they may just as easily run into your vehicle as run away from it.

There are a number of accident and breakdown services but the biggest is the National Road and Motorists' Association (www.nrma.com.au) but the Australian Automobile Association (www.aaa.com.au), and Royal Automobile Club of Australia (www.raa.net) have a huge presence.

Australia has a 0.05% blood alcohol limit for drivers holding open class licences. Contact the police in the state in which you are travelling on limits applying to other classes of licences.

Fuel prices differ within each state and territory and although they fluctuate these were the prices at the time of writing:

ACT: $1.37	SA: $1.36
NSW: $1.36	TAS: $1.35
NT: $1.38	VIC: $1.34
QLD: $1.27	WA: $1.39

LOCAL GOVERNMENT AND VOTING

Below the level of state government, the administration of local areas is undertaken by an elected town or shire council. This body is responsible for the provision and maintenance of public facilities and amenities, such as leisure centres, libraries, and rubbish collections. Payments for all housing rates, and even dog licences, are made to the local government. Planning permission for new buildings, demolitions and extensions are also the responsibility of the local government, and vocal public meetings are frequently held to hear public discussion over topical local issues, such as town planning and new developments. The local government level is the only one at which voting is not compulsory and, in general, most Australians are somewhat apathetic and avoid close involvement in local government decisions.

Local Government websites

Australian Capital Territory: www.directory.act.gov.au.

Northern Territory: www.nt.gov.au/ntg/localgov.

New South Wales: www.dlg.nsw.gov.au.

Queensland: www.lgp.qld.gov.au.

South Australia: www.sa.gov.au.

Tasmania: www.service.tas.gov.au.

Victoria: www.doi.vic.gov.au/councils.

Western Australia: www.dlgrd.wa.gov.au.

Registering a Vote

Enrolment on the Commonwealth electoral role has been compulsory in Australia since 1911. Failure to do so is punished on conviction by a fine of up to $50. If you were a British subject on a Commonwealth electoral roll as at 25 January 1984 you are eligible to enrol as an Australian voter even if you are not an Australian citizen.

You can pick up an enrolment form from any post office, AEC office, state/territory electoral office, or online. Once processed, the AEC will send you an acknowledgement card. This will advise you of the name of the federal electoral division that you are enrolled in. More information is available from the Australian Electoral Commission (AEC), ☎02-6271 4411; e-mail info@aec.gov.au; www.aec.gov.au.

Maintaining Your UK Vote

If you are a British citizen living abroad you can apply to be an overseas voter in UK Parliamentary and European elections. You have to have appeared on the electoral register in the UK within the previous 15 years.

You can register as soon as you move abroad by completing an Overseas Elector's Declaration form from your nearest British consular or diplomatic mission. More information is available at www.aboutmyvote.co.uk, or for Northern Ireland www.electoralofficeni.gov.uk.

RELIGION

In the 18th century when the English first settled in Australia, they established churches under the Bishop of London. Over the next two centuries the Anglican Church of Australia moved towards independence, which only came in 1962. Today, almost all denominations are represented in the Australian population: Catholic 26.4%, Anglican 20.5%, other Christian 20.5%, Buddhist 1.9%, Muslims 1.5%.

At the time of European settlement, the indigenous Australians had their own religious traditions and although there was contact from explorers, fishermen and survivors of shipwrecks there was no significant European influence on the religion of indigenous Australians. The Aborigines believe that the individual is part mortal, part spiritual. Their fundamental principle rests on their dependence on nature and each clan has a special relation with certain animals, plants and other natural objects.

Useful Contacts

Catholic Church: www.catholic.org.au.

Anglican Church: www.anglican.org.au.

Lutheran Church: www.lca.org.au/lutherans/.

Presbyterian Church: www.presbyterian.org.au.

Australian Pentecostal Churches: www.ministryblue.com/church-pentecostal.htm.l

Buddhism in Australia: www.buddhistcouncil.org/.

Australian Federation of Islamic Councils: www.afic.com.au.

Quality of Life

CHAPTER SUMMARY

O Seniors and retirees in Australia are eligible for a range of concessions including discounts on vehicle registration, dining out and reduced fares on trains and buses.

O A 'new residents' or 'community' information pack will give you information on sporting and other clubs.

O Australians are fanatical about their sport, whether participating or from the armchair.

O *Birdos* have 800 different kinds of birds to look out for and identify.

O Australia's 37,118 miles (59,736 km) of coastline means there are an abundance of diving sites, including the famous Great Barrier Reef.

O There is an enormous choice as far as holiday destinations are concerned, from the 'touristy' to the unknown.

WHERE TO GET INFORMATION

O *The Seniors Enquiry Line:* ☎1300 135 500; www.seniorsenquiryline.com. au, links you to a range of community information.

O *www.seniors.gov.au:* the Australian government's premier source of information for the over 50s, including health, lifestyle, care, finance, work and legal rights.

O *Australian Retired Pensions Association (ARPA):* ☎03-9650 6144; www. over50s.asn.au, is an independent national organisation assisting members in quality of life issues, such as employment, social security, taxation, safety and security.

O *COTA National Seniors:* ☎02-6282 7677; www.cota.org.au, is Australia's largest seniors organisation.

Tourist Offices

Australian Capital Tourism Corporation: 5/2 Brindabella Circuit, Brindabella Business Park, Canberra International Airport, ACT 2609; ☎02-6205 0666; fax 02-6205 0629; e-mail visitcanberra@act.gov.au; www.canberratourism.com.au.

National Capital Authority: Treasury Building, King Edward Terrace, Parkes, ACT 2600; ☎02-6271 2888; fax 02-6273 4427; e-mail natcap@natcap.gov.au; www.nationalcapital.gov.au.

Visit NSW: Sydney Visitors Centre, 106 George Street, The Rocks, NSW 2000; ☎02-9255 1788; www.visitnsw.com.

Northern Territory Tourist Commission: Tourism House, 43 Mitchell Street, Darwin, NT 0800; ☎08-8951 8471; fax 08-8951 8550; e-mail nttc@nt.gov.au.

Tourism Queensland: Tourism Queensland House, 30 Makerston Street, Brisbane, QLD 4000; ☎07-3535 3535; fax 07-3535 5444; www.tq.com.au.

South Australia Tourism Commission: 18 King William Street, Adelaide, SA 5000; ☎08-8303 2220; www.southaustralia.com.

Tourism Tasmania: Level 2, 22 Elizabeth Street, Hobart, TAS 7000; ☎03-6230 8235; fax 03-6230 8353; www.discovertasmania.com.au.

Tourism Victoria: 55 Collins Street, Melbourne, VIC 3000; ☎03-9653 9777; fax 03-9653 9722; www.visitvictoria.com.

Tourism Western Australia: 2 Mill Street, Perth, WA 6000; ☎08-9262 1700; fax 08-9262 1702; www.westernaustralia.com.

MAKING NEW FRIENDS

Friends help to make our lives meaningful and enjoyable and while most of us make friends instinctively, you can feel isolated and vulnerable when you move to a new country – a stranger in a strange land. By joining clubs and associations you can find people that enjoy the same interests and activities. Your local shopping centre, park, library or Community Information Centre are also good places to start. If you contact your local council, you can ask for a 'new residents' or 'community' information pack. This will give you information on your local sporting and other clubs and you will find details of newcomer clubs, where you can join a group of people going to shows, exhibitions, museums and other events. Your local newspaper and church will also have details on social events. Social clubs arrange a host of outings: wine tastings, nights at the cinema, dinners, theatre trips and ski weekends. Lions and Rotary clubs are also have a presence in Australia. Probus Clubs are for retired businessmen and women who wish to keep their minds active and expand their interests with other like mind people. Toastmasters International has more than 500 clubs in Australia divided into three districts. Expat Brian Havard explains his club activities:

At first, we were slightly apprehensive, but within days my doctor introduced me to another of his patients, then President of the local Probus Club, which had some splendid people among its membership, many of whom have become firm friends. My wife became founder member and later President of a Ladies Probus, then she joined a Quilting Group. Now, after 12 years, I have finally resigned my Presidency of the British Australian Pensioner Association (BAPA), which campaigns for pensions parity, and we have a little more time, we have joined the University of the Third Age. I guess we are still settling in.

Some Useful Contacts

Lions Australia: ☎ 02-4940 8033; www.lionsclubs.org.au.
Probus Clubs: ☎ 02-9806 0100; www.probus.com.au.
Rotary Down Under: ☎ 02-9633 4888; www.rotarnet.com.au.
Toastmasters International: www.toastmasters.org.au.
Waverley Newcomers Club: ☎ 03-9511 4430; www.angelfire.com/wa/waverleynew comers/, based in south-east Melbourne.
Welsh Society of Western Australia: ☎ 08-9300 9009; www.wawelshsociety.org.au.

SENIOR CONCESSIONS

If you are aged 60 and over and do not work more than 16 to 20 hours a week you can get a Seniors Card. There are no national senior cards but instead they are issued free by each state and territory government and enable holders to obtain a wide range of discounts on public and commercial activities. Eligible criteria and concessions available vary, so contact your state or territory Seniors Card office for details.

Businesses (including tours, attractions and accommodation) in one state will usually recognise cards from another. Shops frequently display a 'Seniors Card Welcome' sticker. Generally, Seniors Cards will not attract concessions on interstate public facilities but there are exceptions.

Western Australia was the first state to establish a Seniors Card programme followed by the other jurisdictions. The states and territories have worked collaboratively over many years to develop a card nationally recognised by

many private businesses and tourism providers. The private business discounts available to interstate seniors are listed in the Discount Directories published in each jurisdiction.

There have been national efforts to determine the cost of establishing a reciprocal transport scheme. However, trying to find a scheme that can be implemented across the transport and card systems of each jurisdiction has proven too difficult and negotiations with the states and federal governments have now ceased. It is felt that extending concessions to seniors visiting from other states and territories would have a significant cost impact overall and would be detrimental to those jurisdictions providing the greatest range of concessions. Regardless of this, in 2005 the Victorian Government announced concession travel on V/Line passenger services for all Australian pensioners whatever their state or territory of origin.

Seniors Cards Offices:

ACT: ACT Office for Ageing, ☎02-6282 3777; www.ageing.act.gov.au.

NT: Office of Senior Territorians, ☎08-8999 2638; www.seniorscard.nt.gov.au. Application forms are available at your local post office, Motor Vehicle Registry, Community Care Centre, or Office of Senior Territorians.

NSW: NSW Department of Ageing, Disability and Home Care, ☎1300 364 758, www. seniorscard.nsw.gov.au. Application forms are available from local and state government offices, including Department of Ageing, Disability and Home Care regional offices, Government Access Centres, most NSW local council offices and all NSW MP offices.

QLD: Department of Communities, ☎07-3224 2788, www.communities.qld.gov. au. Available for those over 65 and retired residents over 60 who already receive a specified Centrelink or Veterans' payment or concession card. Another card, the Seniors Business Discount Card, is available to all permanent residents who are 60 years or over, regardless of their income or assets, who do not qualify for a Seniors Card. This card gives access to shopping discounts only.

SA: Office for the Ageing, ☎08-8226 6852; www.familiesandcommunities.sa.gov.au. You can also apply at the post office.

TAS: Department of Premier and Cabinet, ☎03-6233 4532; www.dpac.tas.gov.au. On application, you will need to take three current documents as evidence of identity, such as a passport, driver's licence, or credit card.

VIC: Department for Victorian Communities, ☎03-9616 8241; www.seniorscard.vic. gov.au. If you are 60 years or more, a permanent resident of Victoria, and retired or working less than 35 hours a week in paid employment.

WA: Office for Seniors Interests, ☎08-9328 9155; www.seniorscard.wa.gov.au.

Discounts and Benefits for Cardholders

ACT: $1.20 a day Action Bus Travel for travel during off-peak periods, all day weekends and public holidays. Discounts on ACT dog registration through ACT Government Shopfronts. A 10% concession on the registration component of privately registered motor vehicles. A $35 subsidy towards the purchase of spectacles through a provider of your choice; subsidy is available every two years. Concessions can be obtained from ACT Countrylink for travel from ACT into NSW. In some countries, particularly Great Britain and the United States of America, businesses will provide holders of an ACT Seniors Card with discounts on goods and services, although there are no formal agreements in place.

NSW: Thousands of businesses in NSW have discounts and special offers for Seniors Card holders. You are entitled to special concession rates on NSW government transport and half fare travel on many other government and private transport services.

NT: Two business directories are available annually. The *General Business Directory* lists offers available to Seniors Card holders from home maintenance to pet care (updated each August). The *Tourism and Leisure Business Directory* lists discount offers such as accommodation, eating out and sporting activities (updated each May).

QLD: A 50% concession on urban bus services but not on long-distance services. A 50% concession on ferry services. A 50% reduction of the registration fee component of your motor vehicle registration fees. A 50% concession on normal adult rail fares. A rebate of $9.57 a month to the cost of electricity supplied to your home. Free dental treatment and dentures. A 10% annual discount to fish in specific dams throughout Queensland.

SA: You are entitled to some government concessions, such as 50% reduction on state public transport services, as well as discounts on a variety of goods and services including accommodation, sport, retailing, entertainment and culture. When you receive a card you will also be sent a Seniors Card Directory *Your Lifestyle Guide*. This discount directory is updated annually and posted out in October/November each year.

TAS: Discounts are available on many products and services, including accommodation, building supplies, dining out, food and beverages, furniture, hairdressing, tourist attractions and more.

VIC: A range of exclusive discounts are available from more than 3,000 businesses and include: A Seniors Daily (60 Plus) Metcard for all day use on trains, trams or buses across zones 1, 2 and 3 Monday to Sunday. V/Line (☎13 61 96; www.vlinepassenger.com.au) is Victoria's largest regional passenger transport operator and has concession fares (50% to 65% discounts) on nominated V/Line off-peak services. Free admission to the Melbourne and Immigration Museums and Scienceworks. Free fishing in Victorian waters.

WA: Reduced cost of driver's licence and $28 reduction in the annual vehicle registration fee. A rebate on the energy supply charge of 25.57 cents a day and the up-front cost of a meter test is reduced to $139.20; and an air conditioning rebate. A rebate of up to 50% on annual water charges. Up to 25% rebate on local government rates. A maximum subsidy of up to $50 on a pair of spectacles once every two years. Reduced fares of 50% to 60% on bus, train and ferry services (SmartRider). A 50% reduction on coach and rail services fares. A 30% concession on privately operated public buses between towns in WA.

Call the Seniors Card office in the state where you will be travelling and ask them to send you a copy of their *Discount Directory*.

There is also the **Commonwealth Seniors Health Card (CSHC)**, which gives older Australians access to concessions on prescription medicines through the Pharmaceutical Benefits Scheme (PBS) as well as payment of a Telephone Allowance. Many self-funded retirees will be eligible for CSHC. This card is for people of pension age but who do not qualify for the Age Pension and have an income of less than $50,000 per year for singles and $80,000 for couples. The card also offers concessions on Great Southern Railways (Indian Pacific, The Ghan and The Overland).

The Pensioner Concession Card (PCC) enables pensioners to obtain concessions on prescription medicines and hearing services and, in conjunction with a Medicare card, basic hospital and medical treatment. You also get the Telephone Allowance plus concessions on state and local government charges and from some businesses.

The Health Care Card gives concessions on prescription medicines and additional concessions, such as health, household, educational, recreational and some transport concessions. These concessions differ within each state and territory.

Australian Government concessions are available for the holders of the PCC and CSHC as follows:

- ○ Prescription and other medicines listed in the Pharmaceutical Benefits Scheme (PBS) at the concession rate.
- ○ Bulk billed GP appointments, at the discretion of the doctor.
- ○ Reduction in the cost of out-of-hospital medical expenses above a certain threshold through the Medicare Safety Net.
- ○ Assistance with certain hearing services, such as hearing tests and hearing aids (for PCC only).
- ○ Free mail redirection through Australia Post for a maximum period of 12 months (PCC only).

Extra Assistance for Seniors

Seniors Concession Allowance: Assists Commonwealth Seniors Card holders to pay for services that, in most states and territories, are not available at concession rates to these cardholders. These include energy, rates, motor vehicle registration, and water and sewerage. Each cardholder receives $206 a year. The allowance is paid in two separate instalments of $103 in June and December each year.

Utilities Allowance: Assists those older Australians of Age Pension or Service Pension Age receiving income support to pay regular bills such as gas, electricity and water. This allowance is paid in two instalments on 20 March and 20 September each year ($50.50 in each instalment for a couple; and $25.30 for single).

For more information, contact Centrelink (☎1800 050 004; www.centrelink. gov.au).

SPORTS AND LEISURE PURSUITS

Australians are sports mad, whether as a participant or spectator, and there are facilities for almost every sport on earth. It plays a pivotal role in many facets of local lifestyle and the type of sport played varies between regions. The climate is also well suited for playing sport all year round.

Studies have shown that people are now living way beyond 65, which in the past was regarded as aged. Sixty is now being touted as the new 40 and increasingly retired people are pursuing sports and living fit and active lives. Sports are the best way of maintaining a healthy cardiovascular system and a feeling of well-being. A recent report highlighted the fact that a 60 year old can have a cardiovascular system as efficient as that of a 20 year old. Unfortunately, this does not apply to joints as well, so it is important to know your weaknesses and take suitable precautions and medical advice.

Walking

Australia is a vast country to enjoy walking. There are long distances and few towns so you need to be self-sufficient. Winter is the best time for walking as summer temperatures regularly exceed 104 deg F (40 deg C). Remember that water is often hard to find. Recognised trails and bushwalking areas are generally within a day's driving of the major centres of Sydney, Melbourne, Hobart, Perth, Brisbane and Adelaide.

The state-based National Parks Associations (NPAs) has an annual Great Australian Bushwalk (www.greataustralianbushwalk.org.au), which offers a range of walks and outdoor activities for all ages and levels of fitness. There are at least a 100 walks in all states and territories from rolling countryside, beaches and rainforests, and along rivers and bush pools. You can register online or contact the NPA in your state or territory (below).

Major National Parks

New South Wales: Ben Boyd, Blue Mountains, Mungo, Myall Lakes, Sturt, Sydney Harbour, Warrumbungle and Wollemi.

Northern Territory: Kakadu, Litchfield and Uluru-Kata Tjuta.

Queensland: Daintree, Lawn Hill and Simpson Desert.

South Australia: Coffin Bay, Coorong, Flinders Ranges, Lake Eyre and Murray River.

Tasmania: Ben Lomond, Cradle Mountain – Lake St Clair, Franklin-Gordon Wild Rivers, Freycinet, Mount Field, Mount William, Southwest and Walls of Jerusalem.

Victoria: Alpine, Croajingolong, Grampians, Mornington Peninsula, Mount Buffalo,

Port Campbell: Wilsons Promontory and Yarra Ranges.

Western Australia: Cape Arid, Drysdale River, Leeuwin-Naturaliste, Nambung and Stirling Range.

The public reserve system in New South Wales consists of more than 500 national parks and nature reserves covering 6.7% of the region. Victoria has 52 national parks, 30 state parks, three wilderness parks and 11 marine sanctuaries. In addition, there are more than 30 metropolitan parks and about 3,000 smaller conservation reserves. In all, these cover 8.9 million acres (3.6 million ha) or about 16% of Victoria. ACT parks consist of the Namadgi National Park, Canberra Nature Park, Tidbinbilla Nature Reserve, and Murrumbidgee River Corridor. Tasmania has 19 national parks and a range of other reserves protected for their natural and cultural importance. The Bibbulmun Track is one of the world's great long walk trails stretching 621 miles (1,000 km) through the heart of the south west of Western Australia.

National Park Associations

National Parks Association of NSW: ☎02-9299 0000; e-mail npansw@npansw. org.au; www.npansw.org.au.

Victorian National Parks Association: ☎03-9347 5188; e-mail vnpa@vnpa.org.au; www.vnpa.org.au.

National Parks Association of Queensland: ☎07-3367 0878; e-mail npaq@npaq. org.au; www.npaq.org.au.

National Parks Association (ACT): ☎02-6282 5813; e-mail npaact@bigpond. com.au; www.npaact.org.au.

Tasmanian National Parks Association: ☎04-2785 4684; e-mail admin@tnpa. asn.au; www.tnpa.asn.au.

Nature Conservation Society of South Australia: ☎08-8223 6301; e-mail ncssa@ ncssa.asn.au; www.ncssa.asn.au.

Bibbulmun Track Foundation (Western Australia): ☎08-9481 0551; e-mail friends@bibbulmuntrack.org.au; www.bibbulmuntrack.org.au.

Darwin Bushwalking Club: ☎08-8985 1484; www.bushwalking.org.au.

Bushwalking Australia: www.bushwalkingaustralia.org; represents walkers throughout Australia. You can find some useful bushwalking information on its website, including types of walking and walking areas and what to take with you. A list of walking clubs in your area is also available.

The Confederation of Bushwalking Clubs: www.bushwalking.org.au; a New South Wales organisation for bushwalking and outdoor recreation activities. The website lists clubs in your area.

Australia is not particularly known internationally as a hiking destination but it's just that it hasn't been discovered yet. Mt Kosciuszko at 7,310 ft (2,228 m) is Australia's highest mountain and one of the world's Seven

Summits. The most challenging hiking is found in the mountainous region of Tasmania, where it's not unusual to climb and descend 2,500 ft (762 m) in a day. There are also some amazing hikes in the Blue Mountains region of NSW and a mystical hike around the base of Ayers Rock. Gentler hikes are also available, such as Eungella National Park to see the elusive platypus.

Active Australia (www.activeaustralia.com) can organise a suitable trip for you.

Ten Highest Mountains

Mount Kosciuszko 7,310 ft (2,228 m)

Mount Townsend 7,247 ft (2,209 m)

Mount Twynam 7,201 ft (2,195 m)

Rams Head 7,185 ft (2,190 m)

Unnamed peak on Etheridge Ridge 7,152 ft (2,180 m)

Rams Head North 7,142 ft (2,177 m)

Alice Rawson Peak 7,086 ft (2,160 m)

Unnamed peak south-west of Abbott Peak 7,083 ft (2,159 m)

Abbott Peak and Carruthers Peak 7,037 ft (2,145 m)

Mount Northcote 6,991 ft (2,131 m)

All these mountains are situated in New South Wales, within a 12-mile (20-km) radius of Mt Kosciuszko.

Cycling

Australia abounds with many cycling routes, such as along the Great Ocean Road, and many other forest trails and general cycling areas. State cycling organisations provide organised rides as well as advice on what kind of bike to buy and how to maintain it.

Useful Addresses

Bicycle Federation of Australia: ☎02-6249 6761; www.bfa.asn.au.

Bicycle NSW: ☎02-9281 4099; www.bicyclensw.org.au.

Bicycle Queensland: ☎07-3844 1144; www.bq.org.au.

Bicycle Tasmania: ☎03-6266 4582; www.biketas.org.au.

Bicycle Victoria: ☎03-8636 8888; www.bv.com.au.

Birdwatching

There are about 800 different kinds, or species, of naturally occurring birds that have been recorded in Australia and its territories at least once for birders, or birdos, to enjoy. Bird clubs publish newsletters and hold regular meetings, as well as conducting outings to good birding sites. Often they run volunteer-based projects aimed to discover more about birds in their area of concern. You can become physically, mentally and emotionally fitter through birding and it can be one of the most rewarding activities.

Birds Australia (☎03-9882 2622; e-mail mail@birdsaustralia.com.au; www.birdsaustralia.com.au) is dedicated to the enjoyment of Australia's native birds and their habitats. It is Australia's oldest and largest national birding organisation, with more than 6,000 members throughout the country and overseas. It has a list of all the country's birds and information about where to watch and study birds, as well as guidelines for recreational birdwatching. It has offices in New South Wales, Victoria and Western Australia; and regional groups in ACT, Queensland, New South Wales, Tasmania, Victoria and Western Australia. Its two bird reserves are the Gluepot Reserve in South Australia and Newhaven Reserve in the Northern Territory. Observatories are located in Broome and Cockebiddy in Western Australia. Becoming a member enables you to get discounts on accommodation, courses and tours, to receive its regional newsletter, which includes local information, and copies of its quarterly *Wingspan* magazine. Single membership costs $68 a year, concessions $50.

Birdwatching Australia (☎03-9877 5342; e-mail info@ausbird.com; www.ausbird.com) has a directory of Australian birdwatching tours, bird clubs, freelance guides, bird-orientated accommodation and reference material. Information on accommodation, local tour operators and tours, local guides, day tours, local bird clubs and societies is provided by state. You can also buy field guides, books and bird calls on tapes and CDs.

The Bird Observers Club of Australia (☎03-9877 5342; e-mail information@birdobservers.org.au; www.birdobservers.org.au) is a major birding organisation and runs birdwatching activities, outings, camps, local and overseas trips, undertakes bird surveys, and has an extensive library and shop. It publishes the bi-monthly news magazine, *The Bird Observer*, distributed free to all members. BOCA has 38 branches and affiliates in the southern and eastern states of Australia. Membership includes a bonus issue of *The Bird Observer*, a free copy of *The Little Blue Birdlist*, 20% discount on a field guide of your choice, and discounts on binoculars and telescopes. Single membership costs $70 a year, pensioner single $52, pensioner household $79, or Seniors Card single $65, household $97.

The *Interpretive Birding Bulletin* is published six times a year and includes articles to encourage bird enthusiasts. At Interpretive Birding Online (www.ibirding.com) you can submit your personal field observations and interpretations.

Guides

Field Guide to the Birds of Australia, by Graham Pizzey and Frank Knight (Angus & Robertson, $29.95), a classic field guide.

Field Guide to Australian Birds, by Michael Morcombe (Steve Parrish Publishing, $45).

Hotlines

Birdline NSW: ☎02-9439 9536.

Birdline VIC: ☎03-9882 2390.

Canberra Hotline: ☎02-6247 5530.

Special Interest Groups

Australasian Raptor Group (ARP): Victoria, ☎04-2733 8898; e-mail president@ ausraptor.org.au; www.ausraptor.org.au.

Australasian Seabird Group (ASG): ☎03-5678 2240.

Australasian Water Studies Group (AWSG): Victoria, e-mail ken@gosbell.id.au.

Birds Australia Parrot Association (BAPA): Victoria, e-mail Ian.Temby@dse. vic.gov.au.

Golf

The Australian Golf Club in Sydney and Royal Melbourne Golf Club are the two oldest clubs in Australia, while Bothwell Golf Club in Tasmania is the oldest course. Golf was first played here by Alexander Reid, who came from Scotland, in the late 1820s. Australia has a national, computerised handicapping system where a central computer calculates and maintains your handicap. Golfers are issued a personalised individual swipe card and are able to access the system. Male golfers obtain a handicap through a golf club that must be a member of the Australian Golf Union (AGU). Handicaps for women are issued by Women's Golf Australia. Handicapping is based on the course rating of the course played; not its par.

○ Ausgolf (www.ausgolf.com.au) is Australia's most informative golf website and features course ratings and reviews, travel, equipment, information on handicaps and much more.

○ Iseekgolf (www.iseekgolf.com) features details of more than 1,800 golf courses in Australia, 1,300 items of golf equipment to read and review, clubfitting and repairs, travel, latest golf news, players interviews and golf classifieds.

Scuba Diving

With a coastline of 37,118 miles (59,736 km), including islands, Australia has some of the most diverse diving locations in the world: the most popular, of course, being the Great Barrier Reef, off Queensland. However, other spots, such as the Kelp Forest off the Tasman Peninsula, as well as wreck and shark cage diving are all popular pursuits. Whether a novice or experienced diver, contact Dive-Oz (☎mobile 0414 604 853; www.diveoz.com.au) or Diving Australia (☎0408 – diving; www.diving-australia.com) for more information on locations, trips and equipment.

Fishing

Fishing is one of the biggest and most economically viable recreations in Australia. The national annual expenditure on the sport is almost equal to the total annual income from casinos and is ahead of horse and dog racing. Between 37% and 42% of the adult male population fishes at least once a year; female participation ranges from 16.9% to 21%.

Recreational fishing is a statewide activity and the season extends from August to May, with the best fishing normally between October and April. However, many waters are now open for all year round angling.

The Australian National Sportfishing Association is the peak body of sportfishing in Australia representing all levels, from beginners to the experienced angler, through its branches and affiliated clubs. Clubs usually meet once a month to plan competitions and fishing trips.

Fishnet (www.fishnet.com.au) is the largest and most comprehensive online recreational sportfishing information resource in Australia. It includes a comprehensive database of fish species in Fish File, countrywide fishing reports from members, and listings for fishing clubs and associations.

When you decide where you would like to go and fish, you can check out the location's current weather conditions on Fishnet's weather service. This includes wind speed and direction, air temperatures, humidity, dew point and even the latest barometric pressure readings, all updated every half an hour. You can also access day forecasts and the latest radar and satellite images for metropolitan and regional areas throughout the nation.

Licence Details

Government Fisheries Agencies will be able to give you information on recreational fishing rules, licences, bag and size limits, protected species, closed seasons, fishing tips and hotspots. Contacts are as follows:

New South Wales: ☎02-6391 3100; www.fisheries.nsw.gov.au. It's estimated that one million people fish in NSW at least once a year. If you go fresh and saltwater fishing in NSW, you will need to pay the NSW Recreational Fishing Fee and carry a receipt showing payment. A three-day licence costs $6, one month $12, one year $30, or three years $75. This fee goes towards improving recreational fishing in the state.

Northern Territory: ☎08-8999 2144; www.fisheries.nt.gov.au. NT has a limit on how many fish you may have in your possession at any time. Darwin Harbour is a popular fishing spot and is in close proximity to the central business district (CBD). You do not need a licence for recreational fishing in the Northern Territory but neither can you sell or barter your catch.

Queensland: ☎07-3404 6999; www.dpi.qld.gov.au. More than 700,000 fish are caught recreationally in Queensland each year. Anglers take home about 8,500 tonnes of finfish, crabs and prawns. Saltwater fishing is currently the most popular; while 40% of anglers own a boat. No licence is required for recreational fishing in Queensland.

South Australia: ☎08-8347 6100; www.pir.sa.gov.au. A quarter of South Australians fish each year. There are regulations governing fishing activities in the state and you should familiarise yourself with these. Legal minimum lengths apply.

Tasmania: www.fishonline.tas.gov.au. It's generally accepted that at least one in three Tasmanians fish each year. Tasmania is also recognised internationally for its game fishing. Fish Online gives you a complete guide to fishing in Tasmania. A licence is required to fish all inland waters in Tasmania. The cost of a licence varies from $57 for an annual season (concessions for pensioners and Seniors Card holders) to $17.50 for a 24-hour licence. There are regulations on inland fishing, including minimum legal sizes, bag limits and closed seasons on species and waters. More information on inland fishing is available from the Inland Fisheries Service (☎03-6233 4140; www.ifc.tas.gov.au).

Victoria: ☎03-5332 5000; www.dpi.vic.gov.au. Victoria's recreational fishing opportunities range from freshwater fishing in its lakes and rivers to estuarine and saltwater fishing in oceans, inlets and bays. There is good fishing for native species, such as golden perch, Murray cod and Australian bass. Illegal fishing is an offence and you should stick to the recreational fishing regulations. A Recreational Fishing Licence (RFL) covers all recreational fishing in Victoria's marine, estuarine and fresh waters. A 48-hour licence costs $5.50, 28 days $11 and one year $22 (senior concessions are available). You must carry your licence with you at all times.

Western Australia: ☎08-9482 7333; www.fish.wa.gov.au. About 34% of the state's population are involved in recreational fishing. There are five licence categories in Western Australia: rock lobster $32 a year, marron $22, abalone $38, net fishing $27 and freshwater angling $22; all categories costs $75.

Badminton

There are badminton clubs all over Australia, either connected to universities or private. Try the University of Sydney Badminton Club (www.usydbadminton.com) or the PAOC Badminton Club (www.paocbadminton.com.au) in Adelaide.

Sailing

Yachting Australia (☎02-8424 7400; www.yachting.org.au) is the peak body for all forms of yachting, both power and sail, throughout Australia. Yachting Australia, together with its eight state and territory Member Yachting Associations (MYAs), provides various services to affiliated clubs, members and the general public. They assist people of all ages to become involved in this recreational sport. The Yachting Australia website has information about training, racing, cruising, and a calendar of events. You can also search its database for clubs, instructors and recognised teaching establishments.

Tasmania supports both recreational and competitive sailing. Bass separates Tasmania from Victoria by 160 nautical miles, with King Island on the western end and Flinders Island on the eastern. It contains some ideal cruising grounds among the many small islands.

The Derwent River, on which Hobart is situated, has large cruising grounds that lead south to the D'Entrecasteaux Channel which has sheltered cruising waters inside Bruny Island. Also from Hobart, you can cruise south and round the bottom of Tasmania to some of the most beautiful cruising waters in the world: Port Davey and Bathurst Harbour in the far south west. The only access to this area is by boat, plane or a week-long hike on the South West Track.

Another popular cruising ground is on the east coast of Tasmania from Flinders Island in the north to Tasman Island in the south. Coles Bay, Freycinet National Park and Wineglass Bay are the most popular spots.

The Sydney to Hobart Yacht Race, held on Boxing Day every year, is one of the most popular yacht races in Australia and has become an icon of the country's summer sport. Over Easter there is the annual Three Peaks race from Port Dalrymple, to Flinders Island, to Coles Bay on the east coast, and then on to Hobart. It is based on the UK race from Barmouth to Corpack.

There are about 24 yacht/sailing clubs around Tasmania, ranging from the major clubs with their own marinas to small off the beach sailing clubs, affiliated to Yachting Tasmania (☎03-6383 4719; www.tas.yachting.org. au). You are not required to be a member of any club to own a mooring in Tasmania.

For spectacular scenery and magic places to sail in New South Wales, try Hawkesbury River, Pittwater, Jervis Bay or Port Stephens. Learning to sail is done through commercial schools from which you can gravitate on to clubs who have a register of people wishing to crew. There are about 120 small, family oriented clubs sailing dinghies affiliated to Yachting New South Wales. The bigger clubs with facilities are all based in the Sydney metropolitan area. The smaller dinghy clubs are always looking for members while the larger ones may have a waiting list and are usually quite expensive to join. The smaller clubs may close for winter but the bigger clubs are open all year round and club racing is held in summer and winter. For more information contact Yachting New South Wales (☎02-9660 1266; www.nsw.yachting.org.au).

There are 35 sailing clubs and several sailing centres in South Australia, which conduct regular 'Learn to Sail' courses for new members and people interested in trying this leisure activity. If you wish to join a club in South Australia, the sailor registration fee is $40 and club fees range from $100 for a club with less than 100 members to $655 for a club with more than 1,000 members. More information from Yachting South Australia (☎08-8410 2117; www.sa.yachting.org.au),

Yachting Queensland (☎07-3393 6788; www.qld.yachting.org.au) is responsible for about 10 sail training centres and promotes the sport of 'boating' within Queensland. The Whitsundays, a group of 74 tropical islands, is a popular sailing hotspot and more information is available at www. whitsundaysailtraining.com.

For sailing in the other states and territories contact Yachting Victoria (☎03-9597 0066; www.vic.yachting.org.au) and Yachting Western Australia (☎08-9386 2438; www.wa.yachting.org.au).

Fitness Centres

The number of fitness centres opening across Australia has soared; up to 20% in five years. There are now an estimated 1,200 fitness centres in Australia.

Fitness Australia (www.fitnessaustralia.com.au) represents about 12,000 registered trainers and businesses and sets a voluntary code of practice outlining basic standards and conditions for members. Many centres now offer accredited personal trainers and instructors, a variety of aerobic and yoga classes, a crèche and a café. An average membership costs about $600 to $700.

One of the largest fitness chains is Fitness First (☎1300 55 77 99; e-mail enquiries@fitnessfirst.com.au; www.fitnessfirst.com.au) which has about 50 clubs; 28 in New South Wales. One of the top three privately operated chains is Zest Health Clubs (☎02-9026 8600; e-mail info@zesthealthclubs.com.au; www.zesthealthclubs.com.au). Healthy Inspirations (☎03-6224 0300; e-mail Salamanca@healthyinspirations. com.au; www.healthyinspirations.com.au) has opened 22 franchises in six states and is strongest in regional Australia. UK-based Next Generation (☎08-9412 0000; e-mail infops@nextgenerationclubs.com.au; www. nextgenerationclubs.com.au) is a contemporary country club concept and has expanded rapidly since opening its first club in Adelaide in 1999. Its clubs in Adelaide, Perth and Sydney now have a café and bar, squash and tennis courts, crèche, swimming pools, hairdresser, spa and beauty treatment facilities and aqua aerobics for seniors. Membership is from $59 (off-peak). Pension concessions are catered for in the Classic membership: $45 for individuals, $81 for couples.

Arts and Culture

There are 29 museums in ACT; 34 in NT; 341 in NSW; 236 in Queensland; 147 in SA; 80 in TAS; 295 in Victoria; and 140 in WA. For information about daily arts and cultural activities in the ACT, visit www.artsaroundcan-berra.com.au.

Cultural Contacts

The National Museum of Australia: ☎02-6208 5000; www.nma.gov.au. Situated in Canberra, 'explores the land, nation and people of Australia'. It is open 9am to 5pm daily.

The National Gallery of Australia: ☎02-6240 6502; www.nga.gov.au. In Canberra, it has 90,000 pieces of art, including Australian art, Aboriginal and Torres Strait Islander art, international and Asian. It is open 10am to 5pm daily.

The Museum of Contemporary Art in Sydney: ☎02-9245 2400; www.mca.com.au. Contains Australian art, including an extensive collection of Aboriginal art. It is open 10am to 5pm daily; admission is free.

Art Gallery of New South Wales in Sydney: ☎02-9225 1700; www.artgallery.nsw. gov.au. One of Australia's foremost cultural institutions. It is open every day from 10am to 5pm with a late closing of 9pm every Wednesday.

National Gallery of Victoria: www.ngv.vic.gov.au. Has a rich treasury of more than 500 works and has been displaying art works since 1861.

Australian Museums & Galleries Online: www.amol.org.au, lists about 1,000 museums and galleries.

Aboriginal Australia Art Centre: www.aboriginalart.com.au. Offers a variety of cultural tours in the Northern Territory where you can experience Aboriginal life, music and dance.

Aboriginal Fine Arts Gallery: ☎08-8981 1315; www.aaia.com.au. An Aboriginal–owned art gallery in Darwin. It focuses on works by prominent artists from the central and western desert regions and Arnhelmland in the 'Top End.' It also has a huge selection of artefacts and didgeridoos. It's open 9am to 5pm, Monday to Friday; and 9am to 2pm, Saturday; and 10am to 2pm on Sunday from June to September.

National Library of Australia: www.nla.gov.au. An enormous repository of information.

The Australian Music Centre at The Rocks in Sydney, New South Wales: ☎02-9247 4677; www.amcoz.com.au. Established in 1974 to facilitate and encourage the creation, performance and understanding of Australian music, composers and sound artists. It is open Monday to Friday from 9am to 5pm.

Opera Australia has a centre in Sydney: ☎02-9699 1099, and Melbourne: ☎03-9685 3777. Opera Australia's OzOpera performs year-round in small and large communities across the country. More information on OzOpera's performances is available at www. opera-australia.org.au.

State Opera South Australia: www.saopera.sa.gov.au, is an innovative performing arts company, which entertains all sections of the community.

More information on galleries and museums; indigenous arts, culture and heritage; performing arts; and visual arts and crafts is available at www. cultureandrecreation.gov.au.

South Australia is widely regarded as the creative and artistic centre of the nation. The Adelaide Festival Centre (☎08-8216 8600; e-mail afct@afct.org. au; www.afct.org.au) is South Australia's home for the performing arts. It has pioneered seasons of drama, major musicals, contemporary dance and other theatre. It also houses the state's Performing Arts Collection. Its schedule of events is chosen to appeal to as many people as possible. It has four theatre venues – the Festival Theatre, Drama Centre (including Dunstan Playhouse), Space and Ampitheatre.

As well as managing the theatres and environs of the complex, the centre has a history of being one of Australia's most active theatrical producers and currently presents a wide range of shows and events in Adelaide, as well as touring them throughout the country.

Best Available Seating Service (BASS) was Australia's first computerised ticketing agency and provides services to a variety of venues and events in Adelaide and South Australia. You can buy tickets by phone, fax, mail, or in person (BASS Box Office, Adelaide Festival Centre, King William Road, Adelaide SA 5000; ☎08-8205 2300; fax 08-8231 0550; www.bass.net.au). It offers a one-stop ticketing and bookings shop for accommodation, dining, car parking and merchandising and is the only company in the country specialising in arts ticketing but also able to manage major sporting events.

Dancing

Ballroom dancing is being seen as the new worldwide glamour sport. If you want to meet new friends or enjoy a good night out, ballroom dancing is great for people of any age. It's good exercise and good fun. You can find out more information on social dancing and studios at www.ballroomdancing.com.au.

Modern square dancing is another dance phenomena providing light exercise for the body and mind. In Australia, a National Square Dance Convention is held every year and most states also hold a State Convention. The National Square Dance Society of Australia (☎1800 643 277; www. squaredanceaustralia.com) will be able to give you details of classes and clubs in your region.

Latin Motion is a Salsa dance company pursuing the growth of Salsa, Mambo and Rueda in Australia. Details on the world of Salsa, classes and events can be accessed at www.latinmotion.com.au or contact ☎02-9557 7751, e-mail info@latinmotion.com.au.

Photography

You can share your enjoyment of photography with other members of the Australian Photographic Society (☎03-5243 4440; e-mail a-p-s@bigpond. net.au; www.australianphotographicsociety.org.au). The society offers extensive services to its members to improve their photography and photographic skills. Membership is open to beginners, amateurs, or professionals. APS has four divisions and you can join as many as you wish. They are: print, slide, nature, contemporary: audio-visual and electronic digital. It also has information on camera clubs in each state and territory.

TAKING COURSES

If you want to extend the perimeters of your knowledge, now is the time. Throughout Australia, there are many courses on offer for the older student and you can delve into some subject that you have never had the time to pursue in greater depth.

Australian Correspondence Schools (☎07-5530 4855; e-mail admin@acs. edu.au; www.acs.edu.au) offers a range of full-time, part-time and Internet delivered courses.

Open Universities Australia (www.open.edu.au) has courses provided by seven Australian universities. These universities provide the course materials and academic support, assess your progress and award your qualifications. You can study throughout the year and for entry level courses there are no pre-requisites.

Adult Learning Australia (www.ala.asn.au) is the national peak body for adult learning in Australia.

The University of the Third Age (U3A: ☎07-3211 8117, is a self-help adult education movement. It is a good place to learn, make friends and keep active. No qualifications are required and no qualifications are awarded. It began in France in the 80s and has been in Australia since 1984, providing a variety of courses, crafts, field trips and social activities. Courses are held during term time on a weekly basis. The word 'university' applies in a classical sense to groups of students participating and sharing knowledge rather than to the modern concept of higher learning. Instruction is informal and dependent on volunteer tutors. U3A Online, www.u3online.org/, offers short courses covering a range of interests for older people who want to study online. This is ideal for people who are isolated geographically or through physical or social circumstances.

Computer Courses

There are a plethora of institutions offering computer courses and local libraries around Australia run internet training for seniors. You can also get free access to the internet at these libraries, although booking in advance is essential.

Australian Seniors Computer Clubs Association (ASCCA): ☎02-9286 3871; e-mail ascca@seniorcomputing.org; www.seniorcomputing.org. A non-profit organisation for seniors who are interested in using a computer. It includes information on computer clubs for seniors throughout the country where you can learn at your own pace. These clubs have low fee structures so classes are not prohibitive.

Department of Education, Science and Training: www.itskills.dest.gov.au. Has a Basic IT Enabling Skills (BITES) for Older Workers training programme for those aged 45 years and over. It helps older people, who are in the labour force, to gain nationally accredited skills in information and communication technology. To see if you are eligible contact the hotline at ☎1800 800 618. Their *Connecting with Computers* video and DVD is available through the Australian Government's seniors portal at www.seniors. gov.au.

SeniorNet: www.seniornet.com.au. Offers internet training for seniors in Brisbane, Ipswich, Canberra and the Hunter Region.

Skills.net: www.skills.net.au. Provides free, or affordable, internet training and access for people who do not have it in Victoria.

Melbourne PC User Group: www.melbpc.org.au. Australia's largest PC user group.

Seniors-On-Line: www.seniorsonline.com.au. Specialises in introducing the over 50s to computing through a well-tested, innovative and user-friendly teaching program. It includes 'taster sessions' for novices and a classroom location map. Courses are run at their computer learning centres where one-on-one assistance is provided.

Computers for Seniors: ☎03-9720 3161; www.users.bigpond.net.au/attc. An online learning site for seniors and offers free lessons and help.

GARDENING

Gardening has many health and therapeutic benefits, keeps you fit and healthy and is a stimulating physical activity that can be enjoyed by all. There are many nurseries and garden centres in Australia, able to help keen gardeners.

Gardening Australia (www.abc.net.au/gardening/) is the online version of ABC's gardening TV programme. You can download programme transcripts, review gardening fact sheets, check out the events diary and shop for gardening gear, books and magazines. You can also obtain tips on such things as plant division, versatile sunflowers, composting and loads more. By subscribing to the free online newsletter you can keep up-to-date with gardening issues. Gardening Australia can be contacted at ☎03-9524 2875; e-mail gardening@abc.net.au.

The Horticultural Therapy Association of Victoria (☎03-9848 9710; www.htav.org.au) has information on horticultural programmes, workshops and activities.

More information on a fauna-friendly garden can be obtained from www.floraforfauna.com.au.

Organic Gardening From Down Under (www.organicdownunder.com) encourages organic vegetable growing. The website includes a planting guide for Australia and information on growing root crops, onions, tomatoes and more.

TRAVELLING IN AUSTRALIA

Seniors have a higher propensity to travel, due mainly to having more free time, and they form the biggest travel market demographic in Australia. They enjoy different activities on a state-by-state basis: the most popular are walking in New South Wales and Tasmania, going to the beach in Western Australia and Queensland, visiting museums in ACT, and gazing at the stars in the Northern Territory.

Popular Destinations

NSW: Blue Mountains, wineries of the Hunter Valley, and Port Stephens, the dolphin-watching capital of Australia.

NT: Uluru and Kata Tjuta, tabletop Mount Connor, Alice Springs and the Simpson Desert.

QLD: Whitsundays, Gold Coast and Sunshine Coast, Fraser Islands, and the Great Barrier Reef.

SA: Flinders Ranges, Coober Pedy, Baross Valley, and Fleurieu Peninsula.

TAS: Tasman Peninsula, Mount Field National Park, Flinders Island, and Port Arthur, the infamous convict settlement.

WA: Albany, Esperance, Shark Bay, Ningaloo Reef, and Nullarbor Plain.

Holiday programmes specifically designed for seniors are available in most states. Generally, the fees are reasonable and cater for groups of up to 20 people. However, they are also available to couples or single people. In NSW you can contact Sport & Recreation, Holidays for Seniors (☎13 13 02; www.dsr.nsw.gov.au) in Tasmania, Life Be In It (☎03-6245 0034) and Western Australia, Outdoors Western Australia (☎08-9408 5632. Groups only).

If you wish to extend your intellectual interests, MindVentures (☎07-3878 4077; www.mindventures.com.au) has learning and leisure holiday packages for retired and semi-retired people. Subjects include history, literature, science, health, and politics. Presenters are drawn from universities, educational and cultural institutions, the media, literary and artistic communities.

> If you are travelling between South Australia, Victoria and New South Wales, make sure you eat or dispense with all fresh fruit. Drivers can be fined $200 on-the-spot at random roadblocks for bringing fruit into a Fruit Fly Excursion Zone (FFEZ). All types of maturing ripe fruit, as well as some vegetables, are hosts of fruit fly, which could infest valuable production areas. You may even end up in court where fines of $20,000 can be imposed on those spreading fruit fly into this tri-state FFEZ. More information is available at www.agric.nsw.gov.au/fruitfly, www.pir.sa.gov.au/fruitfly, or www.dpi.vic.gov.au.

Good Breaks: Tips from Retirees

Joan Riddle says:

We love touring around Australia. The Great Ocean Road, a visit to Phillip Island to see the Fairy Penguins, a day at Healesville Zoo, where all native species are well cared for and well 'housed.' The Goldfields and a visit to Ballarat where a gold mining town is portrayed and you can pan for gold. The Aquarium is another must see as is the Sydney Harbour Bridge and Opera House in News South Wales and Dubbo Zoo. Adelaide is the City of Churches and boy are they wonderful. Queensland is another story: so much to see – Surfers Paradise, the beaches. The Red Centre (Uluru). There is something for everyone in Australia. The beaches everywhere and the green of mountains. I could go on all day.

Ian Lewthwaite prefers to stay away from the crowds:

We go twice a year to Sandy Point, near Wilsons Promontory. Sometimes for a break we just go up to the big town like Ballarat, Aubrey-Wodonga and Bendigo for a few days in a motel to look around the area. There is so much recent history. Tasmania is like the curates egg, good in parts. It's a bit cooler than the mainland so the wine is a lot drier and not to my taste. Launceston and Hobart are both worth a stay. Cairns and Port Arthur we stayed at some six years ago but it has all changed now and is very commercialised. We used to like Port Fairy but this has also changed dramatically. Malaccota was very rural last time we went 10 years ago. As you can see we didn't come to Australia for the crowds.

Brian Havard has been more adventurous:

Retiree holiday destinations are many and varied dependent on state of health and bank balance – it's a big country. In my state, South Australia, many will go to the south coast resorts around Victor Harbour. However, much favoured is Queensland – Gold Coast and Sunshine Coast, Cairns, the Daintree, or the coast of New South Wales. People from WA equally go south to Esperance, which is beautiful, or fly up to Broome. Many retirees go right round Australia by caravan taking months over it. Others even sell their bricks and mortar and live permanently on the road. My wife and I once drove from Adelaide via Alice Springs to Darwin, then over to Broome, all down the WA coast to Perth for a couple of weeks (another wonderful city), on further south to the south coast and back across the Nullarbor Plain and home – 17,000 km in three months. What an adventure.

Mike Osborne says:

For Queensland retirees, Byron Bay on the border of NSW is quite popular. Sunshine Coast and Gold Coast for day trips. Coral Coast (Hervey Bay and Fraser Island) for an extended weekend. Obviously, Cairns for the coral must also be worth mentioning. In South Australia, Victor Harbour is popular (called God's waiting room by many). Port Vincent found favour with many locals for a while until prices went sky high and folk realised there was no hospital.

Kathleen Kalver's highlights for the last 40 years have been:

Surfers Paradise in Queensland, now extended to what is termed the Sunshine Coast, stretching around south Queensland and New South Wales. Other huge areas are Cairns, the Great Barrier Reef, Green Island and the Whitsunday Islands. In NSW, the first thought would be Sydney and the fantastic harbour and beaches. Each state has a festival of some importance. There are so many vineyards and wineries now and that is a huge industry for commercial and tourist reasons. In Tasmania, the wineries have increased enormously. Alice Springs and Uluru is always a tourist destination and the Ghan train goes from South Australia to Darwin. And much, much more. Australia is quite different to Britain and distances are enormous in comparison. Outdoor interests are legion. I guess it is right to say 'there is something for everybody.

Jane Knight believes that:

In Victoria, there are good weekend breaks in Portsea, Sorrento, Lorne, Apollo Bay, Daylesford. Others may travel further to Merimbula or Echuca Moama. I think the most popular retiree holiday destinations are Broome, Hervey Bay, Port Douglas, Cairns, Noosa and the Whitsundays.

Rail

Great Southern Railways (www.gsr.com.au) operates Australia's great train journeys:

- ○ *Indian Pacific:* Spans 2,704 miles (4,352 km) across Australia, Sydney-Adelaide-Perth. Twice weekly; three nights on train in either direction.
- ○ *The Ghan:* 1,851 miles (2,979 km) through the heart of Australia, Adelaide-Alice Springs-Darwin. Two nights; once a week Adelaide-Darwin and twice a week Adelaide-Alice Springs.
- ○ *The Overland:* Daylight service Adelaide-Melbourne, Melbourne-Adelaide (514 miles/828 km). Three times a week in both directions.
- ○ The Sydney-Canberra service runs three times daily to and from the capital, passing through the scenic Southern Highlands.

Other local and interstate travel is provided by: CityRail (www.cityrail.nsw. gov.au) and CountryLink, (www.countrylink.nsw.gov.au) in New South Wales; Queensland Rail (www.qr.com.au); TransAdelaide (www.transadelaide.sa.gov.au) in South Australia; V/Line (www.vlinepassenger.com.au) in Victoria; Transperth (www.transperth.wa.gov.au) in Western Australia.

Coach and Bus Services

Greyhound Australia (☎07-4690 9950; www.greyhound.com.au) offers a network of 1,100 destinations across mainland Australia (not Tasmania). The Aussie explorer pass offers set itineraries that take in the most popular centres. Greyhound Australia offers a 10% discount off the full adult fare for pensioners. A valid Pension Card must be presented when buying a ticket to be eligible for this discounted fare.

Internal Flights

Qantas and Virgin Blue and their subsidiaries operate services between all state capital cities and regional centres. Australia's regional airlines connect metropolitan, regional and leisure centres.

Useful Addresses

The Qantas Group(Qantas Airlines, Australian Airlines, QantasLink and Jetstar): ☎13 13 13; www.qantas.com.au.

Virgin Blue: ☎13 67 89; www.virginblue.com.au, Australia's regional low fare airline. You can check fare prices, routes and special offers.

Cruises and Ferries

International cruise companies, such as P&O, Holland America, Hapag-Lloyd, Saga Shipping, Star Cruises, Seabourne, Silversea and Cunard Lines call into various Australian ports. There are other cruising options available, ranging from paddlewheelers to houseboats.

Travelling to Tasmania is made more exciting on board the *Spirit of Tasmania* (☎1800 634 906; www.spiritoftasmania.com.au), which crosses to Devonport from Melbourne and Sydney. Concessions for seniors and pensioners apply. You can book online.

Accommodation

Farmstays are a rural alternative to a traditional bed and breakfast and are generally cheaper than B&Bs. For details, contact Australian Bed and Breakfast and Farmstay (☎1300 888 862; www.australianbedandbreakfast.com.au).

AAA Tourism manages the Australia STAR Rating Scheme, which involves sending inspectors with a 1,000-point checklist to some 11,000 properties around Australia. Each category (hotel/motel, backpacker, bed and breakfast, caravan park, houseboat, park cabin, resort, and self-catering accommodation) is assessed and then awarded one to five stars. The hotel and tourist park guides, incorporating the star ratings, are available (discounted for members) from state motoring organisation or www.aaatourism.com.au.

Travel websites

www.travelmate.com.au. Here you can find good year-round rates on accommodation, search for flights, search for great getaway specials, car hire and campervan rentals.

www.solotraveller.com.au. An online singles travel agency with a wide range of destinations without the dreaded single supplement.

www.exploreoz.com. An interactive site for those interested in camping, four wheel driving and caravanning in Oz.

www.auscamps.asn.au. At this Australian Camps Association (ACA) site you can look for a campsite, check availability and book accordingly.

www.avalook.com.au. Outback travel tips for independent over-50 travellers who prefer not to take a packaged tour.

www.takeabreak.com.au. Accommodation for seniors; you can search by region, locality, type of accommodation and theme.

www.travelaustralia.com.au. Search for accommodation throughout Australia.

www.walkabout.com.au. An A-Z travel guide where you can search by region or theme, also details on flights, top deals, cruising and car hire.

www.ozbedandbreakfast.com. A comprehensive B&B directory for each region.

www.cheaperthanhotels.com/Australia/. Here you can search for accommodation in Australia that is cheaper than staying in hotels.

www.budgetmotelchain.com.au. Motel accommodation at an affordable tariff.

www.forgetmenotcottages.com.au. Luxury, boutique B&B accommodation for that special occasion.

In Australia, membership of the National Trust of Australia (www.nsw.nationaltrust.org.au) gives you free access to more than 170 properties (galleries, house museums and gardens). The Trust also organises a range of holidays, short breaks and day tours when you can visit museums, historic sites and conservation areas.

If you prefer house swap holidays, you can access Aussie House Swap (www. aussiehouseswap.com.au). It is a home exchange database where you can stay in someone's house and they stay in yours, for an agreed length of time, at no cost. If you would like to put your home on the website, you must become a member which costs $48 a year. As a member, you are in control of who you want to swap with. It's a way of holidaying on a limited budget.

Get Up & Go is the official Seniors Card travel magazine. It is published quarterly, available from newsagents throughout the country, or on subscription: one year costs $25, or two years $48. Written for the mature traveller, *Get up & Go* includes the latest discounts for seniors, tours, hotels, airlines, self-drive itineraries, rail, cruise, Australian short breaks and overseas trips.

Caravanning and Motorhomes

There are more than 330,000 registered caravans and campervans in Australia. Research also shows, that those who live in Victoria and New South Wales are the most committed caravanners in the country. The Northern Territory outback, Queensland, South Australia and Western Australia are the top destinations.

Campervan & Motorhome Club of Australia (www.cmca.net.au) is the largest motorhoming (RV) club in Australia. It offers such benefits as insurance, free monthly magazine and social events.

Caravan, RV & Accommodation Industry Australia, (www. welovethiscountry.net.au) has information on where to go caravanning, camping and motorhoming, plus tips on tents, trailers, caravans, campervans and motorhomes.

To check on road conditions and trouble spot information, access the following:

NSW: www.rta.nsw.gov.au/trafficreports/index.

NT: www.dpi.nt.gov.au/whatwedo/roadreport/.

QLD: www.racq.com.

SA: www.transport.sa.gov.au.

VIC: www.vicroads.vic.gov.au.

WA: www.mainroads.wa.gov.au.

PUBLIC HOLIDAYS AND FESTIVALS

Public Holidays (2006)	
New Year's Day	1 January
Australia Day	26 January
Good Friday	14 April
Easter Saturday	15 April
Easter Monday	17 April
Anzac Day	25 April
Queen's Birthday	12 June
Labour Day	2 October
Christmas Day	25 December
Boxing Day	26 December

Apart from these national public holidays, each state and territory has local public holidays of their own (some of which are holidays in particular council areas only):

ACT: *Canberra Day,* March.
NT: *May Day,* first Monday in May; *Picnic Day,* first Monday in August.
NSW: Council area holidays (see *Celebrations and Festivals*).
QLD: *Royal Queensland Show,* August.
SA: *Adelaide Cup,* May.
TAS: *Eight Hours Day,* second Monday in March.
VIC: *Melbourne Cup Day,* November.
WA: *Foundation Day,* June.

Queensland has at least 139 annual agricultural, horticultural and industrial shows held throughout the state. Show holidays are also public holidays in that particular district, for example the Gold Coast Annual Show on 1 September, which is a holiday in the City of Gold Coast district.

In Tasmania, a major event in a particular municipal area is a public holiday in that area:

o   Devonport Cup, January.
o   Royal Hobart Regatta, February.
o   Launceston Cup, February.

○ King Island Show, March.
○ Agfest, May.
○ Burnie Show, October.
○ Royal Launceston Show, October.
○ Flinders Island Show, October.
○ Royal Hobart Show, October.
○ Recreation Day, November.
○ Devonport Show, December.

The same applies in New South Wales, where local holidays are attached to council shows or race days, for example the Mussellbrook Cup Race Carnival on 7 November.

The Northern Territory has show days in Alice Springs (July), Tennant Creek (July), Katherine (July), Darwin (July) and Borroloola (August) and a public holiday is observed in that region only.

More information is available from:
ACT: www.workcover.act.gov.au.
NT: www.nt.gov.au.
NSW: www.industrialrelations.nsw.gov.au.
QLD: www.wageline.qld.gov.au.
SA: www.eric.sa.gov.au.
TAS: www.wst.tas.gov.au.
VIC: www.information.vic.gov.au.
WA: www.docep.wa.gov.au.

Celebrations And Festivals

Information on local events can be obtained from tourist information centres located throughout Australia. There are too many to mention here but if you contact the main state and territory tourist offices they will be able to give you details of their regional offices. Local councils will also help, contact the Local Government Association (☎02-6122 9400; www.alga.asn.au) for a list of councils in your area.

ACT
Canberra District Wine Harvest Festival, April, ☎1300 554 114; www.canberrawines.com.au. Celebrate Autumn at various vineyards around the ACT

when the grapes are harvested.

Floriade, ☎02-6205 0666; www.floriadeaustralia.com, is the largest flower festival in the southern hemisphere and takes places each Spring.

National Folk Festival, ☎02-6249 7755; www.folkfestival.asn.au, cultural celebration of traditional and contemporary music, dance, poetry and storytelling.

Canberra International Chamber Music Festival, ☎02-6230 5880; www.cicmf.org.

NT

Alice Springs Cup Festival, ☎08-8952 4977; www.alicespringsturfclub.org.au, Carnival of racing over four days.

NSW

Sydney Festival, www.sydneyfestival.org.au, takes place throughout January every year.

Sydney Gay and Lesbian Mardi Gras, ☎02-9568 8600; www.mardigras.org.au.

QLD

Gladstone Harbour Festival, ☎07-4972 5111; www.gladstonefestival.com, a week of celebrations marking the end of the Brisbane to Gladstone yacht race.

Great Barrier Feast, ☎1300 720 651; www.hamiltonisland.com.au, is held annually on Hamilton Island and is the ultimate food and wine weekend.

SA

The Adelaide Fringe, run side-by-side of the Adelaide Festival every second year, is the largest arts event in Australia and is rivalled only by the Edinburgh Fringe in Scotland. Artists from across the world take part alongside homegrown talent in all art forms. More information is available from the organisers at ☎08-8100 2000; www.adelaidefringe.com.au.

Adelaide also plays host to the *Adelaide Film Festival,* held every year, which includes films from around the world as well as Australia. For more information on dates and times, ☎08-8271 1488; e-mail info@adelaidefilmfestival.org; www.adelaidefilmfestival.org.

Adelaide Cabaret Festival, www.afct.org.au, held annually, it is a niche festival showcasing world-class cabaret artists.

Adelaide Hills Harvest Festival, ☎08-8388 1185; www.adelaidehillswine.com.
au, tastings and gourmet experiences.
Tastes of the Outback, ☎08-8642 4511; www.tastesoftheoutback.com, nine
days of wining and dining at various venues in the Flinders Ranges.
Mount Barker Jazz and Heritage Festival, ☎08-8391 7238; www.dcmtbarker.
sa.gov.au, jazzfest at a range of venues, as well as a memorabilia exhibition.
Penola Coonawarra Arts Festival, ☎08-8737 2855; www.penolacoonawarraf-
estival.org, entertainment for all tastes, as well as art exhibitions, dance, literary and history tours and a farmers' market.
Mclaren Vale Sea and Vines Festival, ☎08-8323 9944; www.mclarenvale.info,
a combination of seafood and wines listening to blues, rock and jazz.

TAS

The annual *Taste of Tasmania* food and wine festival takes place on the Princes
Wharf and runs for a week over the New Year period. About 70 stalls sell food
and drink from around the world.
Antarctic Tasmania Midwinter Festival, ☎03-6233 5949; www.antarctic-tas-
mania.info, winter solstice marks the annual celebration of Hobart's links with
the Antarctic. Huskies' Picnic, exhibitions, lectures and demonstrations.

VIC

Riverboats Jazz, Food and Wine Festival, ☎1800 804 446; www.echucamoama.
com/jazz, an array of food and jazz bands beside the Murray River in Echuca
Yackandandah Folk Festival, ☎02-6027 1988; www.folkfestival.yackandan-
dah.com, annual festival held in this historic town, including international,
national and local performers in a rural setting, with food, wine, dance, markets and a buskers competition.
The Working Horse Festival, ☎03-9802 7996, is a two-day event held on
Churchill Island every April. It celebrates the natural and cultural values of
the island. You can watch Clydesdale horses ploughing paddocks, sowing seed
and making hay bales; marvel at spinners, weavers, blacksmiths and wood
turners.

WA

Minnawarra Festival, ☎08-9399 0148; www.visitarmadale.com.au, WA's premier arts and crafts festival.
Ningaloo Whaleshark Festival, ☎08-9949 2135, festivities linked to the arrival
of whalesharks at Ningaloo Reef.

Fremantle Heritage Festival, ☎08-9432 9888; www.fremantlefestivals.com, a celebration of the city's past with lectures, public art and heritage walks, workshops and seminars.

KEEPING IN TOUCH

Wherever you are in the world today, it has never been easier to keep in touch with family and friends. Modern technology is making it possible for us to communicate via e-mail and internet telephone calls or VoIP (Voice over Internet Protocol) and enables us to dispense with high telephone bills.

Telephones

Telstra (www.telstra.com.au) is 51% government-owned and is the main telecommunications provider in Australia. Other landline providers/operators are AAPT, B Digital, Dodo, Ecomtel, Encircle, GOTalk, Optus, Powertel, Primus, Southern Phone, Speek, TeleOne and TransACT. There is tremendous competition between the phone companies in supplying international calling rates. It's worth checking the internet or the newspapers for special offers. Local calls in Australia are not charged on a timed basis but instead a single connection charge of about 25 cents on a domestic phone allows you to talk for as long as you wish. Public telephones are still used and phone cards are available from selected newsagents and stores; some also accept credit cards.

PhoneChoice (www.phonechoice.com.au) provides details on a range of information about the telecommunications industry. It includes details on mobile phones, dealers and network information; residential phone rates (international, long distance and local); broadband plans; and VoIP.

Mobile Phones. Australia's mobile network operates on the 900 and 1800 bands for the European GSM technology. Communic8, Optus, SIMplus Mobile, Telstra, Virgin and Vodafone are the main networks. Customers can swap networks and keep the same number and text messages can be sent between networks. Competition is fierce and you can buy a pre-paid mobile for as little as $50.

Internet and E-mail

The proportion of people in older age groups using a computer and accessing the internet is increasing all the time. According the Australian Bureau of Statistics, 92% of older persons are most likely to use their home computer for personal and private purposes. A key requirement for many new retiree migrants is to get online as soon as possible after their arrival for e-mail, banking, real estate and to keep in touch with those left behind.

There are more than 800 ISPs operating in Australia and a vast number of plans to choose from. You can set up an ISP account over the phone or you could choose a prepaid account until you've had a chance to study all the alternatives offered by the ISPs. In the meantime, for about $20 you can buy 20 hours access.

You can also access the internet from some public places such as libraries, hotels and airports using coin-operated kiosks. They cost about $1 for 10 minutes ($6 per hour) which is more expensive than your ISP plan, but not too bad for a few hours work each week to check your e-mail or websites.

Not all kinds of broadband connections are available in all areas and your provider may have to test your existing equipment. This is a normal procedure that should be covered as part of the installation cost. Most plans are a fixed-monthly price. An Internet Tool Kit and a list of ISPs are available online from the Australian Communications and Media Authority at www.toolkit.acma.gov.au, where you'll also find help for the best value mobile and fixed line products; for a list of broadband service providers visit www.broadbandexchange.org, or under internet access providers in the Yellow Pages.

A list of ISPs is available from the Australian Government Directory, www.agd.com.au, but a few of the more obvious ones are:

- Australia Online, www.australiaonline.net.au.
- Internode, www.internode.on.net.
- Ozemail, www.ozemail.com.au.
- Pacific Internet, www.pacific.net.au.
- Primus Telecom, www.primustel.com.au.
- Telstra Bigpond, www.bigpond.com.

Internet Phone Calls. With the convergence of computer and telephones, call traffic is moving to one simple network – the internet. VoIP are voice calls over the Internet and the rates for long-distance and international calls are a fraction of normal charges. This is because the internet protocol is much more efficient way to transmit data than a traditional landline. VoIP is at its most competitive (effectively free) where you and the person you are calling are either on the same private network, a broadband connection, or within a local call of your nearest VoIP exchange. Australian VoIP providers offer untimed long-distance calls between capital cities, for example calls between Sydney and Melbourne cost around 10 cents. Choose a VoIP provider that is based in Australia to ensure you are protected by Australian consumer and telecommunications laws. The most popular VoIP provider is Skype (www.skype.com) and all you have to do is download the software, register and install it, plug in your headset and speakers and start calling.

Post

The postal system throughout Australia is run by Australia Post. At www.auspost.com.au you can check postage costs, obtain postcodes, find out about services and special offers and locate your nearest office or agency. Post offices and PostShops are open from 9am to 5pm Monday to Friday and 9am to 11am on Saturday; closed Sunday and public holidays. Australia Post also offers a telephone bill paying service.

WORKING, VOLUNTEERING AND STARTING A BUSINESS

There are only so many golf and fishing days one can have during retirement before it actually becomes quite dull. Finding a part-time job is an ideal way to keep yourself busy and stimulated.

Close to a third (32%) of people in the labour force are aged 45-64 years. Much debate has focused on the issues associated with the ageing Australian population. According to the Australian Bureau of Statistics (ABS), between 2011 and 2030, the baby boomer generation will be aged 65 years and over. This brings the possibility of a labour shortage with such a large number of people set to retire.

In recent years, the retention of mature age workers in the labour force has been highlighted as a potential solution. These mature age workers bring their skills, experience and maturity to potential employers. Paid work results in a higher retirement income and provides a sense of self worth. The education industry employs the highest proportion of mature age workers, followed by health and community services; electricity, gas and water supply; government administration and defence; and, finally, agriculture, forestry and fishing industries. With the federal government's passing of the Age Discrimination Bill in June 2004, employers are no longer able to discriminate on the basis of age.

Job vacancies are advertised in the local newspapers and on community notice boards in shopping centres and libraries.

You may be interested in working for the Grey Army (☎13 11 98; www. greyarmy.com.au) who has a network of mature tradespeople offering maintenance services available on call out.

Useful Websites

The internet is useful to research organisations and check out employment prospects. Mature age jobseekers should access the following:

Jobwise: www.jobwise.gov.au. Promotes mature age employment and is part of the Australian Government's Mature Age Employment and Workplace Strategy (MAEWS) which seeks to improve the labour force participation of mature age Australians.

The Australian Government, through Centrelink Employment Services: ☎13 28 50; www.centrelink.gov.au. Has a Transition to Work programme available to mature age people, 50 years and over, who are starting work for the first time or are returning to work after an absence of two years or more. It offers practical help, such as training and funding to help you develop your skills.

Working Connections: www.workingconnections.com. Part of ARPA Over 50s Association and connects mature jobseekers with income generating opportunities. It has an office in Melbourne (☎03-9650 6144) and Sydney (☎02-9286 3864).

Voluntary Work

Volunteers play a crucial role in Australian society in sport, health and welfare services, arts and culture, the environment, education, emergency services, politics and advocacy. Many organisations throughout Australia also rely on these volunteers to help run their aid, development and conservation programmes.

Conservation Volunteers Australia, (☎03-5330 2600; www. conservationvolunteers.com.au) is the country's largest practical conservation organisation. It has offices in every capital city and regional centre across Australia. CVA completes more than 1,500 week-long conservation projects across the country each year. These projects involve the community in conservation in urban, regional and remote Australia from tree planting, seed collection, endangered species protection, weed control, flora and fauna surveys, walking trail construction, fencing and environmental monitoring. If a project includes an overnight stay, $30 is payable, which covers accommodation and meals.

Australian Business Volunteers (ABV), www.abv.org.au, is a non-Government organisation whose aim is to contribute to reduce poverty, create sustainable development and good governance by providing volunteers who assist business and organisations in developing countries to grow and thrive. Volunteers are mostly retired and assignments are short-term.

Australian Volunteer Search, www.volunteersearch.gov.au, is an online search tool for those looking for volunteer opportunities. They are listed nationally or by state and territory.

FIDO (Friends in Deed Organisation), www.fido.com.au, provides volunteering opportunities for those with professional or other skills to offer. It facilitates the matching of skills provided by volunteers with the needs and requirements indicated by non-profit organisations. Assignments can be one-off, one hour, one day or one week.

Opportunities may also be available from Volunteering Western Australia (☎08-9482 4333; www.volunteeringwa.org.au).

Indigenous Community Volunteers (☎1800 819 542; www.volindigenous. org.au) is a national, not-for-profit organisation assisting indigenous communities and organisations through skills transfer projects undertaken by volunteers. 48% of its 500 strong volunteer base are seniors.

Expat Mike Osborne became involved in volunteering during his retirement in Australia:

I had long planned doing something that would be a challenge and I selected being an ambo volunteer. I had to get a South Australian licence but within a few weeks of being here I was into the training programme. I had no previous experience with health services or first aid – I thought Band Aid was a pop group. I have been qualified for more than three years now and it's one of the most worthwhile things I've ever done. There are sad times and humorous ones. I've learnt to deal with situations I would never have dreamed about. When a person comes up to you and says that you have saved their life or that of a relative, it makes you feel pretty humble.

Starting a Small Business

It's reported that 488,000 small business operators are more than 50 years old. However, setting up a small business in retirement does attract the same regulations as at any other age. There are tax consequences and you have to decide on the structure: sole, trader, partnership, or trust.

However, if you are not yet ready to retire fully and would like to operate a small business, the Australian Government's Business Entry Point, www. business.gov.au, and the Small Business Development Corporation (SBDC), www.sbdc.com.au, have almost all the information you will need.

Australia has a complex network of procedures and formalities, too many to cover adequately in this book, but detailed information can be found in *Starting a Business in Australia* published by Vacation Work Publications (www.vacationwork.co.uk).

Personal Finance

CHAPTER SUMMARY

- The amount one needs to retire on depends largely on your lifestyle; 70% of retirees in Australia claim some form of government income support.
- Banks fees are the norm in Australia whereas, in the UK, you may be used to fee-free personal banking.
- Remember that your UK pension is frozen at the rate you receive when leaving and you may not be eligible for an Australian state pension.
- What to do if a loved one dies while in Australia.

There is really no answer as to how much an individual needs to retire on; it depends largely on your lifestyle and what is important to you. Research done by CPA Australia suggests that around $20,000 a year should provide a modest but adequate lifestyle. However, the Department of Family and Community Services has stated that the number of seniors now relying on the government to support them has reached its highest levels, with almost 70% of retirees claiming some form of government income support. On the other hand, research in the UK shows that retirees save similar levels to people working; they have adjusted their lifestyle accordingly and maintained a savings element even though they are retired. There are many retirement income calculators available online to assess what is needed to support you through the later stages of life.

A specialist advisor who understands the financial systems of both countries can offer invaluable pre-emigration advice on your finances and transferring you pension. One such organisation is Prism XPAT (☎0945 450 4004; www. prismxpat.com).

BANKING

The current or cheque account (also known as a transaction account) is the way to go for day-to-day banking. This type of account provides a cheque book, ATM access, direct debit facilities and telephone banking. You can also open a savings account (also known as a deposit or investment account) for long-term savings.

Account holders are issued with a cash card for ATM withdrawals, debit card (EFTPOS) for use in general retail, credit and charge cards (*Bankcard*, *MasterCard* and *Visa*), depending on your requirements.

Electronic banking is alive and well in Australia and includes automated bill payment (BPAY), automated computer banking through dial-up services, automatic teller machines (ATMs), electronic funds transfer, internet banking, smart cards, stored debt cards, telephone banking, and touch-screen customer service terminals. Chip and Pin, recently introduced in the UK, has been in use in Australia for 20 years.

When you open a bank account in Australia you will have to provide proper identification to meet with the '100 points system.' Under this system you must demonstrate your identity and place of residence by providing different forms of identification, which are scored. For instance, a passport will provide you with 70 points, a Visa or Mastercard (25 points), a birth certificate (70 points) or a driver's licence (50 points).

According to Westpac, bank fees are a major concern for people migrating from the UK where they are accustomed to 'fee free' personal banking. All the high street banks in Australia have a fee-based structure for personal accounts. Fees are based on the level of activity on the customer account and the type of transactions used. Electronic transactions are cheaper than manual ones as they are less expensive to process and there is less chance of fraud. Westpac offers a single flat fee of $5 a month, regardless of the number of transactions. If you have other business with Westpac, such as insurance, investments, loans and mortgages, they will lower the fees applicable: to the point where you may pay no fees at all.

The four largest banks are Australian and New Zealand Banking Group (ANZ) (www.anz.com.au), Commonwealth Bank of Australia (www.commbank.com.au), National Australia Bank (www.national.com.au), and Westpac Banking Corporation (www.westpac.com.au).

Other Australian Banks

Adelaide Bank:, www.adelaidebank.com.au.

Advance Bank: www.advance.com.au.

AMP Banking Australia: www.amp.com.au.

BankSA: www.banksa.com.au.

BankWest: www.bankwest.com.au.

Bendigo Bank: www.bendigobank.com.au.

Citibank: www.citibank.com.au.

Deutsche Bank: www.deutschebank.com.au.

HSBC Bank: www.hsbc.com.au.

Macquarie Bank: www.macquarie.com.au.

St George Bank: www.stgeorge.com.au.

SunCorp Metway Bank: www.suncorpmetway.com.au.

Other Services. Australian permanent building societies represent only 5% of the national financial services market but are an alternative banking option. *giroPost* is a banking service offered at more than 3,000 Australian Post outlets.

Banks are generally open from 9am or 9.30am to 4pm on Monday to Thursday and from 9.30am to 5pm on Friday. Some banks and building societies open on a Saturday morning. Many have extended opening hours in the cities, at shopping centres and international airports. The majority of banks and building societies have 24-hour ATMs for account balances, deposits and cash withdrawals.

Investments. If you have extra capital you wish to invest in higher returns in Australia, you should seek professional advice. All licensed advisors are listed at the federal government's investors site at www.fido.asic.gov.au. There are also many reliable investment services.

Transferring UK Funds

Once you receive your Australian account information after opening an account from the UK you can then go into your bank in the UK and arrange the transfer of funds to your new account in Australia. Westpac maintains that the safest and speediest means of transfer is by 'telegraphic transfer' whereby the funds are remitted electronically. Your UK bank will charge you for this transaction; a fee of £20 to £25 is normally charged regardless of the amount transferred. It takes three to four days for the funds to arrive in your account in Australia where it will immediately start earning credit interest. Generally, people have their UK bank convert the funds to Australian Dollars but Westpac will convert your funds in Australia (see *Housing Finance*).

There are advantages to using a currency specialist to transfer your funds from the UK (see *Transferring Money* in *Housing Finance*).

Further Financial Information is Available From:

National Information Centre on Retirement Investments: ☎02-6281 5744; www. nicri.org.au, is a free, independent and confidential service.

Australian Investors' Association: www.investors.asn.au, an online 'investors helping investors' portal.

AXA: ☎03-9287 3333; www.axa.com.au, financial and investment advisors.

Australian Securities & Investments Commission: ☎03-5177 3988; www.asic. gov.au, enforces and regulates company and financial services.

Financial Review Smart Investor: ☎02-9282 2822; www.afrsmartinvestor.com.au, published by Fairfax, includes loads of information and analysis on investing; 12 issues cost $77.

The Department of Families, Community Services and Indigenous Affairs: www. facs.gov.au, offers a free publication entitled *Investing Money – Your Choices*, designed to help you with your retirement planning.

Useful Contacts

Centrelink, Financial Information Service: ☎13 23 00; www.centrelink.gov.au.

Financial Planning Association of Australia: ☎03-9627 5200; www.fpa.asn.au, recommends member financial services companies.

National Seniors: ☎07-3211 9611; www.nationalseniors.com.au, offers a range of services, including financial.

UK PENSIONS AND BENEFITS

Nowadays, it is possible to claim a UK state pension from almost anywhere in the world. However, pensioners retiring to most Commonwealth countries, including Australia, have their state pensions frozen at the date they first emigrated or become eligible after emigration. This means that over time their pensions decline further and further against the uprated (the difference between your frozen pension and the current full pension) version.

This is a contentious issue among retired UK pensioners living in Australia. According to the British Australian Pensioner Association (BAPA), this is 'unjustifiable discrimination. Britain first froze the pensions of overseas residents in the early 1950s because the economy was in dire straights following World War II. However, today Britain is one of the strongest economies in the world, yet pensions paid to Britons in Australia remain frozen'. Brian Havard elaborates:

A very high percentage of UK pensioners here, despite qualifying for the Australian tax-funded means-tested pension system, are living on the poverty line if they have no company pension or significant assets. Britain is the only country to discriminate against its own expatriate pensioner nationals. The federal government here appears genuinely concerned about older people, which is a welcome relief from the cynical indifference of our mother country whose high principles many of us in the older generation fought to defend. The government says it would cost £400 million to update the final 500,000 pensioners but the pension budget is £46 billion. Step away and consider the human cost; last year we lost a 96-year-old colleague with a 100% contribution record who, at the time when the weekly Basic Pension was above £80, was being paid a contemptible £6.75. A Battle of Britain hero was in the same straits.

Receiving Your UK State Pension in Australia

You can make arrangements to have your UK pension paid directly into your Australian account. To do this you need to contact the pensions service (☎0845-606 0265; www.thepensionservice.gov.uk) and ask or search for details of Overseas Direct Payment. As Australia has a tax treaty, also known as a double tax agreement, with Britain, you can arrange for your pension to be paid gross. If you complete form P85 from the Inland Revenue, available at your local tax office, you should only pay tax in Australia.

Those who move to Australia before reaching retirement age, but do not intend to work, should arrange to continue paying national contributions in the UK to qualify for a British state pension when they reach 65. Failure to do so may result in not being eligible for a UK pension on reaching retirement age. Advice on this issue is available from Inland Revenue National Insurance Contributions Office (☎0845-302 1479; www.hmrc.gov.uk/nic/).

If you visit the UK while being a pensioner in Australia with a frozen UK pension you are able to claim uprating of your pension for the period you are visiting the UK. You may also claim full uprating for the duration of your visit to any one of the 25 European Union member states. This uprating also applies if you visit Barbados, Bosnia-Herzegovina, Croatia, Israel, Jersey, Mauritius, Sark, Switzerland, Turkey, Guernsey, Philippines, Yugoslavia and Macedonia.

Private Pensions

Private UK company pensions are paid as per the rules of the individual company. Some insist payments go into a British bank account. You will then have to use a cash machine to access your money or set up a foreign account and transfer it over. Many banks charge either £2 or a 2% fee to withdraw money from a foreign cash machine. There can also be another 2.75% foreign currency loading fee so a bank-to-bank international transfer is probably more cost-effective.

UK Private Pension Transfer System

According to Global Pension Transfers, over recent years the whole notion of transferring your UK pension to Australia has become much more common than it ever was in previous times. Historically, it was not possible to transfer UK pension funds to Australia because the requirements that had to be satisfied by the receiving Australian scheme had to mirror the rules for UK pensions. No Australian fund matched those rules and, therefore, transfers would not be approved by the UK regulators.

In 1994, the Australian Government introduced a new taxation provision, which effectively imposed a tax on the growth of earnings of overseas pension schemes that were not transferred or repatriated to an Australian fund within six months of taking up permanent residence in Australia. This, among other things, brought pressure to bear on regulators and pension fund providers alike, with the result that there was a release of an Australian superannuation fund that met the UK rules.

In other words, the UK authorities allowed the transfer of UK pension funds to any complying Australian superannuation fund, recognising that they should accept transfers and allow the receiving country regulations to apply. As people had left the UK permanently, it was reasonable that they should be regulated in their new country rather than having to be in some way tied to their old country rules.

From the Australian perspective, the tax law changes allowed any accrued taxation liability to be charged to the pension scheme at the time of transfer at a rate of 15% *in lieu* of the previous marginal tax rate, which could be as high as 48.5%. Clients had to either elect for the tax to be paid by the fund or to have the growth declared as personal income. Realistically there was no decision to make, no one wants to pay more tax that they should, and the rate of 15% within their fund, as opposed to 48.5% personally.

As from 6th April 2006, known as "A Day" to financial observers in the UK, a new set of rules was introduced which placed some significant requirements on the receiving Australian schemes to avoid a massive tax grab out of the funds before they leave the UK. The proposed changes under the framework of simplification are as follows:

A new lifetime allowance of £1.5 million is being introduced as the maximum amount an individual can have in their pension funds and still retain the full tax benefits in the UK. There are transition rules for those who already hold this amount, or more, in their pension funds.

Pensions will need to be transferred to a QROPS (qualifying recognised overseas pension scheme). However, few Australian funds will go to the trouble of amending their trust deeds and their processes to satisfy the new UK rules. They will also not be interested in meeting the reporting requirements back to the UK regulators once the funds have been transferred. A transfer to a QROPS will generally incur no penalty in the UK. At the time of writing, only two have indicated that they will endeavour to meet the new rules and become a QROPS.

In the event that funds are transferred to a non-QROPS, then tax, initially at the rate of 40%, will be debited with a further 25% tax for amounts over 25% of the funds that are being transferred. The process of transfers will generally remain the same. You will need to declare that you have become a permanent resident and do not intend to return to the UK to live or to work, that you are gainfully employed or self employed, and that your UK pension funds have not commenced to pay a pension income stream.

If you can satisfy these basic criteria, you will be eligible to transfer your funds. However before you make the decision to transfer you need to assess whether it will be financially beneficial or detrimental to physically transfer the funds. There may be significant locked in benefits within your existing scheme, which may or may not be matched by the proposed new scheme.

These benefits may be financially determined to then demonstrate what earning rate you will need to earn in a new scheme to offset the lost benefits from the existing scheme.

You will also need to assess the taxation implications of drawing an income from the UK scheme as opposed to drawing an income stream from an Australian fund. Typically, income from a UK based fund is fully taxable, whereas an Australian pension fund income can be almost tax free. These tax considerations are an important aspect of the assessment process and can make the final decision that much easier. The decision to transfer or not is one that most certainly needs to be properly investigated before any long-term decisions are made.

A simple example of how the pension system operates in Australia is if you assume an amount of £150,000 is transferred from a UK pension scheme to an Australian superannuation fund. The client almost immediately retires, having turned age 55 years, which is the minimum preservation age that you can retire in Australia at this time (this age is increasing to 60 years over the coming years).

The life expectancy of the client will have to be determined from the government actuarial tables. For this purpose, 20 years has been used. The sum of £150,000 is divided by the life expectancy, which gives a figure of £7,500. This amount will be the tax free component of the pension for each year the pension is paid to the client. The minimum and maximum income levels that can be drawn each year are then calculated, which are based on pension valuation numbers issued by the tax office in Australia. Typically, these will allow a pension to be drawn of between 5% and 9% of the capital, with new pension numbers being assessed at the beginning of each financial year. For this calculation it's assumed you wish to draw £10,000 per annum.

The tax calculation therefore shows an income of £10,000 per annum of which £7,500 is tax-free. The balance of £2,500 is taxable at the marginal rate for the individual, but a tax credit of 15% is also applied to the taxable component. So the tax credit amounts to £375, being 15% of £2,500. At current exchange rates £2,500 converts to Australian $6,000, which happens to be the tax-free threshold on income in Australia. The £375 tax credit can therefore be used to offset other tax liability for other income earned.

If it's assumed that the client is aged 65 and is entitled to claim the UK state pension, of which 92% is taxable in Australia, the credit of £375 can be used to meet the tax liability of that income. Typically, therefore, all of the pension and state pension would become totally tax-free in Australia.

Naturally, when you compare the outcome of leaving the funds in the UK you have a series of 'what ifs' to consider before you can realistically decide which option will be the most beneficial. There are a few other significant aspects of having the funds in Australia, which need to be understood.

The provisions of Section 27CAA will still apply in Australia if the funds are not transferred within six months of taking up permanent residency. This aspect will need to be factored into the equation when assessing the viability of transferring or not. Of equal importance is the fact that on the death of the pension owner the treatment is very different in both countries.

In the UK, on death of the pension owner, there is a pension reversion to the spouse of 50% of the pension amount. Then, on the death of the spouse, the pension fund is retained by the pension scheme with no benefits passing to beneficiaries. In Australia, when the pension owner passes away there is a 100% reversion to the spouse, totally tax free. When the spouse passes away the funds pass to the estate subject to some lump sum tax liability, which may or may not be applicable. Over the years this has been seen as a huge benefit to people who wish to provide some long-term benefits to their children by having the ability to pass on their pension funds.

Australia has no inheritance tax, and you are also able to include what is known as a binding death nomination to your Australian funds, which effectively removes it from any estate determination, or the need to obtain probate over the estate. All in all, in spite of the new rules that came into effect on the 6th April 2006, you should not make a blind decision one way or the other. A full and proper assessment is essential.

Other matters worth noting are the different structures offered by Australian funds. Many Australian funds operate on the same structural basis as those of a Self Invested Personal Pension (SIPP) in the UK. These funds are also portable, in that when you leave an employer in Australia your fund is not frozen, but rather it is your own fund into which a future employer can contribute. You do not need to use the employer pension fund if you decide not to and you can also include your life insurance cover into your superannuation fund to gain the maximum taxation benefits.

As far as taxation is concerned, when you contribute to a pension scheme in the UK the Inland Revenue adds the tax component to your contributions. In Australia, when you invest into a superannuation plan you are able to claim the amount as a tax deduction from your income tax. At the same time, however, the tax office will take a 15% tax charge out of the contribution you make. The tax charge taken up front allows the tax office to provide the tax credit on income drawn and gives the tax office the benefit of the cashflow up front and not at the back end of the equation.

Other major differences between the two countries involve UK state pensions and social security age pensions in Australia. The UK system is based on contributions and number of years, with a pension determined by these two factors. However, when you begin drawing your UK state pension in Australia you will pay tax on 92% of the income, but the pension amount will be frozen from that time forward.

The Australian system of Age Pension is a non-contributory system which is means tested. It is there to provide a safety net for those without the means to support themselves and is certainly not there as an additional benefit for all retirees. When a UK migrant has lived in Australia for 10 years they will become eligible for the Age Pension if their assets and income are below the set thresholds that apply.

Clearly, the two pension systems are very different, each with it's own good and bad points. To get the best of both worlds, the ideal scenario is one where you accumulate most of your pension funds in the UK with the tax benefits at that end. Then relocate to Australia just before retirement to satisfy the transfer criteria and begin a pension in Australia and take the tax benefits available in the pension phase at that end.

Exportable UK Benefits

On top of your UK pension, once you have received Australian residence, you are still entitled to some UK benefits such as any Bereavement Allowance (payable for up to one year), and Widowed Parent's Allowance. However, there are a number of benefits that you can no longer receive once living abroad. These include Disability Living Allowance, Income Support, Pension Credit, Attendance Allowance, and Carer's Allowance. Some pensioners therefore find their income substantially reduced on moving to Australia. For clarification, contact the International Pension Centre, DWP, Tyneview Park, Benton, Newcastle-upon-Tyne NE98 1BA; ☎0191-218 7777; fax 0191-218 3836; www.dwp.gov.uk.

Australian Pensions

The Age Pension has been the cornerstone of Australia's retirement income system since 1909. It provides a modest retirement to those unable to fully support themselves and is not designed to provide a replacement for income. Currently, the maximum single rate pension is $11,772 a year ($19,656 for a couple) but the actual amount you receive depends on your assets and income. It is means-tested, therefore if you have significant resources you must draw on them before applying for an Age Pension.

You only become eligible for an Australian pension after 10 years of residency. However, the Social Security Agreement between Britain and Australia terminated on 1 March 2001, therefore you are disqualified from entitlement to an Australian pension for as long as your assets and income, including your British pension, exceed the limits specified in the Australian means test.

PERSONAL TAXATION

If you decide to take on paid employment in Australia then you will need to register with the Australian Taxation Office (ATO) and apply for a tax file number. The amount of tax you will have to pay will depend on the amount of money you earn, the more money you earn the higher your average tax rate rises. For the financial year 30 June 2005 to 30 June 2006, the following tax rates apply:

Taxable Income	Tax on this income
$0-$6,000	Nil
$6,001-$21,600	15c for each $1 over $6,000
$21,601-$63,000	$2,340 plus 30c for each $1 over $21,600
$63,001-$95,000	$14,760 plus 42c for each $1 over $63,000
Over $95,000	$28,200 plus 47c for each $1 over $95,000

Australian taxation law allows the Undeducted Purchase Price (UPP) of all pensions originating in the UK to be taken into account when calculating taxable income.

The UPP of any pension is the total value of all contributions made over the years during which you were earning entitlement from that fund. This total value is divided by the number of years during which you are likely to receive payments from the fund. If the pension is to be paid for life, the term will be based on the life expectancy of the pensioners, as set out in the Australian Life Tables. If, on the pensioner's death, the pension reverts to another person, that person's life expectancy will be used, if it is longer.

The calculations are made in Pounds Sterling, the original currency of the pension, while the annual deduction for tax purposes will be the agreed amount converted into Australian currency at the average rate of exchange for the year in question.

The UPP deductions can be applied to all pensions received from the UK, whether private or government. If you have not claimed this form of deduction of your pension or pensions in the past, you can backdate your claim for a maximum of three years.

In order to claim for UPP deductions you will need to provide documentary evidence of your contributions. A letter to your Pension Fund Manager or the Department for Work and Pensions in the UK should get you all the information you need.

In the case of the UK Government National Insurance or Age Pension, you also have the option of calculating the annual deduction on the basis of 8% of the annual pension received (expressed in Australian currency).

If you keep your pension rights in the UK, you may become liable for tax on the growth of the fund under the Foreign Investment Funds (FIF) legislation. This is a very complex issue but the Australian Tax Office publishes a FIF guide, which you can view at www.ato.gov.au.

An overseas pension may have a deductible amount if you made contributions towards it. An arbitrary deduction of 8% of the pension received during the financial year is available in respect of British National Insurance Scheme pensions.

WILLS AND INHERITANCE

When you move to Australia it is probably a good idea to make a new will, or a codicil, because there are some variations in law, which could affect your estate. If you decide to do this, the Public Trustee Office in each state and territory specialises in the drawing and storing of wills. Some state offices do not charge for this service. Government approved charges are incurred when the estate is administered and are only charged on solely owned assets. Typical charges are 4.4% for assets up to $100,000; 3.3% from $100,001 to $199,999; 2.2% from $200,000 to $299,999; and 1.1% for $300,000 and above. If the value is less than $100,000 there is a minimum fee of $1,100 or

2.2% of the value. The minimum charge for administering an estate is $200. You should enquire about other charges with the Trustee in your state or territory. Solicitors can also carry out the task, for a fee. They advertise on television, in the printed media and telephone directories, so are easily found.

Public Trustees

The Public Trustee for the ACT: ☎02-6207 9800; www.publictrustee.act.gov.au.

Public Trustee: ☎08-8999 7272; www.trustee.nt.gov.au (Northern Territory).

The Public Trustee of New South Wales: ☎02-9252 0523; www.pt.nsw.gov.au.

The Public Trustee of Queensland: ☎07-3213 9288; www.pt.qld.gov.au.

Public Trustee South Australia: ☎08-8226 9204; www.publictrustee.sa.on.net.

The Public Trustee Tasmania: ☎03-6233 7598; www.publictrustee.tas.gov.au.

State Trustees: ☎03-9667 6444; www.statetrustees.com.au (Victoria).

Public Trust Office: ☎08-9222 6777; www.justice.wa.gov.au (Western Australia).

Bereavement

Although most people prefer not to think or talk about it, funeral arrangements should be made and, possibly, paid for in advance. After a death has occurred you should notify the family doctor to obtain a medical death certificate, the executor of the will, and the chosen funeral director. Contacts for registered funeral directors are available from the Australian Funeral Directors Association (AFDA), ☎03-9859 9966; www.afda.org.au.

Funerals

A prepaid funeral and a funeral bond are the two arrangements that allow you to put money aside for funeral expenses. A prepaid funeral can be arranged by a funeral director but paid for at a later date, which offsets future costs. If you enter into this type of arrangement, make sure the contract is covered under the Funerals (Prepaid Money) Act, so that your contributions are paid into a trust fund. You can pay in a lump sum or in instalments.

A funeral bond means you are not committed to a particular funeral director. The bond is like any other managed fund and you will pay management fees. You can pay by instalments and up to $5,000 can be saved without affecting any asset and income tests. The proceeds of funeral bonds must go towards the funeral expenses of the holder.

If the death occurred in Australia a burial can take place at a location of the family's choice in accordance with Australian state laws. There are no restrictions based on birthplace, ethnicity, or reason for being in Australia. The same applies to a cremation, as long as it's in accord with family wishes and Australian state laws. Australian cremation documentation requires a government medical officer to authorise cremation in addition to a general medical practitioner or coroner.

Ashes may be mailed, preferably by registered/insured mail, and should be accompanied by a Certificate of Cremation issued by the Cremating Authority and a Certified Copy of the Death Certificate. There have been some problems sending ashes by mail to the extent the ashes did not reach their destination, but it is rare. Ashes can also be sent by courier; not all wish to do this, but those that do can do so door to door and will incur a cost of about $104. If you carry ashes as hand luggage, you should ensure you have the above mentioned certificates in case of any query by Customs Officers.

The AFDA stresses that it is difficult and not advisable to give an average cost of either a burial or cremation as written $values can immediately become out-of-date. It is also worth noting that the AFDA and other industry organisations are not allowed to prescribe fees as it breaches Australian government law. However, a typical funeral would cost between $5,000 and $8,000 (this includes a burial plot or cremation costs).

In addition to the option above, you can pay in full immediately at the time of arrangement, pay a required deposit and thereafter the terms and conditions of the funeral director's contract, by credit card or combination of all. It is usual that funeral companies ask for a deposit at the time of the arrangement.

Repatriation

The deceased can be returned to the UK in accordance with the family's wishes, airline regulations and some state regulations. While in some states embalming is not compulsory, in issuing the Health Department certificate for exporting human remains, the Environmental Health Officer must sight an embalming certificate or a statement of 'other means of embalming' should arterial embalming not be possible.

Although there are very prescriptive requirements for repatriation to the UK, in reality some find that the UK Consul in Sydney does not take any part in the process so there are no Consular Bills of Loading and funeral directors hermetically seal the embalmed body in a polythene liner of a thickness of no less than 0.26mm and enclose the sealed body in a wooden coffin. Most international airlines require the body to be embalmed. The consigner must declare that nothing other than the human remains are contained within the coffin.

As well as the Funeral Director's fees, the freight charges from Sydney to London (Heathrow) are $15.35 per kilo as at 16 March 2006 and are subject to change. You will also have to pay the airway bill fee, export documentation fee, export security fee, fuel surcharge and the airline insurance surcharge. These extras typical cost approximately $190 on top of the per kilo cost.

Healthcare

CHAPTER SUMMARY

○ The Australian health system is generally regarded as being world class. Contribution to this system is made through taxes and a Medicare levy.

○ Only permanent residents are eligible to enrol in Medicare, the name by which the national health system is known.

○ A revamp of the system is being considered and may provide a free yearly check-up for those aged 45 and over.

○ As a retiree migrant, it is essential you take out some form of private medical insurance cover.

○ Care in the home and residential care is one of the many good services Australia has to offer.

○ Be aware of the mozzies, creepy crawlies, crocodiles and sharks.

THE AUSTRALIAN HEALTHCARE SYSTEM

A combination of public and private sector health service providers, medical practitioners and a multitude of insurance schemes make up the Australian health system, which is widely regarded as being world-class. The national government-run healthcare scheme is called Medicare. Contribution to this health care system is made through taxes and the Medicare levy based on an individual's income.

The government also subsidises the cost of medication through the Pharmaceutical Benefits Scheme (PBS). The patient contribution per PBS prescription is $29.50 (adjusted annually at the beginning of the year). Not all medicines are listed on the PBS scheme and some medicines may include a brand price premium, which is not subsidised by the PBS. When the total contribution reaches $960.10 (also adjusted annually), that is 33 PBS prescriptions at $29.50 each, a concession card is issued by the pharmacist and the contribution for subsequent prescriptions reduces to $4.70.

To find out if you are eligible, and to enrol in Medicare, you should wait about 10 days after you arrive in Australia and then go to a Medicare office with proof of your status. If all eligibility requirements are met, you will be advised of your Medicare card number. Generally, only permanent residents are eligible for Medicare. However, Australia does share a reciprocal health agreement with the UK and Northern Ireland and, therefore, you may be eligible. However, there are specific rules, so check with Medicare first.

Under the Medicare scheme you will receive free treatment as a public patient in a public hospital; free or subsidised treatment by doctors in a general practice; subsidies on some treatments by participating specialists, optomerists and dentists. Some GPs 'bulk bill' Medicare, so you don't pay anything; others charge more than the Medicare schedule fee and you will have to pay the difference.

Free annual check-ups for people over 45 years of age are being considered as part of a revamp of the nation's health system. It's designed to deliver longer term savings by promoting preventative health care. Medicare now only pays rebates for health assessments if the patient is 75 or older. The current rebate for a 15-minute consultation is $31.45; for longer consultations $59.70 for 20 to 40 minutes; and $87.90 for 40 minutes. A national telephone line for initial health concerns to take the strain off emergency departments by directing some cases to after hours GPs or to wait until the next day is also being planned.

For comprehensive information on health matters, contact the Department of Health and Ageing (☎02-6289 1555; www.health.gov.au), or the state/ territory government departments, as follows:

ACT: ACT Health, ☎13 22 81; www.health.act.gov.au.

NT: Department of Health and Community Services, ☎08-8999 2400; www.nt.gov. au/health.

NSW: NSW Health, www.health.nsw.gov.au.

QLD: Queensland Health, ☎07-3234 0111; www.health.qld.gov.au.

SA: Department of Health, ☎08-8226 6000; www.health.sa.gov.au.

TAS: Department of Health and Human Services, ☎03-6233 3185; www.dhhs.tas. gov.au.

VIC: Department of Human Services, ☎03-9616 7777; www.health.vic.gov.au.

WA: Department of Health, ☎1800 022 222; www.health.wa.gov.au.

The ADCIS Directory (www.adcis.org.au) provides access to information on health services throughout Tasmania.

The Australian Medical Association (☎02-6270 5400; www.ama.com.au) is the doctor's representative but has information on primary health care and other issues.

The Royal District Nursing Service (☎03-9536 5222; www.rdns.com.au) delivers 24-hour nursing and healthcare services to people in their homes.

Health *Insite*, an Australian Government initiative, is an online entry point to information from leading health information providers, health organisations and government agencies. It includes up-to-date information on many health topics, such as asthma, cancer, diabetes and hypertension.

A list of Australian medical websites (too many to mention), plus private and public hospitals in each state and territory, is available at www.drsref.com.au/ausmedsite.

Medicines Line is a National Prescribing Service (NPS) telephone service (☎1300 888 763), providing independent and accurate information about the safe and effective use of your medicines, including prescription, over-the-counter and complementary medicines. Details are provided by experienced medicine information specialists and clinical pharmacists.

People aged 65 years and older are able to get free influenza and pneumonia vaccines. For more information contact the Immunisation Infoline: ☎1800 671 811, your GP, or local health centre.

PRIVATE MEDICAL CARE

Only 43% of Australians have private health insurance but as a retiree you will need to take out and maintain an adequate health insurance policy. This covers some or all of the cost of treatment as a private patient in private or public hospitals, and can extend to some services that Medicare does not cover, such as dental and optical services.

The government has introduced financial incentives aimed at encouraging people to take out private health insurance. This includes a 30% rebate for people under 65 on private health insurance premiums and an additional 1% tax levy on high-income earners who don't take out private health insurance. As from 1 April 2005, people aged 65 to 69 receive a 35% rebate and people 70 and over receive a 40% rebate.

There is also Lifetime Health Cover under which the cost of private health insurance differs depending on the age at which people first take out hospital cover. People who delay taking out hospital cover pay an extra 2% loading for each year they delay joining after 30 years of age, up to a maximum loading of 70% that applies to someone who first takes out hospital cover at 65 years.

There are many forms of private health insurance but comprehensive cover is advisable. Other options include private hospital cover, where you can choose which hospital to go to and when to have your treatment; or ancillary cover, which covers treatments that Medicare does not, such as dental, optical, podiatry and physiotherapy.

All health funds have qualifying periods, where new customers must wait a specified period before being eligible to claim benefits. These can vary but a typical example is a six-month waiting period before claiming for spectacles or contact lenses.

Health cover is a complex issue and there are more than 38 registered health insurance funds in Australia and selecting one can be confusing. iSelect (☎1300 735 255; www.iselect.com.au) is a free, impartial advisory service that is independent of any participating insurer. It can identify a health insurance policy that best meets your needs and budget. According to expat, Mike Osborne:

Pretty well everyone here pays to see a doctor, with a basic fee of between $40 to $45 in many places in South Australia. If you have a Medicare card, they reduce this but you pay what they call 'the gap.' This is the difference between what the system gives the practitioner and the fee he wants. Australians will often get their gap paid for them but for non-residents you are stuck with paying. Health insurance is a major worry for most older folk, especially temporary residents.

Private Health Insurers

Healthcare Assist: ☎1300 725 909; www.healthcareassist.com.au.

HBA: ☎13 12 43; www.hba.com.au.

HBF: ☎13 34 23; www.hbf.com.au.

HCF: ☎13 14 39; www.hcf.com.au.

MBF: ☎13 26 23; www.mbf.com.au.

Medibank Private: ☎13 23 31; www.medibankprivate.com.au.

NIB: ☎13 14 63; www.nib.com.au.

SGIO: ☎13 32 33; www.sgio.com.au.

HOSPITALS AND EMERGENCIES

Hospitals

State and territories provide public hospital services, free of charge, to public patients. The Australian Government dispenses funds to support free services to public patients through an agreement with each state and territory (Australian Health Care Agreements). However, if you are not eligible for Medicare you have to pay for your own public or private hospital costs, so make sure you are adequately covered in your health insurance policy.

Australia has 759 public hospitals and 298 private hospitals. Each public hospital is different in size and the range of services they provide. Generally, the larger the public hospital the wider the range of services it provides. These may include organ transplants, major surgery and chemotherapy. You can also access the widest range of outpatient and diagnostic services in the larger hospitals, which are not available in the smaller regional or remote centres.

Emergencies

Hospital emergency departments are set up to assist people who are experiencing a medical emergency that is life threatening or could cause serious disability. A nurse will assess your medical condition and assign you to one of the five 'triage' categories. You are not necessarily seen in the order in which you arrive at the emergency department. If someone arrives after you and is assigned to a more urgent triage, they will probably be treated first. Outpatient services are also provided by all hospitals.

Most retirement villages and an increasing number of private residences operate emergency call systems, which allow you to summon assistance by means of a personal alarm that you carry with you or wear.

SmartLink is a telephone based emergency call system featuring a lightweight water resistant transmitter worn as a pendant on a neck chain, on the wrist using a wristwatch strap, or on a keyring. It is designed to help people who are at home alone to call for assistance, when required, 24-hours a day. More information is available from LifeTec Queensland (☎07-3553 9000; e-mail mail@lifetec.org.au; www.lifetec.org.au).

*Care*CALL (☎1300 130 100; www.carecall.com.au), provides personal emergency alarm monitoring 24-hours a day.

MedicAlert (www.medicalert.com.au), the internationally-recognised emergency patient protection, can help you when a diagnosis is needed in a hurry. MedicAlert provides health professionals with your vital medical information when it's needed the most.

The emergency number throughout Australia is 000.

According to Mike Osborne:

Each house pays about $60 a year for the emergency services but it does not include ambulances – don't know why. Ambulance cover is vital because you can get big bills. Many health insurance schemes will pay for emergency call outs but often with a limit of $1,000. With an average call now costing $600 you can see where the problem lies. Also, the health funds will not always cover ambulance costs from one hospital to another, say for x-rays or other treatment. In South Australia, you can get ambulance cover for about $100 a year per family.

The Flying Doctor

The Royal Flying Doctor Service (RFDS), www.flyingdoctor.net, is a regular lifesaver in remote and rural parts of Australia. In 2005, the RFDS last year evacuated an average 91 patients a day and flew almost 12 million miles (20 million km) to give emergency medical treatment to people in the bush. It now covers 80% of Australia, an area greater than Europe, and treats an average of 642 patients a day. For those living in the bush, the service is often their lifeline to primary health care.

As rural doctors drift towards the cities, the RFDS acts as ambulance, general practitioner, chemist, cardiologist, health clinic and specialist for people at remote homesteads, mines and Aboriginal communities. It has 23 bases located around Australia and is the largest aero-medical service in the world.

The RFDS is a national body made up of four sections that operate independently. The southeast section covers New South Wales, Victoria, Tasmania and parts of South Australia. The central section covers the Northern Territory and parts of South Australia. Queensland and Western Australia have their own sections.

RETURNING TO THE UK FOR TREATMENT

Under the current Department of Health regulations anyone who spends more than three consecutive months living outside the UK, with the intention of permanently living abroad, is no longer entitled to free NHS hospital treatment in England, except in the case of an emergency. This includes people in receipt of UK state retirement pensions. If you once again take up permanent residence in the UK, you are entitled to the full range of free NHS treatment.

CARE IN THE HOME AND RESIDENTIAL CARE

In Australia the aged and community care industry includes home care and nursing services, residential and aged care homes, care package providers, retirement villages, independent living units and seniors' housing. Currently, there are about 142,806 residential care places in Australia for both high- and low-level care.

Community Care

The main aim of community care is to enable people to stay in their own home. The Australian Government, assisted by state and territory governments, funds a range of community care services allowing many aged people to continue with an independent life. The need for community care is growing and expanding and will be a major force in the future. The following separately funded government programmes, to best meet these changing needs, are currently available:

Community Aged Care Package (CACP). Offers services for frail aged people ensuring that they can remain at home rather than enter residential care. Services include help with bathing, meals, shopping and getting around. You have to have an assessment by an Aged Care Assessment Team (ACAT) to determine if a CACP is appropriate for your needs. The maximum care recipient contribution is currently $5.89 a day (this is based on 17.5% of the maximum basic rate of pension currently $471.40 fortnightly).

Day Therapy Centres (DTCs). Available throughout Australia and provide a range of therapy services to assist the frail aged to either maintain or recover a level of independence, which will allow them to remain either in the community or in low-level residential care. The services may include occupational therapy, physiotherapy, podiatry and speech therapy. There may be a small fee for these services. There are 155 throughout Australia, mostly located at aged care homes. More information and locations of DTCs is available from the Aged and Community Care Information Line, ☎1800 500 853, or www.health.gov.au.

Extended Aged Care at Home (EACH). Provides an option for older people with high care needs to be supported in their own homes. Services can include domestic assistance, in-home respite, nursing, personal care, social support, and transport. Aged Care Assessment Team (ACAT) assessment is a prerequisite. Your maximum care recipient contribution is currently $5.89 a day (this is based on 17.5% of the maximum basic rate of pension currently $471.40 fortnightly). There are 56 service providers nationally and a full list is available from www.health.gov.au.

Home and Community Care (HACC). Provides care services to people in their own homes. While it is for people of all ages who require assistance, most HACC recipients are pensioners and about 40% are over 80 years old. Services include allied health care, counselling, support, information and advocacy, domestic assistance, home modification and maintenance, meals, nursing and personal care, respite care, and transport. Some services charge a small fee depending on your ability to pay. This varies within each state and territory. There are about 3,100 HACC organisations and more information is available from www.health.gov.au.

Aged Care Assessment Teams (ACAT). Help you to work out what kind of care will best meet your needs when you are no longer able to manage at home without assistance. An ACAT assessment and approval is required before you can access residential aged care, CACPs, or EACH packages. There are ACATs in each state and territory. Contact details can be obtained from the Aged and Community Care Information Line, ☎1800 500 853, or www. health.gov.au.

Residential Care

If you think you need help with everyday tasks, assistance with personal care, or 24-hour nursing care, you should think about choosing your aged care home. If you need less care an independent living unit or retirement village (see *Your New Home in Australia*) may be for you.

Residential aged care is offered either on a permanent or short-term (respite care) basis. There are two types of aged care: low-level and high-level care. Low-level care homes, formerly known as hostels, generally provide accommodation and personal care. High-level care homes, formerly known as nursing homes, care for people with a greater deal of frailty who need continuous nursing care.

All care homes must provide a specified range of care and services to its residents, including 24-hour help from staff, assistance with daily living activities, meals and refreshments. Some aged care homes offer an *extra service*, which means they provide you with a higher standard of accommodation and services but cost more. A list of homes with *extra service* is available at www.health.gov.au.

All government-funded aged care homes must meet required accreditation standards assessed by the Aged Care Standards and Accreditation Agency (☎ 02-9633 1711; www.accreditation.org.au). While the government provides funding, most residents will also pay a number of fees and charges. These fall into two categories: daily care fees and accommodation payments. The amount you pay will depend on your income and assets.

Respite Care. Provides short-term care when you need it and if you intend returning to the community. It can also be provided in your home or in a respite care centre. More information can be obtained from a Commonwealth Carer Respite Centre (☎ 1800 059 059) near you. You will be asked to pay a basic daily care fee. The maximum fee is set at the pensioner rate of basic daily care fee, which is currently $28.62. You may have 63 days of respite care in a financial year, with the possibility of 21 days extension.

Aged and Community Services Australia (ACSA), www.agedcare,org. au, represents more than 1,200 church and charitable and community based organisations, about two thirds of the aged care industry, providing accommodation and care services for older people.

Aged Care Network (☎ 1800 266 606; www.agedcarenetwork.com.au) provides information on residential aged care and accessibility of care.

The website www.agedcare.com.au, has a list of aged care facilities, retirement villages, and community care in each state and territory available online.

Costs

Accommodation payments are based on the level of care required and the value of your assets. If you need high-level care you may need to pay an accommodation charge. Alternatively, if you need low-level care, or are going into an extra service plan then you may need to pay an accommodation bond.

Basic daily care fees are for living expenses such as, meals, laundry, heating/cooling and also your nursing or personal care. This fee is paid at either a lower pensioner or higher non-pensioner rate but is currently up to $28.62 a day. If you are a part-pensioner or a non-pensioner, you may also have to pay an income tested daily fee to your care service provider which is up to $22.08 a day.

LOCAL HEALTH ISSUES

Australia has the highest incidence of skin cancer in the world. The sun produces ultraviolet (UV) radiation that can cause serious burns to your eyes and skin and can be an invisible killer. The Bureau of Meteorology now issues a SunSmart UV Alert when the UV Index is forecast to reach three, a level that can damage your skin and lead to skin cancer and melanoma. The alert is reported in most newspapers and some television and radio weather forecasts, or can be accessed at www.bom.gov.au. For more information check www.sunsmart.com.au.

Both direct and reflected radiation causes burning, so to avoid exposure wear sunglasses with polarising lenses and use sunscreen on your exposed skin. Various products are available that contain agents to block UV radiation but it's advisable to use a SPF30+ sunscreen at all times. Also remember, an increase of 1,000 ft (300 m) in elevation causes an increase in UV radiation of 4%. High altitude results in high UV exposure year round. UV radiation causes most damage between 10am and 3pm when the sun is highest in the sky.

Heat stroke can be life threatening and may demand immediate medical attention.

Mosquitoes. Warnings about disease-bearing mosquito outbreaks come with recommendations about precautions from the state or territory governments. Diseases transmitted by mosquitoes in Australia include Japanese encephalitis, dengue fever (restricted to Queensland), Murray Valley encephalitis virus, Kunjin virus, Ross River virus disease and Barmah Forest virus. Malaria in Australia has been endemic, but was declared eradicated from the country in 1981. However, about 700 cases are imported annually from travellers infected elsewhere.

Sensitivity to mosquito bites varies from person to person; most people have only a mild reaction but others can have severe symptoms from the saliva of mosquitoes. Simple measures can be taken by individuals to limit their contact with mosquitoes. Areas that are known to be infested with large numbers of mosquitoes should be avoided. Activities that are scheduled for outdoors, especially around dusk, should be limited. A chemical repellent that contains about 20% DEET (diethyl toluamide) should be used on exposed areas of the skin.

Australian mainland and coastal waters have a large variety of venomous creatures that may be of risk to humans. These venomous creatures include snakes, spiders, ticks, wasps, bees, scorpions, ants, centipedes, millipedes, jellyfish, octopus, cone shells and sponges. Sharks and crocodiles are predators to be wary of. Some hazards are very region specific. For example, some pests are only in the tropical regions and there are no crocodiles in Tasmania.

Snake Bites. Australia is home to 21 of the world's 25 most deadly snakes. Death adders are 28 times as venomous as a rattlesnake. If you are able to identify the snake, it will help the doctor pick the right anti-venom straight away. Don't guess though; doctors can use a venom-detection kit. If bitten, stay still and apply pressure to the bitten area. Splint the whole area to immobilise. Don't try and force the venom out of the bite as it will only push it further into the bloodstream. Australian snake bites are often not painful, so contact a doctor immediately if you have the following symptoms: continued bleeding from bite site; tender or painful lymph nodes; headache, nausea, vomiting, abdominal pain; abnormally low blood pressure; blurred or double vision; facial paralysis; muscle weakness.

Spiders and Other Crawlies. Australia has some of the most venomous spiders in the world and, in general, can be rather large: huntsman spiders grow as big as your hand. Do not attempt to handle any spider, even if it is small. It also has some very large species of centipedes and Bull ants. Both have nasty bites, as do scorpions, which live in most areas. Be careful where you choose to sit.

Leeches, Ticks and Other Vectors. Most leeches are blood sucking parasites and some feed on humans. When a leech bites it holds its sucker in place and then makes an incision in the skin and excretes a mucous. Most are freshwater animals, living in still or slowly flowing waters, but many terrestrial and marine species occur. Land leeches are common on the ground or in low foliage in wet rain forests.

When walking in the bush and rainforest be sure to wear boots, thick long socks and long trousers. Leeches and ticks are common so check your body thoroughly after walking. Ticks can be removed with kerosene or methylated spirits and leeches with salt or heat.

Tick typhus occurs down the east coast, Bass Strait and Tasmania. Lyme disease is reported but its presence is controversial. Fleas were responsible for an outbreak of murine typhus in Western Australia. Mites cause scrub typhus and there has been a fatality in the Northern Territory.

Ants. Fire Ants, found mostly in Queensland, inflict a painful, fiery string. They look like ordinary house or garden ants and are coppery-brown in colour. The sting causes a small blister at each sting, which become itchy and prone to infection if broken.

Bluebottles. Several species of harmful jellyfish can be found off the north Queensland beaches during the warmer months of November to May, the least dangerous of which is the Bluebottle. Bluebottle tentacles will, however, cause a sharp, painful sting if they are touched, which is aggravated by rubbing the area. Intense pains may be felt from a few minutes to many hours and develops into a dull ache, which then spreads to surrounding joints. The affected area develops a red line with small white lesions. Asthmatics and people with allergies can be badly affected and suffer from respiratory distress. Bluebottles are not always obvious in the water and dead specimens stranded on the beach can still cause stings. Bluebottles are more common on exposed ocean beaches after strong onshore winds and are rarely found in sheltered waters. Special exclusion nets are placed on beaches in populated areas during the warmer months and bathers are recommended to swim inside these nets.

Sharks. Almost half of the world's shark species are found in Australian waters. Many people believe that sharks are a threat to human life but the majority of the 370 species are harmless. However, a shark attack was recently reported near North Stradbroke Island, Queensland, where shark safety equipment is in place. Bull sharks, believed to be responsible for this attack, are aggressive and unpredictable. They are common in waterways, such as channels, canals, rivers and lakes during the hot, wet months. Others to look out for are Tiger sharks, the Great Hammerhead and some reef whalers, such as Bronze, Grey and Silvertip.

Areas of danger, especially those involving sharks, crocodiles and stingers, have clearly marked signs. The signs have clear illustrations of the potential dangers of an area. When swimming, swim between the flags and where a lifeguard is present. Scuba diving can be treacherous so follow recommended precautions and never dive alone.

Crocodiles grow to more than 19 ft (6 m) and are protective of their turf. They occasionally attack people wading and swimming in estuaries and rivers. A "Croc Smart" brochure is available for you to read before travelling within Australia, especially along the Wet Tropics coast.

MENTAL HEALTH

There have been recent reports that Medicare will be expanded to allow more people to see psychologists on referral from the family doctor as part of a $1.5 billion plan to tackle the nation's mental health crisis, a disorder that effects one in five Australians a year. At the moment, the Medicare rebate is available only on a limited basis for people visiting psychologists. In addition, as part of the health reform programme, there will be a national health telephone network and a major component of this will include support services for mental health.

Depression. The Australian Government also has a National Depression Initiative to provide national awareness, prevention and early intervention of depression and related disorders. On average, one in five people in Australia will experience depression at some point. Depression is not always detected in older people but help is at hand with *beyondblue* (☎13 11 14; www.beyondblue.org.au) an independent company formed to progress the government's initiative and offer help to the public.

The Mental Health Foundation of Australia (Victoria) (☎03-9427 0406; www.mentalhealthvic.org.au), is an organisation of professionals, sufferers, families of sufferers and related organisations concerned with mental health.

Relationships. Settling in another country at any time in one's life can place extreme pressure on your marriage and other relationships. If you find you have sudden need of marriage counselling, Relationships Australia (☎1300 364 277; www.relationships.com.au) provides professional services to help and support relationships.

Alcoholism. Misuse of alcohol is a major preventable risk factor for a wide range of diseases and injuries. In Australia, the mortality rate due to alcohol is estimated to be in the order of 3,000 per annum and responsible for 4.9% of the total disease burden. Road accidents, family violence, health care costs, mental disorders, suicides and drowning are all problems impacted by the misuse of alcohol.

Advice and information is available from the Alcohol Education and Rehabilitation Foundation (☎02-6122 8600) and from the government's information site at www.alcohol.gov.au.

Health Organisations

Alzheimer's Australia: www.alzheimers.org.au.

Arthritis Australia: www.arthritisaustralia.com.au.

Australian Dental Association: www.ada.org.au

Australian Hearing: www.hearing.com.au.

Australian Homeopathic Association: www.homeopathyoz.org.

Australian Kidney Foundation: www.kidney.org.au.

Australian Osteopathic Association: www.osteopathic.com.au.

Australian Physiotherapy Association: www.physiotherapy.asn.au.

Cancer Council Australia: www.cancer.org.au.

Chiropractors' Association of Australia: www.chiropractics.asn.au.

Diabetes Australia: www.diabetesaustralia.com.au.

Heart Foundation: www.heartfoundation.com.au.

Multiple Sclerosis Australia: www.msaustralia.org.au.

National Asthma Council: www.nationalasthma.org.au.

National Herbalists Association of Australia (NHAA): www.nhaa.org.au.

National Stroke Foundation: www.strokefoundation.com.au.

Parkinson's Australia: www.parkinsons.org.au.

Crime, Security and the Police

CHAPTER SUMMARY

○ Crime rates are lower in Australia than in the UK but boosted in the tourist season.
○ Police forces are the responsibility of each state and territory.
○ Look out for scammers, they are as present in Australia as anywhere else in the world.

Street crime, burglaries and car thefts are the most common crimes in Australia. They are often crimes of opportunity and most intruders find a house left open or unlocked. Precautions are necessary: you can use deadlocks and grills on doors and windows; do not hide extra keys under mats; do not give your key to trade persons; have adequate lighting outside; and lock wheelie bins away (they make good stepladders).

While Australia has an anti-gun policy, weapons are increasingly used in such crimes, which also may be associated with drug trafficking and usage. Appropriate common sense should be taken, especially at night, to avoid becoming a target of opportunity.

Personal alarms are used to deter would-be attackers and are compact and easy to carry. When activated they emit a loud, piercing noise. They are used in an emergency and are tied into a fixed base alarm system or connected to a phone system to call for help.

Police forces are the responsibility of state/territory governments, and are headed in each state by a Commissioner for Police. Regulations for each force vary and some may carry guns on duty, depending on the state. The Australian Federal Police (AFP) is the nation's multi-faceted law enforcement organisation, policing representative, and the chief source of advice to the Australian Government on policing issues. It enforces Commonwealth criminal law, and protects Commonwealth and national interests from crime in Australia and overseas. In general, the police enjoy a good public profile and maintain open communications with the community.

Australia is on a medium level of terrorism alert. Security has been heightened at airports and major sporting and public events. The 24-hour national security hotline is ☎1800 123 400 and more information is available from www.nationalsecurity.gov.au.

Useful Contacts

Dial 000 for Police, Ambulance or Fire Brigade.

Ring 13 14 44 to report information that is not an emergency.

Police numbers in each capital city:

Canberra, ACT: ☎02-6256 7777.

Darwin, NT: ☎08-8981 1044.

Sydney, NSW: ☎ 02-9286 4000.

Brisbane, QLD: ☎07-3222 1222.

Adelaide, SA: ☎08-8416 2811.

Hobart, TAS: ☎03-6231 0166.

Melbourne, VIC: ☎03-9607 7777.

Perth, WA: ☎08-9320 3444.

SCAMS

In Australia, as anywhere else, there are people trying to cheat you out of your money. From door-to-door scams, phoney bank e-mails (phishing), investment scams, internet fraud, pyramid and self-employment schemes, many scammers target older people. Research shows that up to 60% of all people targeted are over 60 years of age.

The Australasian Consumer Fraud Taskforce (☎1300 795 995; www.scamwatch.gov.au) is a group of 18 government regulatory agencies and departments who have a remit for consumer protection in relation to frauds and scams. One of these is the Australian Securities and Investments Commission (www.asic.gov.au), which acts against scams involving financial products and services. Scams involving other products and services are covered by police and other state and Commonwealth consumer protection regulators.

The Office of Fair Trading in Queensland produces *The Hard Sell*, a 54-page free guide to help consumers identify common scams and deal effectively with high-pressure sales techniques in different situations. It covers mobile phones, real estate, motor vehicles, credit, the internet, interest-free offers, door-to-door sales and itinerant tradespeople. In New South Wales, the Office of Fair Trading has a *Scam Smart* kit which you can download from the website or call ☎ 13 32 20 for a copy.

Mail Scams. Fraudulent schemes using the post are common and come in many forms: a letter claiming you have won an overseas lottery or one claiming that by recruiting and selling a 'selling scheme' to others you'll get rich; a chain letter; donations to a charity; and some asking you to provide your bank details to help move money out of a foreign country. These offers are unlawful as are pyramid schemes.

Amazing Offers Scams. Free goods, winning tickets, or invitations are used to entice you to go with a scam. You may be asked to pay a joining fee or call 190. The advance fee or Nigerian scam is an offer to participate in the transfer of overseas funds to Nigeria, other African countries, or Iraq. This type of scam dates back to 1588 when it was called the 'Spanish prisoner' scam where a letter was written by a supposed prisoner requesting money to be paid to the jailer to release him. Today, it's from a fictitious Nigerian exile wanting to move millions out of the country.

Investment Scams. Telemarketing, or cold calling, can be used. To attract and hold your curiosity, the scammers may pretend to be investment advisers or community workers from a religious organisation.

Many scammers use the internet to promote fraud through spam. The Australian Government introduced anti-spam legislation in 2003, which targets Australian-originated spam and the technology spammers use to send unsolicited e-mails. The Australian Communication and Media Authority monitors compliance and more information is available from www.spam. acma.gov.au.

New Zealand

Part one

Before
You Go

Setting the Scene
Basics

Setting the Scene

CHAPTER SUMMARY

○ For the many Britons who draw their pension abroad, retirement can come as a relief. Freed from the confines of the 9 to 5, they have the chance to enjoy a new life-style in a warmer climate.
○ The outstanding quality of life sees many ex-pat New Zealanders return home in later life.
○ The New Zealand lifestyle is much more relaxed and geared towards the outdoors.
○ Non-residents are able to buy property in New Zealand.
○ It will be much easier to make friends as unlike retiring to a Mediterranean hotspot, you won't have to learn a new language.

REASONS TO RETIRE TO NEW ZEALAND

Where better to retire than a peaceful, uncrowded and beautiful country, far away from the world's trouble spots. With a summer that lasts at least twice as long as that in the UK, New Zealand is the ultimate get-away-from-it-all retirement destination. With a warm and sunny climate and the wine and food to match, the great advantage of New Zealand over many other warm countries is that you can instantly communicate with the locals without the need to grab a phrase book every time you want to make yourself understood.

This is a country where the living is easy and where there is none of that petty, time-wasting bureaucracy that is a factor of daily life in some European countries. Even though the strong ties between Britain and New Zealand have started to unravel in recent years, the two nations have much in common and share many of the same values. Shared values mean that you will find it much easier to make new friends and integrate into society. Whether your passion is watching rugby, going to the theatre or discussing the merits of Pinot Noir, your retirement lifestyle in New Zealand will be the envy of your friends and family back home.

PROS & CONS

Pros

O Making new friends and creating a new social life for yourself will be much easier in a country which shares not just a language but many similar values with the UK.

O Land and property are cheaper than in the UK, as is the general cost of living.

O New Zealand is roughly the size of Italy but with fewer people than Ireland and you are bound to find your perfect home, be it a beach house, a villa in the country, or a luxury retreat in the mountains.

O The New Zealand lifestyle is much more relaxed and geared towards outdoor activities.

O Abundant fresh produce and great cuisine and wine at a more reasonable cost than in the UK.

O Buying property in New Zealand is relatively straightforward particularly as the legal system is based on English law.

Cons

O Unless you have immediate family in New Zealand who can sponsor your residency application anyone over the age of 55 may need to buy an established business or set one up to gain residency.

O Distance. Fares may be cheaper than they once were but it still takes 24 hours to fly back to the UK. Friends and family need to be in good health to make the journey.

O Property prices in the most popular areas have risen rapidly in recent years with waterfront property now prohibitively expensive.

O Some of the cheaper regions in which to buy property may be too remote and quiet during the winter.

O There is no universal free public health system as there is in the UK and you have to pay to visit a G.P.

INTRODUCING NEW ZEALAND

Historians still don't know for sure, exactly where in the Pacific the first settlers came from and when they arrived. Below is a chronology of some pivotal events in New Zealand history, which may help to set the scene of the country you have adopted for retirement.

Key Dates Of New Zealand History

1200 – 1300 AD The first Maori settlers arrive from Polynesia.

1642 *The First European Encounter* – Abel Tasman's triumph at being the first recorded European to sight the South Island turns to tragedy as local Maori are killed.

1769 Captain Cook spends six months charting the coast of the two islands. Cook's careful observation of local protocol enables him to successfully trade with Maori.

1773-4 Cook's second visit.

1777 Cook's last visit.

1790s Sealers and whalers start to exploit New Zealand waters.

1814 Christian missionaries arrive in the Bay of Islands to try to convert Maori to Christianity.

1840 Treaty of Waitangi signed by the Crown and Maori chiefs.

1840-50 *The First Settlers* – Over 22,000 immigrants arrive from England through the New Zealand Company

1844-75 Hone Heke's symbolic gesture of defiance at breaches of the Treaty starts a revolt over land rights which erupts into the New Zealand Wars which lasts until 1875.

1882 Refrigeration sees the start of New Zealand's export lamb trade to England.

1893 *Votes for Women* – New Zealand is the first country in the world to give women the vote.

1914-1918 Australian and New Zealand Army Corps (ANZACS) formed to fight in World War I. The loss of life per capita was greater than any other nation.

1947 *An Independent Nation* – New Zealand gains full independence from Britain.

1973 Britain joins the Common Market. This has a huge negative impact on New Zealand's economy as the country is forced to find other markets for its butter and lamb.

1975 Waitangi Tribunal is set up to consider Maori land claims.

1985 *New Zealand says no to nuclear ships* – The Greenpeace flagship *Rainbow Warrior* is blown up in Auckland harbour by French intelligence agents. Nuclear-powered and nuclear-armed vessels banned from New Zealand ports.

NEW ZEALAND TODAY

New Zealand is admired by many nations around the world as a country that has not only begun a reconciliation process with its indigenous population but as one that is not afraid to stand up for itself when it has to. Since the establishment of the Waitangi Tribunal in the mid 1970s the country has begun the process of paying compensation to its native people for seizing their land unlawfully. New Zealand has emerged as a stronger more confident nation since it has established successful trading partnerships within the Asia-Pacific region. New Zealand has the lowest unemployment rate in the OECD beating even South Korea. For a small nation with a relatively recent settlement history, New Zealand has achieved a remarkable amount in a short time.

The Current Government and the Future

New Zealand's system of government is a parliamentary democracy with Queen Elizabeth II as the Head of State and the Governor-General appointed as her representative. The two main political parties are the centre-right National and Labour on the centre-left.

The 1996 election was the first to use proportional representation (Mixed Member Proportional – referred to as MMP). Under MMP voters have two votes, one to elect their MP and the other to choose a party.

Since 1999 a Labour-led coalition headed by Helen Clark has been in power. Although the 2002 election saw the worst election defeat of National in 70 years, the results of the September 2005 election were so close that Labour's victory was not confirmed until some weeks afterwards, when the special votes were counted. Out of a total of 121 seats, Labour won 50 and National 48.

Labour's coalition partners are United Future and New Zealand First. The biggest challenge facing the current government over the next term will be the economy as rising oil prices start to bite.

Population

The current population of New Zealand is around 4.2 million. However there is a wide disparity in the population density between the two islands; nearly three million live in the North Island with over a million living in the Auckland region. In the South Island it is a different story. When you consider that of the 1.2 million people, over 500,000 live in the Christchurch area, it should be easy to find a place all to yourself in the South Island.

Geography

The size of the United Kingdom, Italy or the US state of Colorado but spread across two main islands, the total land mass of New Zealand is 104, 454 square miles/270,534 sq. km. The Cook Strait, a body of water as wide as the English Channel, separates the two islands. There are numerous offshore islands, the largest of which is Stewart Island, at the southern tip of the South Island.

Lake Taupo in the central North Island is the largest lake at 235 square miles/607 sq. km. and is the source of the longest river, the Waikato, which runs for 264 miles/425km.

Packed within this one small country is a diversity of landscape that is generally only found in entire continents, with lakes, mountains, volcanoes, sub-tropical beaches and rainforest.

Climate Zones

Being surrounded by the Pacific Ocean to the north and east and the Tasman Sea to the west, New Zealand has a maritime climate. At sea level temperatures never get too hot or too cold. But as more than 75% of the country is over 200 metres high, temperature, rainfall and wind varies significantly.

In all there are nine climate zones, ranging from sub-tropical in the north to cool and temperate in the far south to alpine conditions in the Southern Alps. These microclimates occur because of proximity to the west or east coasts, how close they are to mountains and whether there is any shelter from the winds. Nelson and Marlborough at the top of the South Island enjoy some of the best weather New Zealand has to offer yet barely less than 75 kilometres away across the Cook Strait, Wellington can be buffeted by gales.

AVERAGE MAXIMUM TEMPERATURES

Area	Jan	Apr	Aug	Nov
Bay of Islands	25°C	21°C	17°C	19°C
Auckland	24°C	20°C	16°C	18°C
Napier	23°C	18°C	14°C	19°C
Wellington	20°C	17°C	12°C	15°C
Nelson	23°C	18°C	13°C	17°C
Christchurch	22°C	18°C	12°C	16°C
Queenstown	22°C	16°C	10°C	14°C

Most of New Zealand has more than 2000 hours of sunshine a year with Nelson and Marlborough vying for top spot as the sunniest places in the country.

Retiree Sheila Gavin who moved to Arrowtown in the South Island, says *'in Aberdeenshire we had one or two barbecues in the summer. Although I haven't had a winter yet in Arrowtown, I know the cold will be nothing like winters where I used to live in Scotland'.*

CULTURE SHOCK

Many people choose to live in New Zealand because they like the climate and the kind of lifestyle that they have experienced whilst on holiday there, believing that it is a similar country to Britain but with a better climate. While there are many similarities to the British way of life, there are a great many differences too and these can come as a shock to those who wrongly believe that New Zealand is like Britain was forty years ago. New Zealand is a Pacific country, not a European one and that is reflected in the diversity of the population, especially in Auckland.

The major differences between the two countries are that New Zealand has an indigenous population and was not founded on a class system. As a result New Zealanders tend to treat each other equally and do not stand on ceremony. They call each other by their first names, even in business meetings and are warm and friendly especially towards those who praise their country. They are sensitive to criticism especially when anyone compares New Zealand unfavourably with anywhere else.

Rugby is a national obsession and the mood of the country is determined by whether or not the All Blacks win or lose against France, South Africa or any other rugby-mad nation.

Basics

CHAPTER SUMMARY

O Whether or not it is cheaper to live in New Zealand will depend upon your lifestyle.

O Unlike Australia, New Zealand has no special visa category for retirees as the immigration policy specifically targets young professionals.

O There are numerous alternatives to moving full-time which include renting and house swaps.

O The best way to avoid a costly, abortive move to New Zealand is to have a trial period.

O Before you depart the UK permanently you should arrange to have your UK pension paid into your bank account in New Zealand.

O Only cats and dogs are allowed to be imported into New Zealand and they must be micro-chipped and vaccinated.

O Getting rid of non-essentials before you go could save you thousands in shipping costs.

THINGS TO CONSIDER

Is it Affordable?

Those who can afford retirement in the UK will certainly be able to afford it in New Zealand. The cost of living in New Zealand is around 20% cheaper than in Britain. However, the gap is certainly closing and it would be a mistake to assume that you will be far better off if you live in New Zealand – it depends entirely on where you choose to live, your lifestyle, how regularly you want to make trips back to the UK, and whether your pension and any other income amounts to a secure, regular long-term income.

One factor that people fail to consider is the fluctuation of the exchange rate. The majority of migrants have enough funds to live on, but anyone with a state or a private UK pension is subject to the strength of the British pound.

Note that British state pensioners who retire to New Zealand, (or any other Commonwealth country) do not receive index-linked increases or Christmas bonuses. The UK state pension is frozen at the rate when the person first qualified. At present New Zealand Superannuation 'tops up' any shortfall but there is no guarantee that a future government may not reduce New Zealand Super to an amount less than the UK DSS pension.

There are 550,000 British pensioners who are affected by this ruling. The anomaly is that 400,000 other British pensioners do get the increase because they happen to have retired to other countries. Annette Carson, a British pensioner living in South Africa, with a frozen pension, has taken legal action in the British courts. She lost her appeal in the House of Lords. Her only recourse now is the European Court of Human Rights. Mrs Carson and many retired women (especially widows), live in reduced circumstances in countries where there is no social security top up system.

If you intend to rely heavily on your state pension, it is a good idea to get a forecast of exactly how much you will receive (see below).

UK Retirement Pension Forecast

Those who have not yet reached retirement age, but plan to start receiving their UK state pension in New Zealand need to take advice on whether they should continue to pay National Insurance contributions in the UK. Should your circumstances change perhaps later on in life, and you want to retire to a third country, by keeping up National Insurance payments you will not be financially penalised.

You should request a Retirement Pension Forecast. This tells you the amount of state pension you have already earned and the amount you can expect to receive upon reaching pension age. To receive a forecast, obtain form BR19 from your local social security office or contact the Retirement Pension Forecasting and Advice Unit: ☎ 0845-3000 168.

Cost of Living in New Zealand Compared to the UK

NB The figures quoted below were collated in April 2006.

Food. Grocery items in the supermarket cost about the same as in the UK but there are many discount shops that offer very good value for fresh produce. Buying fruits and vegetables when they are in season will reduce your food bills.

Product	New Zealand price ($)	UK price (£)	New Zealand price in £ sterling equivalent
Semi-Skimmed Milk (1 litre)	1.95	0.53	0.64
Eggs (6)	1.95	0.94	0.64
Orange Juice (1 litre)	3.99	1.62	1.32
Butter (250g)	1.20	0.76	0.40
Marmalade (454 g)	2.79	0.77	0.92
Multigrain Bread (1 kg)	3.45	0.88	1.14
Ground Coffee (250 g)	5.10	2.49	1.68
Tea bags (100 bags)	4.23	1.88	1.39
Fresh Chicken (1 kg)	9.00	1.78	2.97
Potatoes (2 kg)	2.99	1.50	0.99
Sugar (500g)	0.95	0.45	0.31
Onions (1kg)	1.99	0.64	0.66
Table Wine (750 ml)	12.25	4.99	4.03
Beer – 6 x330ml	9.20	2.59	3.03
Daily local newspaper	1.50	0.60	0.49
Unleaded petrol (1 litre)	1.62	0.90	0.53

Healthcare. The cost of healthcare is an important consideration when retiring to New Zealand. Unlike the UK there is no universal National Health Service although there are some core publicly funded health services. Visits to the doctor and prescriptions have to be paid for although reduced fees exist for eligible pensioners who are on a low income and in receipt of a Community Services Card. Dentists and opticians in New Zealand are private and this is an extra cost that should be factored in.

Product	New Zealand price ($)	UK price (£)	New Zealand price in £ sterling equivalent
Routine checkup at family doctor	50	85	16.48
Single prescription	15	6.65	4.94
Visit to dentist (one x-ray and one filling)	240	60	79.09
Painkillers (20 tablets)	2.38	1.50	0.78

Utilities. Electricity is less expensive in New Zealand and gas is slightly cheaper than electricity. Mains gas is only available in the North Island. In the South Island your heating bills will be more expensive than in the North Island as you will need to use it more often. Note that many councils include the cost of water charges in their rates and the costs will be cheaper than those quoted below.

Product	New Zealand price ($)	UK price (£)	New Zealand price in £ sterling equivalent
Phone line – average monthly rental	42.20	10.66	13.91
Phone – average charge per local call from home (3 mins)	Free	0.14	Free
Electricity, monthly bill for family of four	150	45	49.44
Gas, monthly bill for family of four	135	45	44.49
Water, monthly bill for family of four on mains water supply	120	25.83	39.55

Leaving Family and Friends

As well as sufficient funds, you will also need the resolve to cope with the move practically and emotionally. Moving house down the road can be stressful enough, but moving halfway across the world is another matter entirely. Before you start a new life you have to let go of the old one and for many people the feelings of loss and isolation can be difficult to deal with. Uprooting yourself from friends and family and assimilating into a new culture is a challenge. You know why you are making the move but not everyone else can be expected to understand. Leaving children and grandchildren behind might be difficult but it also allows them the opportunity to escape the dreary British winter and visit you in your new home 'Down-Under.' The biggest test for any relocation is the ability to deal with emergencies that may arise in the UK when you are living in New Zealand. There is no point in moving to somewhere beautiful with a lovely climate if you have no one to share it with. This is one of the reasons why a trial period (see below) is such a good idea.

Looking Ahead

It is also vital to consider whether you will be able to cope with your new life in New Zealand if in the future you become seriously ill or are no longer able to care for yourself. New Zealand is a very family focused society and although there are nursing homes and personal home care services these are generally supplemented by support from the extended family.

If you are a couple, you must also consider what will happen if one of you dies or becomes seriously ill. In the case of bereavement it is vital to consider whether the other one will want to stay on or return to the UK. This ties in with whether or not you sever all links with the UK tax and national insurance system. If you have wholly left the British system and then want to return to it, you may find it financially punitive to do so, unless you have made plans for this contingency.

ALTERNATIVES TO PERMANENT RETIREMENT IN NEW ZEALAND

Because of the distance involved and the cost of moving it may be worth considering one of the alternatives to permanently uprooting your life. Retiring to New Zealand will not be for everybody and there are a lot of advantages to keeping your UK property and simply taking extended holidays in New Zealand. Instead of shivering indoors in the bleak northern winters you could be sitting on a beach soaking up the New Zealand summer sunshine. Because there are no restrictions on non-residents owning property you could still buy a holiday home, as even a Visitor's Visa would still give you enough time to enjoy it during the best part of the year (the usual maximum stay is nine months in an eighteen month period).

For some people though, retirement is an opportunity to eliminate stress and responsibility and rather than buying a property why not rent one or take advantage of timeshare and home-exchange deals. Being a free agent will allow you to take extended holidays and explore new regions each time you visit.

Holiday Homes. Renting a holiday home allows you to get to know an area, meet the locals and make new friends and gives you a far better idea of what permanent residence might be like.

Timeshare. The average timeshare costs around $10,000 (£3,485) approx). However, the New Zealand Consumers Organisation offers some great tips on the purchase of timeshare. Buy a second-hand timeshare, they suggest, it's much better value.

Timeshares have had a very bad reputation in the past so make sure you do your research before buying, and try not to be taken in by the latest high-pressure sales tactics. Marketeers have come up with a catchy new name for timeshare – 'premiere vacation clubs'. But whatever they are called, the risks of buying into a timshare yet to be built are enormous. Timeshare is regulated in New Zealand although only if the company is a member of the New Zealand Holiday Ownership Council. The 'cooling off' period is only five days but this should still give you sufficient time to pull out of the contract should you change your mind. Contracts should give the identity and address of the sellers, all the costs involved, the location and description of the property, and the number of weeks a year you can use it. It is important to be fully informed of management fees payable on a property as these can add considerably to the initial outlay. For further advice contact the Timeshare Consumers Association (☎01909-591100; 24hr advice line: ☎0901-607 0077; www.timeshare.org.uk) or in New Zealand: Commerce Commission (☎04 924-3600; www.comcom.govt.nz).

Home Exchanges. Even though your small flat in Edinburgh might not seem like fair exchange for a three bedroom beachside house in Auckland's sought-after eastern suburbs, the UK is a popular destination for New Zealanders wanting to visit family and friends. The New Zealand dollar doesn't go all that far in Britain and the price of hotel accommodation in tourist areas is prohibitive. Many Kiwis would probably love to stay in a home rather than a cramped hotel.

Exchange websites now offer instant communication, virtual tours and thousands of homes worldwide.

O Most agencies charge an annual fee of around £50-£120 which covers the cost of promoting your home.

O Check with your insurer that your policy covers home exchanges.

O Usually both parties continue to pay their own rates and utility bills.

O House swapping gives you the chance to get to know the area and help you decide if you would like to buy your own property there.

Exchange Agencies

Home Exchange:	www.homeexchange.com
HomeLink International (UK):	☎01962-886882; www.homelink.org.uk.
Exchanges Worldwide:	www.exchangesworldwide.com.

A TRIAL PERIOD

Given the stringent immigration conditions involved in being accepted as a permanent resident in New Zealand, as well as the distance and the expense in getting there, such a life-changing decision should never be rushed into. Moving to New Zealand is not a panacea to all of life's problems – even if the weather is a lot better than in the UK. People who fail to settle are usually those that have never experienced living away from friends and family for long periods at a time, have unrealistic expectations of their new destination and are unable to make new friends in their new home. The simple way to avoid an abortive move to New Zealand, which could end up costing you a great deal of money, is to have a trial period. This can take the form of several 'look-see visits' staying in different regions.

Because New Zealand is a long-haul destination across many time zones, the minimum amount of time you should allow for the trip is three weeks. Ideally, you should plan to stay for several months at a time, (as your visa conditions allow), by renting either in one location or several different ones. It is essential to spend a winter in the place where you intend retiring to as many areas undergo a complete change of character in the 'off-season' months. Winter north of Auckland might not be cold but it can still be wet and miserable as that sub-tropical climate causes frequent rain between June and September. A trial period will give you the time to get to know the facilities and attractions of the region where you intend living. And most of all, it allows you to make social contacts so that you have a network of people in place before you take the final plunge.

RESIDENCE REGULATIONS

New Zealand's current immigration policy, which is unlikely to change much in the foreseeable future, is weighted towards young professionals with job offers, preferably highly educated, who can come in under the Skilled Migrant category. There is no specific immigration or visa category for retirees, like the 4 year retiree visa in Australia, nor are there are reciprocal rights to retirement between New Zealand and the UK, the way there are within EU countries. In fact there are only three ways where applicants over the age of 55 can apply to become a New Zealand resident. One of these, the Family Category is open to those with immediate family who are either New Zealand residents or citizens. Generally only a spouse/partner, child, sibling or parent is eligible for sponsorship. Entry is not guaranteed as applications may be subject to a quota or a lottery.

If you have no immediate family in New Zealand and are over the age of 55 you may be eligible to apply for New Zealand residence as an Entrepreneur. You must invest in a business, either an existing one or be prepared to set up your own and the application must include a business plan. The business must be one that will benefit New Zealand and must be run and operated successfully for a minimum of two years. However, this does mean that your retirement plans will have to be delayed while you set up the new business.

For the semi-retired who have considerable capital to invest, one other way of gaining residency is to come into New Zealand under the New Investor category. However, this category is restricted to those under 54 who must invest NZ$2 million in an eligible investment for five years. The return of the invested funds is based on the rate of inflation as determined by the New Zealand Consumer Price Index. The return of the principal sum is guaranteed.

According to the April 2006 edition of *New Zealand Insider*, for the really determined over 55s, who want to get round the age bias and who do not have formal business experience, one option is to purchase and run a successful franchise in the home country for a minimum of two years. That way you could use this success to establish a similar business in New Zealand and thus make an application for a Long Term Business Visa or apply under the Entrepreneur category.

One final category that those over the age of 55 can apply for residence is that of Employee of a Business Relocating to New Zealand. If you are coming to New Zealand as a couple and one half of the partnership is under 55 then they can become the principal applicant where more immigration options are available. All migrants, no matter what their age have to pass a medical and undergo police checks.

Emigration Consultants

Professional assistance can ease the process of settling in New Zealand. The Migration Bureau (Argyll House, All Saints Passage, London SW18 1EP; ☎020-8875 5442; fax 020-8875 5443; e-mail london@migrationbureau. com; www.migrationbureau.com) is one of the largest and longest-established, private immigration consulting groups. They are officially recognised specialists in obtaining permanent residence visas for New Zealand and offer a complete personalised service including professional assistance with residence visa processing and re-settlement services.

> **Immigration New Zealand:**
> **New Zealand Immigration Service:** PO Box 3705 Wellington (for all paper correspondence including the sending of original documentation); ☎0508-558 855; www.immigration.govt.nz.
> **Immigration New Zealand (UK):**
> **Immigration NZ London:** Mezzanine Floor, NZ House, 80 Haymarket, London SW1Y 4TE; ☎09069-100100.

Embassies And Consulates

Once resident in New Zealand, as anywhere in the world, it is advisable to register with your embassy or consulate.

> **British High Commission and Consulates in New Zealand**
> **Honorary Consul – Christchurch:** 1st Floor, Harley Chambers, 137 Cambridge Terrace, Christchurch; ☎03 374 3362.
> **British High Commission:** 44 Hill Street, Thorndon, Wellington; ☎04 924 2888; www.britain.org.nz.
> **New Zealand High Commissions and Consulates in the UK and Ireland**
> **New Zealand High Commission:** 80 Haymarket, London SW1Y 4TQ; ☎020-7930 8422.
> **Consulates:** 37 Leeson Park, Dublin 6; ☎01-660 4233; nzconsul@indigo.ie.
> **Balance House:**118a Lisburn Road, Glenavy, Co. Antrim BT29 4NY; ☎0289 264 8098.
> **Rutland Square:** Edinburgh EH1 2AS; ☎0131-222 8109.

GETTING THERE AND AWAY

Even though there is a proliferation of airlines clamouring for your business, the fastest way to New Zealand is still either via a South East Asian hub like Singapore or through Los Angeles in North America. When searching for air-fares, the cheapest fare may involve much longer routings. If you have never flown as far as New Zealand before and you are flying economy, it is worth paying extra for the fastest route possible.

The Airlines

Please note that airline services can and do change frequently so it is best to check current routes on the internet and to keep an eye on the travel press.

Air New Zealand: ☎0800-737 000; www.airnz.co.nz. Destination: Auckland from London Heathrow via LA or San Francisco or various Pacific Island destinations.

Emirates: ☎0870 -243 2222; www.emirates.com. Destinations: Auckland, via Dubai/ Singapore. Christchurch via Dubai and Melbourne.

Qantas: ☎020-8846 0466; www.qantas.com.au. Destinations: Auckland, Christchurch, via Bangkok or Singapore.

Singapore Airlines: ☎01784-266122; www.singaporeair.com. Destinations: Auckland or Christchurch, from Manchester or London Heathrow.

Other carriers include British Airways, Cathay Pacific, Jal, Malaysia and Thai Air.

WEBSITES SELLING FLIGHTS

www.austravel.net	www.lastminute.com
www.b-t.co.uk	www.statravel.co.uk
www.ebookers.com	www.trailfinders.com
www.expedia.msn.com	www.travelbag.co.uk

PREPARATIONS FOR DEPARTURE

You should begin the essential preparations several months in advance. Some essential tasks are listed below.

Banking

Whether you intend to live in New Zealand permanently or simply spend a lot of time there, opening a New Zealand bank account will allow you convenient access to your money. For short-term visits you can withdraw money from your UK bank account from a New Zealand ATM. Opening an account before you go means that once you start looking for a property to buy, the financial part of the process can take place quickly and smoothly. One bank, the ASB, owned by the Commonwealth Bank of Australia, has a UK (London) office. They will advise you on the forms you need to complete.

New Zealand and Australian Banks in the UK

ASB London Representative Office: Commonwealth Bank of Australia, Financial and Migrant Information Service, Senator House, 85 Queen Victoria Street, London EC4V 4HA; ☎020-7710 3990; www.migrantbanking.co.uk.

For details on banking once you have arrived in New Zealand see *Personal Finance*.

Medical Matters

You have to be in good health to move to New Zealand as not only is passing a medical a minimum entry requirement, the health system is a 'user pays' system for day-to-day healthcare such as visits to the GP, prescriptions, visits to the dentist and optician. You should certainly ensure that you know what the New Zealand equivalents are of any regular prescriptions that you are taking. It will not be possible to take your medical records away with you, but once you have found a doctor in New Zealand these can easily be forwarded on. If you are visiting New Zealand be sure to take out a comprehensive travel insurance policy before you leave.

Further information on all medical matters can be found in *Healthcare*.

Mail Forwarding

Post can be re-directed through The Royal Mail at any post office or apply by post to Royal Mail Redirection Centre, P.O. Box 944, Stoke on Trent, ST1 5DB. From abroad: ☎+44 1752 387 116. The time limit for redirecting post is two years and it costs £67.20 per surname, per year. Special Delivery and signature required mail cannot be forwarded.

Pensions

You should arrange for your state pension payments to be paid into your bank account in New Zealand. To do this you need to contact the pensions service in the UK (www.thepensionservice.gov.uk; ☎0845 60 60 60) and search/ask for details of Overseas Direct Payment in local currency. For occupational and private pensions contact your provider.

Those who move to New Zealand before reaching retirement age, but do not intend to work, should seek advice on whether to continue paying national insurance contributions in the UK. Contact the Inland Revenue National Insurance Contributions Office (☎0845 302 1479; www.hmrc.gov. uk/nic/).

Sheila Gavin from Arrowtown reports that so far her two letters to the UK have gone unanswered and she has had to get in touch with the Department of Work and Income in New Zealand to sort out the teething problems she has experienced in getting the correct amount of pension paid from the UK. For more details see Pensions and Exportable UK Benefits in the *Personal Finance* chapter.

Pets

With very few exceptions, only cats and dogs are allowed to be imported into New Zealand and there are restrictions on certain breeds of dog deemed dangerous – banned not only by the New Zealand government but by the airlines. Some airlines place restrictions on certain breeds of snub-nosed dog because of animal welfare concerns as these dogs are prone to increased respiratory problems when stressed. Dogs coming into New Zealand must be nine months or older to travel and no more than 42 days pregnant.

While there is no official upper age limit for pets to travel, they do have to be given a clean bill of health from the vet first. The journey is a long one and may entail your pet being in his travelling cage for at least 25 hours. You might want to consider carefully whether or not it might be kinder to leave an elderly or nervous dog behind with friends or relatives.

The airlines do say that flying is a safe way for pets to travel. According to estimates, out of a million pets a year transported by air only 30 deaths or injuries occur. Most of these fatalities are preventable as they are mainly due to over sedation. Vets do not recommend sedation as there is no way to judge how your pet will respond to the potentially dangerous combination of sedatives and high altitude.

Although pets are checked and watered at the stopover en route to New Zealand, they are unsupervised during the flight. Pets should only be given a light meal before they fly and not fed again until they reach their destination.

No quarantine is necessary, but a series of tests, injections and procedures, including microchipping are required for dogs, before the animal is allowed to be imported. You should check with your vet before the microchip is implanted that it can in fact be read by New Zealand scanners which have a standard of 134.2kHz.

Airlines flying to New Zealand will only take pets as unaccompanied cargo through a specialist shipper as they claim that too many amateur shippers fail to fill out the accompanying paperwork correctly. Long haul pet transport is not cheap. Large dogs cost much more than their human owners to fly. In New Zealand dogs have to be registered and must wear an identification tag on their collar. Information on dog registration once in New Zealand will be found at the local council offices.

Useful Contacts	
Pet Travel Scheme:	Department for the Environment, Food and Rural Affairs, Area 201, 1a Page Street, London SW1P 4PQ; ☎0870-241 1710; fax 020-7904 6834; e-mail pets.helpline@defra.gov.uk; www.defra.gov.uk.
Airpets Oceanic:	☎01753-685571; www.airpets.com. Pet exports, boarding, transportation by road/air to and from all UK destinations.
Skymaster Air Cargo Ltd:	Room 15, Building 305, Cargo Centre, Manchester Airport, Lancashire, M90 5PY; ☎0161-436 2190; www.whitwam@hermanshermits.co.uk. Pet exports, boarding and delivery.

Removals

When considering what to take with you and what to leave behind or sell at a car boot sale, start with a list of essential items and then try and cut this down again. Anything one decides to take must be carefully considered to ensure that it really is practical, and necessary. For instance, only if they are antique or heirloom pieces should you bother bringing wardrobes as built-in wardrobes are standard in modern New Zealand houses. Should you want to live in an older house, there are plenty of second-hand wardrobes available for purchase. Anything else of substantial weight will be very expensive to ship abroad and it may be cheaper to replace these items in New Zealand.

1st Contact Migration offer a useful ready reckoner on the approximate charge for transporting belongings from the UK to New Zealand. (www.1stcontact. co.uk – click on 'shipping'.) Fifteen tea chests (4.5 cubic ft carton) will cost £920 and fifteen medium-sized suitcases £1430. Don't forget though that you will need to insure your goods and that marine insurance is extremely expensive and could easily double these costs.

There are a number of large companies that specialise in international removals. Look for those who are members of the British Association of Removers (www.removers. org.uk; ☎01923-699480) as these are likely to be more reputable companies. BAR has set up International Movers Mutual Insurance so that clients of any of its member companies will be compensated for loss or damage, or in the case of bankruptcy, the removal will be completed by another BAR member.

Before you start phoning around for quotes, there is a useful website which does the bulk of the work for you: www.reallymoving.com. Simply type in the pick-up and drop-off points and a rough estimate of how many cubic feet you'll be moving (their estimator will work this out for you) and the site will email your request to several shipping companies. Over the following few days personalised quotes will trickle into your inbox.

Removals Checklist

○ Before moving you should compile an inventory of all the goods to be transported to New Zealand as well as photographing them. This will assist the removals company with estimating the insurance on your goods. The removals company will handle most of the paperwork for you.

○ Scrub garden tools and garden furniture, shoes and boots as these items may be inspected the other end. Check cane furniture and antique wooden items for any sign of live insects as otherwise they may be fumigated on arrival in New Zealand.

○ Check with your removal company on which electrical items to take with you. All the plugs will need to be changed and it may be worth paying for someone to do this for you.

Part two

A
New Home
in New Zealand

Where to Retire
Your New Home in New Zealand
Housing Finance

Where to Retire

CHAPTER SUMMARY

- The North Island provides the greatest number of warm-weather retirement options.
- Coastal property particularly waterfront is now some of the most expensive to buy in New Zealand.
- Queenstown and the Southern Lakes area are a great alternative for skiers and walkers although it's one of New Zealand's most expensive areas.
- New Zealand is developing and changing so quickly that wherever you buy, you should consider how the area might change in the coming years.
- A beautiful remote spot might be ideal in your fifties, but as you get older the long trek to the nearest amenities and medical facilities may become a real burden.
- Auckland has an outdoor lifestyle as well as cultural activities and in 2006 was voted by Mercer as the fifth best city in the world for quality of life.
- Napier, Tauranga or Nelson are go-ahead provincial cities that have a great lifestyle but without the downsides of big city living.

CHOOSING THE RIGHT LOCATION FOR RETIREMENT

New Zealand is a diverse country and each area has its own attractions, so where might you find the right place to spend your retirement? Because property prices look set to stabilise you can take your time finding the perfect location by renting in different areas before you buy.

Below are some of the factors that you might want to consider:

Small Beach Resort Vs. Larger Centre

The dilemma about where to live in New Zealand is not so much coast versus interior as nowhere is more than a hour and a half's drive from a beach.

Rather, it is whether you choose a small beach resort over a larger centre that has other facilities as well as an accessible beach. If you make New Zealand your permanent home you have to consider what you will be doing on winter evenings when it gets dark just after 5.00pm and you have a long night ahead of you.

The largest city, Auckland, is a mecca for water sports enthusiasts. Known as the 'City of Sails', Auckland offers some of the country's best opportunities for sailing, kayaking, windsurfing or swimming off one of its superb city beaches. If you prefer the arts to sports, Auckland has art galleries, a fine museum and a great many interesting multi-cultural events.

Christchurch, the South Island's largest city, has a reputation for being rather conservative but it still has a good climate and skiers are barely more than an hour's drive from Mount Hutt, which has the longest ski season in the Southern Hemisphere. Even Wellington, the nation's capital, which is sunny but windier and cooler than Auckland, has the Kapiti coast, which has great beaches and a more benign climate, within a forty five minute drive.

If you have come to New Zealand to escape big city living then a good compromise might be a lively provincial city in the sunshine belt such as Tauranga in the Bay of Plenty, Nelson at the top of the South Island, Whangarei in Northland or Napier in the Hawke's Bay. But there are not just beaches on offer. Some people prefer to make their home surrounded by the stunning lakes and mountain scenery in the Central Otago's Lakes area. But it's already expensive and the resort town of Queenstown now has the highest median house prices in the country.

Summers are extremely pleasant as it only rarely gets too hot and humid for comfort. While it does get busy during the peak holiday time of December and January, only over Christmas and New Year does Whangamata on the Coromandel Peninsula, Mount Maunganui in the Bay of Plenty and Tahuna near Nelson become invaded with partying holiday makers. In the off-season you might have the opposite problem of too much peace and quiet, particularly if you choose an isolated area like Gisborne.

How Might the Area Change in the Future?

New Zealand is going through a period of development and modernisation and wherever you buy, the area will certainly not remain as you found it. Estate agents are constantly looking for the next 'unspoilt beach paradise'

– coastal areas that are less than a two hour drive from a main centre, that have not been over-developed and where prices are still attractive.

Other Considerations

The Climate. Even in the northernmost areas of New Zealand the sea is not warm enough to swim in out of season and in Wellington and the South Island winter temperatures can get distinctly chilly. You will need to pack warm clothes and make sure that the property has adequate insulation and heating. The top areas for climate (sunshine and temperature figures) are the Bay of Islands, Marlborough, Nelson, the Bay of Plenty, Hawke's Bay, Taranaki, Christchurch and Auckland.

Transport and Access. Proximity to an airport is a significant consideration as is the necessity of owning and running a car. Public transport in the regions is almost non-existent as no inter-city train service exists. How easy will it be for you to get to areas of interest, the beaches and the commercial centres bearing in mind that you will have to drive to get there?

Medical Facilities. Isolated rural areas of New Zealand are finding it increasingly difficult to attract young newly qualified medical staff. Rural bliss can soon turn sour if circumstances change and a member of the family requires regular specialist medical treatment which could involve driving long distances.

Planning for the Future. Whilst it may be ideal to live in a beautiful but remote spot in your fifties and early sixties, as you get older the long trek to the nearest shops and amenities may become a real burden.

Leisure Facilities. Depending on what your leisure interests are – golf, sailing, skiing, shopping, water sports, theatres and cinemas, dining out – how close to the property are the nearest facilities?

Communications. Although all major towns and cities now have access to broadband, mobile phone coverage and good television reception, some of the remoter regions may not.

Seasonal Population Fluctuations. Does the area turn into a ghost town during the winter? Try to visit the area in both high and low season.

REGIONAL GUIDE

Although New Zealand might be geographically diverse, the further south you travel the less diverse are its people. New Zealand is officially a bi-cultural society, but only in the North Island is there evidence of bi-culturalism on a day-to-day basis. And even then it is in small parts of Northland, Gisborne,

Waikato and around Rotorua. The majority of the people who live in the South Island are New Zealanders of British descent. Auckland is the only place where there is a real melting pot of cultures.

Listed below in geographical order from north to south are areas that are popular with retirees. Many of these, particularly areas such as the Bay of Plenty and Nelson where schools are good, are just as popular with families so there is no need to worry that you will only have the company of other retirees.

NORTH ISLAND

NORTHLAND

Areas: Bay of Islands, Kerikeri, Whangarei
Main City: Whangarei
Airports: Kaitaia, Kerikeri, Whangarei
Regional tourist office website: www.northlandnz.com
Median House Price: $253,000

Northland runs from Cape Reinga at the very northernmost tip of the North Island in a long thin curve all the way down to the border of Greater Auckland covering an area of 12,600 square kilometres. It has a population of 150,000 and enjoys over 2000 sunshine hours a year.

Tai Tokerau in Maori and known as the 'birthplace of a nation', Northland was the site of the earliest Maori and Pakeha settlement.

In Kerikeri the median house price is higher than the regional median, at $394,000 and in other areas of Northland that will be of most interest to retirees, including the Bay of Islands, Whangarei and Warkworth, house prices tend to be higher.

Russell's pretty setting, nestled beside a tranquil bay and limited availability of property keep prices high. Absolute waterfront property has seen spectacular price rises over the past few years with investors trebling their money in some instances.

However, in 2006 prices began to stabilise and level off. The underlying economic indicators would seem to suggest that prices may soften rather than fall dramatically.

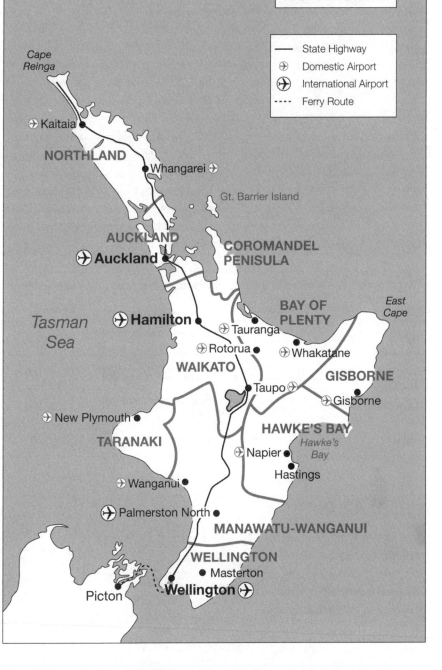

North Island

Legend:
— State Highway
⊕ Domestic Airport
✈ International Airport
---- Ferry Route

Cape Reinga

⊕ Kaitaia

NORTHLAND

Whangarei ⊕

Gt. Barrier Island

AUCKLAND

✈ Auckland

COROMANDEL PENISULA

BAY OF PLENTY

East Cape

Tasman Sea

✈ Hamilton
⊕ Tauranga
⊕ Rotorua
⊕ Whakatane

WAIKATO

Taupo ⊕

GISBORNE

⊕ Gisborne

⊕ New Plymouth

HAWKE'S BAY

TARANAKI

⊕ Napier
Hawke's Bay

Hastings

⊕ Wanganui

✈ Palmerston North

MANAWATU-WANGANUI

WELLINGTON

Masterton

Picton

✈ Wellington ⊕

RETIREMENT HOTSPOT

Kerikeri. With its sub-tropical climate and a median house price of $394,000 Kerikeri was recently voted one of New Zealand's top small towns. Close to the waterfront paradise, the Bay of Islands, which offers all manner of water sports including sailing, fishing and diving, Kerikeri is popular with international buyers as well as former city dwelling New Zealanders. If golf is your passion then the internationally renowned Kauri Cliffs course, voted one of the world's top 100 golf courses by *Golf* magazine in 2005, is close by. The Bay of Islands annual Arts Festival is held in March in Kerikeri's new purpose-built arts and conference centre. Kerikeri has a cinema, cafes and restaurants, vineyards, arts and crafts, farmers markets and sports facilities including a swimming pool. Apartments and a new retirement complex due for completion over the next couple of years will add to the range of properties available which currently consist of small detached houses to larger lifestyle properties and holiday homes on the coast. Keen gardeners can grow practically anything in the dark loam soil and Kerikeri is known as a horticulture area especially noted for its citrus crops.

Typical Properties for Sale in the Bay of Islands, Whangarei and Warkworth

Location	Type	Description	Price
Kerikeri	House	2-bedroom brick house with garden, garage, close to town centre.	$338,000
Russell	House	2-bedroom colonial wooden house with views to delightful bay, close to town centre.	$450,000
Warkworth	House	2-bedroom brick house plus sunroom with private garden and garage.	$359,000
Whangarei	House	3-bedroom renovated villa with single garage	$300,000

AUCKLAND

Areas: North Shore, Eastern Suburbs, Waiheke Island and city centre
Main City: Auckland
Airports: Auckland with both an international and domestic terminal
Regional tourist office website: www.aucklandnz.com
Median House Price: $390,000

The Auckland Region

Auckland sits on a narrow isthmus between two harbours, the Manukau to the west and the Waitemata ('sparkling water') to the east. The contrast between the two coasts is dramatic. Out to the west are the iron sand surf beaches while on the Waitemata harbour is the jewel-like Hauraki Gulf. An area of 5,600 square kilometres, Auckland is home to 1.4 million people but because it is twice the size of greater London it never feels crowded.

With 245 days of sunshine per year, Auckland combines the best of city living but with ready access to the great outdoors. Twenty conservation parks within a 45 minute drive of the city centre keeps walkers and cyclists busy, but the biggest drawcard of all is the magnificent Hauraki Gulf. You can be out on the water on your yacht and away from the city centre within 30 minutes. There are at least two yacht marinas as well as excellent golf facilities, including a course at Gulf Harbour. The Waitemata harbour has safe swimming beaches and caters for all manner of water sports including kayaking and wind surfing.

Auckland really does seem to have it all – fine dining, concerts or any one of a number of cultural events reflecting the city's diversity. Aucklanders are addicted to their cars, although attitudes to public transport are improving as is the system itself. Because the airport is south of the city centre, North Shore residents have to negotiate the Auckland Harbour Bridge. At peak times the bridge can be very congested.

RETIREMENT HOTSPOT

Hibiscus Coast. On the North Shore, a 30 to 40 minute drive north from the Auckland Harbour Bridge, the Hibiscus Coast includes Waiwera, with its hot pools, the beaches at Orewa and the Whangaparoa Peninsula. Housing is a mixture of weatherboard bungalows dating from the 1960s and newer townhouses. Orewa beach has a couple of high rise apartment blocks but the coast is a long way yet from being paved over in concrete. Beach houses on cliff tops cost at least $2 million. The Hibiscus Coast has a bus service into Auckland although the Whangaparaoa Peninsula is a little more cut off by road. There is a ferry service between Auckland and Gulf Harbour. There are plenty of clubs, societies and sports facilities on offer.

Auckland was the first place to experience the boom in prices over the past few years but as the property market begins to cool, it is unlikely that prices will drop significantly for premium property in good areas. Be wary of buying a cheap apartment in the city centre as these will be the first to lose their value if there is a downturn. In the Eastern Suburbs the median house price is around $589,000. House prices overall in Auckland have risen around 5-8% in the past year but properties are taking longer to sell.

Typical Properties for Sale in the Auckland area			
Location	Type	Description	Price
Orewa	Apartment	2 bedrooms, views of the Hauraki Gulf, communal pool, sauna and spa.	$439,000
Eastern Suburbs	House	2-bedroom with sunroom, walking distance to beach and cafes.	$500,000
Waiheke Island	Cottage	2-bedroom house close to beach and shops. 30 minutes by ferry into Auckland.	$290,000
City Centre	Apartment	2-bedroom 2-bathroom apartment with garage.	$650,000

COROMANDEL PENINSULA

Areas: Whitianga, Pauanui

Main Town: Thames

Airports: Whitianga – limited service flying scheduled scenic flights between Auckland and Great Barrier Island.

Regional website: www.newzealandnz.co.nz/coromandel

Median House Price: $329,000

The Coromandel Peninsula is the finger of land that juts out into the Hauraki Gulf, east of Waiheke Island. On the western side is the Firth of Thames and on the east coast the Pacific Ocean. With an area of 23,530 square kilometres the Coromandel is a rugged, mystical place with green wooded hillsides and some of New Zealand's best beaches including Hot Water Beach. Thames is the largest town with a population of 10,000 people and the entire region has just 39,000 people. The area will suit younger active retirees who are keen on the great outdoors or artists and writers. The downsides to living in the Coromandel is that it is relatively isolated (it is a two to three hour drive to either Auckland or Hamilton) and there are limited opportunities for those interested in the arts.

The available property on offer ranges from building plots (known as sections) to beach houses and bungalows. The apartment market is starting to open up in the area.

RETIREMENT HOTSPOT

Whitianga. With a permanent population of 4,000, the attractive little town of Whitianga attracts holidaymakers in the summer, keen to make the most of the surf and white sands of Buffalo Beach. Cathedral Cove Marine Reserve's clear blue waters offer superb diving and snorkelling. Dolphins are frequent visitors to the area around Mercury Bay. Golfers have three courses to choose from including one designed by New Zealand golfer Bob Charles, thirty kilometres north at Matarangi. There are great walks as well as horse riding in the area. At the luxury end of the market a complex is currently under construction which will include a boat mooring – ideal for retirees who may no longer want to be bothered with trailers and boat ramps. There are restaurants and cafes in the area as well as a supermarket and petrol stations.

Typical Properties for Sale on the Coromandel Peninsula

Location	Type	Description	Price
Whitianga	Apartment	2-bedroom apartment on the water overlooking the marina with double garage.	$695,000
Pauanui	Beach house	3-bedroom 2-bathroom wooden bungalow. Short walk across reserve (park) to the beach.	$699,000
Waihi Beach	Beach House	Absolute beachfront 4-bedroom, 2 -bathroom un-renovated house with sea views.	$1,500,000
Papa Aroha	Section (building plot)	4000 sq.m. site with spectacular views of the Gulf Islands for you to build your dream home.	$500,000

BAY OF PLENTY

Areas: Tauranga & Mount Maunganui, Katikati, Papamoa
Main City: Tauranga
Airports: Tauranga, Whakatane and Rotorua. Transtasman charter flights are due to start from Rotorua by Christmas 2006.
Regional tourist office website: www.bayofplentynz.com
Median House Price: $275,000

Situated mid-way down the North Island on the east coast, the Bay of Plenty reaches as far south as the fascinating geothermal region of Rotorua. Joining the Coromandel at Athentree at the western end, the Bay of Plenty hugs the ocean past Whakatane and Opotiki towards the east. With a land area of 12,247 square kilometres, the Bay of Plenty is booming. The coastal area of the Bay of Plenty has a warm and sunny microclimate, which makes it a particularly pleasant place to live.

The Bay of Plenty is the fastest growing region in the country, with a population of 257,600. Tauranga now has 100,000 residents. With over 100 kilometres of sandy ocean beach and more sunshine hours than Biarritz, the area is a mecca for sun worshippers and lotus-eaters. It's no wonder then that the Bay of Plenty is the sun and surf capital of the country. But for those who prefer a menu board to a surf board, the great outdoors can still be enjoyed from the comfort of a pavement cafe or restaurant. Mills Reef in Tauranga and Morton Estate in Katikati combine dining with wine tasting. Music fans will enjoy Tauranga's annual Easter jazz festival.

Tauranga attracts a mixture of retirees and a younger crowd who are attracted to the lifestyle, climate and the work opportunities. The average age is 38 and the area is equally popular with incomers from other regions who have ditched urban living in favour of a better work-life balance, as well as those who have moved from other parts of the globe. Golfers are well catered for with 18-hole courses in both Tauranga and Mount Maunganui. As you would expect in a coastal playground, watersports are the main attraction. If riding is your passion there are horse trekking centres as well as excellent opportunities for walking or hiking.

The housing stock in Tauranga and Mount Maunganui is relatively recent. Anything remotely ramshackle is pulled down and replaced with something newer and glitzier. Under current legislation private developers are unable to build on the beaches as the foreshore area is in the public domain.

In Mount Maunganui-Papamoa the median house price is $391,000. Mount Maunganui (the beach) and Tauranga (the harbour) are where you will find the greatest concentration of apartments which in some cases are in managed complexes. When the owners are away they can put their apartment into a rental pool, safe in the knowledge that the property is being looked after. It's the perfect lock-up and leave lifestyle for those on the move.

RETIREMENT HOTSPOT

Mount Maunganui. Mount Maunganui is Tauranga's ocean beach resort. Mount Maunganui along with Queenstown is the closest New Zealand has to resort-style living but 'the Mount' still (thankfully) has a long way to go before it becomes over developed. At the western end is the magnificent volcano, Mount Maunganui (*Mauao*) which walkers and joggers will enjoy. The beach is wide and sandy and the cafes serve great cappuccino. The only downside to buying in Mount Maunganui is the access as it is cut off from Tauranga by a bridge, which at peak times becomes congested. Although there is a supermarket and restaurants in Mount Maunganui, cinemas and other cultural pursuits are across the bridge in Tauranga. Housing on offer is a mixture of apartments and beach houses.

Typical Properties for Sale in the Bay of Plenty

Location	Type	Description	Price
Mount Maunganui	Apartment	2-bedroom 1-bathroom and 1 carpark with views to the harbour.	$650,000
Katikati	Cottage	3-bedroom 1-bathroom cottage on 6,432 sq.m. Fruit trees and kitchen garden. 30 minutes drive from Tauranga.	$450,000
Te Puna	House	4 bedroom family home on 2000 sq.m. with swimming pool.	$695,000
Lake Rotoiti (near Rotorua)	*Bach* (humble Holiday house)	1019 sq.m with stunning lake views. Use as a basic fishing retreat or pull down and build your dream home.	$600,000

HAWKE'S BAY

Areas: Napier, Hastings.
Main City: Hastings
Airports: Hawke's Bay – Napier-Hastings
Regional tourist office website: www.bayofplentynz.com
Median House Price: $265,000

South of the Bay of Plenty is Hawke's Bay. The Mediterranean style climate makes it one of New Zealand's warmest and driest places. The area contains the Ruahine and Kaweka Ranges – high forested mountains that flatten out to the Heretaunga Plains where the cities of Napier (population 55,000) and

Hastings (59,000) are located. With 14,164 square miles to explore and a total population of only 149,000, Hawke's Bay provides an ideal lifestyle with two small, easily negotiated cities, both with easy access to the great outdoors.

Te Urewera National Park, the largest forested wilderness left in the North Island, borders northern Hawke's Bay and has a variety of long distance walking tracks as does Lake Waikaremoana. The region's many rivers are a great place to fish for trout. The climate combined with the unique soil has made the Hawke's Bay area one of the most productive agricultural regions in the country.

This was the first area in the country to establish a high quality Farmers Market. Orchards, vineyards, olive groves and lavender gardens enhance Hawke's Bay's reputation as New Zealand's premier region for wine and food tourism. With over 40 wineries to visit, as well as events such as the Art Deco Weekend in Napier, the Horse of the Year, The Hawke's Bay Festival including international jazz and opera performers, there is plenty to do in the region.

RETIREMENT HOTSPOT

Napier. Since Napier was rebuilt in the Art Deco style in the 1930s after a devastating earthquake this plucky little city has never looked back. Napier's most recent 'Win a Life' promotion attracted 2700 entries from around the world. The winning family from Britain started a trend with another 50 families emigrating as a result of the campaign. Hawke's Bay wine country is a short drive away where diners can enjoy meals amongst the vines. Napier has a lively café culture with over 30 cafés, a theatre and cinemas. Local parks offer a fitness trail, tennis and petanque. Napier is a walking city and will suit those retirees who do not necessarily want to take the car just to pop downtown.

The beach at Napier is pebbly and is only suitable for good swimmers. Surfers head out to the sandy beaches within thirty minutes drive along the coast at Ocean Beach and Waimarama Beach. Napier and Havelock North attract city dwellers looking to move somewhere smaller, where there is a real sense of community and the pace of life is not so frenetic.

Housing in the region dates from the early 1930s as a massive earthquake flattened all but a few older buildings. Local officials were determined to rebuild their city and chose the Art Deco style. There are streets of Art Deco houses as well as the antique and curio shops in Napier selling the accessories needed to complete the look. Houses are mainly detached, many of which are bungalows although modern architecturally designed houses are beginning to replace them. Apartment living is not as developed as it is in the bigger cities. The median house price in Napier is slightly higher than the regional one, at $285,000.

Typical Properties for Sale in Hawke's Bay			
Location	Type	Description	Price
Napier	House	3-bedroom renovated Art Deco house.	$320,000
Napier Hill	House	3-bedroom 2-bathroom 1980s house with huge terrace with city and sea views.	$765,000
Waipukurau (country town)	House	4 bedroom, 2-bathroom home with in-ground pool and double garage on 800 sq.m.	$400,600
Mahia Peninsula	Bach (older beach house)	3 bedroom older style wooden house just across the road from the beach on subdividable site.	$900,000

WELLINGTON AND WAIRARAPA

Areas: Eastbourne, Kapiti Coast, Martinborough
Main City: Wellington
Airports: Wellington – International and Domestic terminals
Regional tourist office website: www.wellington.nz.com
Median House Price: $316,000

Wellington clings to the edge of a beautiful harbour, surrounded by verdant green hills at the southern tip of the North Island. With its steep streets, wooden houses and a bayside position, perched over an earthquake fault line, Wellington has much in common with San Francisco. Catch Wellington on a fine sunny day with a brilliant blue sky and blazing sunshine and there is no-where else quite like it. But watch out when it starts to blow. When the gales sweep into the harbour from Cook Strait and the southerly winds blow all the way from Antarctica, it's definitely a case of 'Windy Welly'.

Nobody moves to Wellington for the weather but for those that love the buzz of city life, this creative and compact city has a great deal to offer. Wellington, unlike Auckland, has a lively downtown area, which is centrally situated so that it is easily navigable on foot.

The city boasts the most comprehensive public transport in the country, including commuter trains. The compact size of the downtown area or CBD (Central Business District) allows for convenient shopping. Wellington has the best department store in the country (Kirkcaldies and Stains – 'Kirks' to the locals) and a gourmet food shop (Moore Wilson). As the home base of the New Zealand Symphony Orchestra, Wellingtonians can take in a concert or go to the theatre, catch a film in one of the capital's restored cinemas or visit Te Papa, the Museum of New Zealand.

Across the harbour are genteel Eastbourne and Day's Bay (the setting for Katherine Mansfield's short story, *At the Bay*). The weatherboard houses, cottage gardens and seaside location attracts retirees as well as younger families. With its pebbly beach, Eastbourne can at times resemble its English namesake, especially when it rains although the stunning walking tracks up in the tree-fern clad hills behind the village make it uniquely New Zealand.

The Wairarapa, to the north of Wellington, at the foot of the Tararua Ranges means 'Glistening Waters' in Maori. The Wairarapa is separated from Wellington by the rugged Rimutaka hills. In the past ten years the area has become popular with weekending escapees from the capital who cannot seem to get enough of the pretty little country towns like Martinborough and Greytown.

In the Wairarapa, period property is still available for renovation although many wooden *villas* (wooden houses built in the Edwardian era) have already been restored.

RETIREMENT HOTSPOTS

Martinborough. Inland Martinborough and Greytown combine picture perfect country living with city comforts like great coffee, as well as wine and food tourism. Martinborough is only an hour and half's drive away from Wellington for those that crave art galleries, shops and theatres.

Kapiti Coast. If you really cannot do without the beach then the golden sands of the Kapiti Coast, a 45 minute drive north of Wellington may suit. Wildlife watchers will enjoy visits to Kapiti Island, a bird sanctuary where many of New Zealand's most endangered ground-dwelling birds are able to roam in a predator-free environment. Properties are becoming expensive on the coast, particularly anything with a sea view as many commuters have traded in their house in Wellington for a beachside retreat.

Location	Type	Description	Price
Typical Properties for Sale in Wellington and Wairarapa			
Wellington	Villa	3 bedrooms, plus separate studio. Harbour views.	$630,000
Kapiti Coast	Villa	4 bedroom, 1-bathroom Edwardian villa, triple garage and a separate studio on 2000 sq.m.	$465,000
Carterton	Cottage	2-bedroom, 1-bathroom Victorian era country cottage on 2000 sq.m.	$210,000
Martinborough	Homestead	3 bedroom restored homestead with self-contained guest suite. Half a hectare of grounds with tennis court plus 1.6 ha of fenced fields. Mountain views.	$650,000

SOUTH ISLAND

MARLBOROUGH

Areas: Blenheim, Havelock, Picton
Main City: Blenheim
Airports/Ferries: Blenheim. Inter-islander ferry service runs between Picton and Wellington.
Regional tourist office website: www.marlborough.co.nz
Median House Price: $265,500

Marlborough and neighbouring Nelson vie with each other over which is the sunniest and driest region in the country but both have their share of attractions that make them very pleasant places to live. Marlborough's jewel is the Marlborough Sounds, forested inlets and bays that rise steeply from the green waters and in many cases are only accessible by boat. The Queen Charlotte track is an easy flat walk through native forest, a magical place where *tuis* and *bellbirds* sing and the friendly little *fantails* dart between the trees as you walk by. The Marlborough region was the first to produce top quality Sauvignon Blanc and is where *Cloudy Bay* is made.

The region attracts life-stylers, retirees as well as international migrants. Many new residents in Marlborough find that the easy-going rural lifestyle enables them to buy land and become hobby grape or olive growers or create a superb vegetable garden. After all that outdoor activity you can indulge in a vineyard lunch. Although there are no specific retirement hotspots in the region, (the population at 42,300 for the whole region is too small for that), Blenheim (population 27,900) might be worth considering. Housing stock in the region is nearly all detached houses or beach houses with very few apartments available.

Typical Properties for Sale in Marlborough

Location	Type	Description	Price
Blenheim	Historic house	4-bedroom, 2-bathroom house with garage	$500,000
Havelock	Country house	3 bedrooms, 1 bathroom on 2.6ha. with olive trees and spring-fed stream.	$699,000
Picton	House	3 bedrooms. Open-plan dining/kitchen and conservatory.	$250,000
Queen Charlotte Sound	Miner's cottage	2 bedrooms, 1 bathroom on 2.5ha. 15 mins. to Havelock, 30 mins to Picton.	$450,000

NELSON

Areas: Nelson, Golden Bay, Motueka

Main City: Nelson

Airports: Nelson

Regional tourist office website: www.nelson.co.nz.

Median House Price: $265,500

With a land area of 10,200 square kilometers and a population of just 87,000, Nelson, to the west of Marlborough has a climate similar to that of the South of France. With over 2500 sunshine hours a year, the Nelson region really does offer the best of *la dolce vita* 'Down Under'. With a Mediterranean climate (but without the water shortages that usually go with that), the Nelson region is stunningly beautiful with the broad dramatic sweep of sheltered Nelson Bay and Golden Bay set against the backdrop of the mountains known as the Nelson Ranges. The Nelson district is one of those rare places where you really could swim in the sea and climb a mountain in the same day. There are outdoor activities galore with three national parks all within a 90 minute drive of each other as well as two of New Zealand's best long distance walks – the Abel Tasman and the Heaphy tracks.

South Island

Legend
- —— State Highway
- ⊕ Domestic Airport
- ✈ International Airport
- ---- Ferry Route

Tasman Sea

NELSON
- ⊕ Nelson ●
- ⊕ Blenheim ●

Cook Strait

MARLBOROUGH

⊕ Westport ●

Greymouth ●
⊕ Hokitika ●

WEST COAST

Christchurch ✈

Banks Peninsula

CANTERBURY

● Timaru

● Wanaka ⊕
● Queenstown ✈

OTAGO

SOUTHLAND

● Dunedin ✈

Invercargill ⊕

Foveaux Strait

Stewart Island
● Oban

Pacific Ocean

Nelson is not just about the great outdoors. There are over 22 vineyards – including the award winning Siegfried estate. Freshly harvested Nelson scallops make the perfect food match. The Nelson region has long been popular with artists from Europe who have made it their home. As well as painters there are potters, ceramicists, sculptors and glass blowers. But despite the interesting mix of people the area remains primarily an agricultural, horticultural and fishing region.

RETIREMENT HOTSPOTS

Nelson. There is a variety of housing on offer from recently built apartments in the port area of the city to well-tended detached houses, cottages and historic homes. Nelson was one of the earliest cities to be settled by Europeans and Nelsonians seem to take pride in restoring their historic homes, which date back to the 1840s. The median house price in the city is $289,500. Nelson has a thriving arts scene, good restaurants, cinemas as well as the other amenities that a small city can offer, yet you can be out on the water in fifteen minutes of leaving the city centre. There is a long sandy beach at Tahuna, water sports, golf and horse riding in the area.

Typical Properties for Sale in the Nelson Region

Location	Type	Description	Price
Nelson	Cottage	2-bedroom, 1-bathroom un-renovated cottage.	$220,000
Golden Bay	Beach house	4-bedroom, 1-bathroom house 2 minutes walk from glorious beach.	$400,000
Wakefield	Country house	4-bedroom, 1-bathroom house on 3 ha. Pool and landscaped gardens. Double garage.	$585,000
Coastal Mapua	Building plot	Estuary and mountain views from this site. Utilities to the boundary.	$280,000

CANTERBURY AND CHRISTCHURCH

Areas: Christchurch, Geraldine
Main City: Christchurch
Airports: Christchurch – International and Domestic Terminal
Regional tourist office website: www.christchurch.co.nz.
Median House Price: $279,000

Canterbury at 45,346 square kilometers is the largest region in New Zealand. With a population of 520,000, the city of Christchurch accounts for 334,110. Canterbury borders Marlborough to the north, and Westland to the boundary of the Southern Alps. The Waitaki River forms the southern boundary with Otago. It is the driest region in the country but there are many micro-climates in the alpine areas with their own weather conditions.

Along the north Canterbury coast is Kaikoura – the centre for marine ecotourism. It is one of the richest marine feeding grounds in New Zealand waters and this is the place for whale-watching, as well as sighting orca and the rare Hector's Dolphin. To the west of Kaikoura is the Hurunui district in which lies the alpine and thermal village of Hanmer Springs. To the south east of Hanmer Springs is the exciting new wine region of Waipara Valley. Waimakariri, just north of Christchurch and the country towns of Rangiora and Kaiapoi are in Mid Canterbury. This area is known for fishing, beaches, scenic countryside and fine produce. Jutting out into the Pacific is Banks Peninsula, pretty but sparsely populated. Canterbury's oldest village, Akaroa was New Zealand's only French settlement.

RETIREMENT HOTSPOT

Christchurch. Perhaps the most English of New Zealand's cities there are English names on most street corners as well as the River Avon where you can go for a leisurely punt, the Anglican cathedral and public parks and gardens full of annuals and colour. Unlike parts of the sub-tropical North Island, Canterbury has distinct seasons and many deciduous trees. Christchurch's English heritage dates back to 1850 when the Church of England chose it as a place for an ordered settlement and one where the gentry were to be put in charge of running the farms. House prices in Christchurch are at least 20% cheaper than those in Auckland. The median house price in Christchurch is $280,000. Cantabrians take pride in their city and their biggest recent achievement has been the building of the Christchurch Art Gallery.

A large part of Selwyn, extending from the Christchurch border to Arthur's Pass National Park contains high country lakes and forest park. The surrounding areas are sparsely populated. Ashburton to the south is a service town for the farming community. This part of Canterbury includes the popular ski field Mt. Hutt. South Canterbury includes the town of Timaru in the Waimate district. Out west is the pretty little farming town of Geraldine which attracts landscape artists who use it as a base to paint the magnificent Mackenzie mountain scenery. Mackenzie country is home to New Zealand's tallest and most majestic mountain, Aoraki Mt. Cook (3755m), as well as the icy blue glacier fed lakes of Tekapo and Pukaki.

The choices of what kind of property you buy in Canterbury will depend on whether you opt for the city – where houses, townhouses and apartments are available or whether you choose to go rural. You could get a sea view from the Christchurch hills or Banks Peninsula.

Typical Properties for Sale in the Canterbury Region

Location	Type	Description	Price
Christchurch	Apartment	2-bedroom,1-bathroom central city furnished apartment.	$260,000
Christchurch (rural)	Cottage	3-bedroom, 1-bathroom country cottage with open fires.	$169,000
Banks Peninsula	Apartment in complex	1-bedroom, 1-bathroom apartment with spa, terrace and harbour views in managed complex.	$292,000
Geraldine	Farmhouse	4-bedroom 3-bathroom 1920s farmhouse on 3 ha. with paddocks and barn. Mountain views	$600,000

OTAGO – CENTRAL OTAGO AND QUEENSTOWN LAKES

Areas: Queenstown, Wanaka, Arrowtown
Main City: Dunedin
Airports: Dunedin and Queenstown. International flights. Wanaka Domestic only
Regional tourist office website: www.otago.co.nz
Median House Price: $215.000 (Queenstown) $624,900

Sandwiched between Canterbury and Southland, Otago stretches along the coast as far as Oamaru, then reaches inland past Wanaka to its western boundary with the West Coast. Central Otago includes the picturesque settlements of St Bathans and Alexandra. The flat golden plains of the area known as the Maniototo with its old stone buildings and old coaching inns is a reminder of the area's first Scottish settlers. Out in Central Otago you will find little settlements with Scottish names such as Sowburn and Wedderburn. And you can even find the game of curling played out here in winter, when it gets cold enough for the ponds to freeze over.

Otago's main city is Dunedin but unless you have connections with this university town, it is more likely that you will want to head out to the Queenstown Lakes area.

Prices in the region depend on what kind of view the property has and its proximity to Queenstown or Wanaka. The Queenstown Lakes area attracts wealthy second homers from Auckland as well as Australian buyers attracted by there being no stamp duty in New Zealand. Between them they have helped push up median house prices to the highest in New Zealand, pricing local people out of the market. Jobs are not as plentiful as they are in the bigger centres and are mainly at the poorly paid end of the tourism and hospitality sector.

The majestic trio of mountains known as the Remarkables continues to draw visitors to the area from all over the world, offering Australasia's best alpine, cross-country skiing and snowboarding.

RETIREMENT HOTSPOT

Queenstown. Queenstown had a developer-friendly mayor in the 1990s who aroused the ire of some high profile locals who were concerned that their paradise was being spoilt. Property on offer includes apartments and townhouses. This is the one place in New Zealand where new property should come with double glazing, which is needed to keep out the winter chill blowing off the lake. Bars, restaurants, and great local Pinot Noir are the perfect way to wind down after a day out on the ski slopes.

Typical Properties for Sale in Central Otago and Queenstown Lakes

Location	Type	Description	Price
Alexandra	Townhouse	2-bedroom,1-bathroom and cloakroom, centrally heated townhouse. Walk to shops and supermarket.	$295,000
Queenstown	Apartment	2-bedroom, 1-bathroom waterfront centrally heated apartment on the lakeshore.	$499,000
Wanaka	House	4-bedroom, 2-bathroom apartment with terrace and mountain views.	$699,000
Otago Peninsula	House	3-bedroom 1-bathroom waterfront house with conservatory.	$580,000

Your New Home in New Zealand

CHAPTER SUMMARY

o The property market is already starting to soften and beginning to favour buyers rather than sellers. The average time taken to sell a property is rising. Property prices will continue to rise in sought-after areas, but at a slower, more sustainable rate.

o **Estate Agents.** Be aware that cashed-up buyers from the UK are of great interest to New Zealand estate agents and you should be careful not to give out contact details as some agents can be very pushy.

o Luxury retirement villages with top facilities and 24-hour security are a small but growing market in New Zealand.

o There is no stamp duty in New Zealand.

o A building inspector should test a house for moisture levels if it was built between 1990 and 2002 using monolithic cladding.

o Relocating a house to the perfect empty site is a unique way to invest in a home.

o Renting gives you the freedom to try out a new lifestyle before you buy into it.

OVERVIEW OF THE NEW ZEALAND PROPERTY MARKET

Over the last seven years the average property price increase in New Zealand has been 56%, according to one report, and the biggest increases were in coastal, especially waterfront property. The Hauraki Gulf islands, for example rose by 161%, the Queenstown Lakes Region over 100% and Auckland prices by 57%. These price rises though, as many forecasters have predicted are unsustainable and are causing problems of home affordability in a country where the average salary is only £13,000 pa.

As far back as 2003, the volume of house sales was at its peak and it was at that time that prices in one or two of the regions including Nelson began to drop. The key indicator for property prices is in the largest market, Auckland and the question that industry analysts were asking in early 2006 was whether Auckland property prices peaked in December 2005 or in March 2006.

Although there is no doubt that property prices have peaked, the underlying economic factors are still relatively robust (export earnings up, due to the fall in the New Zealand dollar and low unemployment).

The evidence therefore appears to point to a softening if not a downturn in the New Zealand property market, at least in the short term. Given that the underlying economic factors are sound, the indicators are that although property prices may slow right down, they will pick up again but at a more sustainable rate. Immigration has helped keep the Auckland market buoyant and although it is down slightly on previous years, New Zealand's attractiveness as a safe-haven increases whenever there is a significant act of global terrorism in other countries. According to a report in the New Zealand Herald, an emigration seminar in London recently attracted over 6000 people.

A slowdown in the local market coupled with the falling dollar is of course good news for overseas buyers. With a good supply of property and stable prices, buyers should not feel compelled to rush into the market and risk making an unsuitable purchase. While speculators and those that have too many property commitments may feel the squeeze on their profits, for retirees, who are generally buying a place to live or spend holidays, the softening in the market may be no bad thing. If you have sold a property in the UK, which has much higher property prices in comparison, the price of New Zealand property, in most regions, will seem reasonable.

As a retiree you will be more likely to live in your New Zealand home as an owner-occupier, and will be able to make use of the property whilst the market levels out over the coming years. Be aware that estate agents are going to have to work harder to make their sales targets and a foreign buyer with pounds to spend is going to be of interest to them. Keep in mind that buyers are likely to be in a stronger negotiating position than they have been since 2001, as owners, who have been unable to sell their property, may need to be more realistic about their price expectations in order to secure a sale.

FINDING A PROPERTY

Adverts

Moving 'Down Under' is big business and in property magazines and the weekend national newspapers you will find features on buying property in New Zealand as well as sample prices. At the same time you will see advertisements placed by estate agents, removals firms and immigration consultants. Try also the UK-based *Australia and New Zealand Magazine* (☎01225-786800 www.merricksmedia.co.uk).

The Internet

Savvy real estate agents know that the internet is one of their best marketing tools – particularly for 'trophy' property. Below is a list of well-regarded internet sites which display not only photographs but sometimes even on-line tours. The best of these websites will allow you to search for suitable properties by specifying search criteria such as numbers of bedrooms, size of property, as well as the desired region in New Zealand, and of course purchase price.

Internet Sites

www.allrealestate.co.nz:	An easily navigable website.
www.open2view.com:	Another easy-to-use site with photo tours.
www.propertystuff.co.nz:	Nationwide listings from the publisher Fairfax.
www.realenz.co.nz:	Extensive listings on a user-unfriendly website.
www.trademe.co.nz:	Estate agents as well as private sellers list on this site.

Property Exhibitions and Seminars

The *Opportunities New Zealand Expo* (www.smallworldmedia.co.nz), although primarily an employment event, does include presentations by real estate agents. This is your chance to have your questions about New Zealand answered in person.

Estate Agents

Estate agents are perfectly ordinary and decent people, just trying to earn a living. Because there seem to be no restrictions on how many of them are registered, the market place is crowded with far too many agents, who probably earn very little. It is not surprising then that when an agent hears an overseas accent they are keen to do business with you. Be wary about giving an agent your telephone number particularly if you have just arrived as you could be subjected to calls as well as offers to drive you round and show you the area. Agents tend to be slightly more persistent in 'hot' property areas such as Auckland, Queenstown, Tauranga and Mount Maunganui. In rural areas country agents know that if they sell an overseas buyer a house in the district they will be seeing quite a bit of each other around the place.

Real estate agents have to be registered in New Zealand and to have passed a basic qualification which consists of a training course of 40 hours. Despite the minimal training requirements, agents are permitted to not only negotiate contracts on behalf of the vendor but can agree clauses in the Sale and Purchase Agreement which would normally be negotiated by a qualified solicitor in the UK. For more details on this, see the section on *Fees, Contracts and Conveyancing*.

New Zealand agents do not provide the comprehensive flyers that are standard in the UK detailing chattels, building materials, construction and most importantly room dimensions. While you might get an overall size of the property in square metres if you want to know the size of individual rooms you will need to have these measured. More expensive properties are marketed with very flattering photographs taken from the best angles.

If there is one aspect of the house buying process that irks buyers from overseas more than anything else, it is the failure to disclose an asking price for houses that are neither going to auction nor being sold by tender. Because market conditions fluctuate agents will tell you that it is the market, not them that determines price. The cynic might believe that putting a ceiling on the price of a property in fact puts an upper limit on the agent's commission.

Buyers from overseas and sometimes even local buyers are not able to easily gauge market value. Newcomers to an area should check they can afford the median house price first before they start house hunting.

WHAT TYPE OF PROPERTY?

From rural wooden weatherboard villas to luxury new beach houses, there is plenty of comparatively affordable property in New Zealand that will appeal to the British buyer. One popular option, beyond the reach of all but the most wealthy of buyers in the UK, is to find the perfect location to build your dream home and commission an architect.

Before you buy any property it is important that you seek local independent advice on how much the upkeep will be. Then there are considerations regarding local amenities and facilities. Trying to get anywhere by public transport in rural areas is hopeless and unless you are within walking distance of shops, non-drivers may find rural life in New Zealand isolating. If you do have your own transport good road access is very important especially when you are new to the country. Just as you will want to get out and about to visit your new friends, you will want to invite people around to your home. If they have to travel a few kilometres down a dusty gravel road just to get to the house it is not very likely that people will just pop around.

Some of the main types of property for sale in New Zealand are outlined below.

Old Versus New

Any building over fifty years is considered old in New Zealand and even the oldest buildings date only from around 1840. The majority of older buildings were built in the Victorian and Edwardian era. New Zealanders seem to prefer modern houses to older properties as modern houses have a number of built-in comforts that un-renovated villas or bungalows lack. While villas that have been poorly insulated can be cold and draughty to live in, with the addition of thick insulation and heating, they can make very comfortable family homes.

Old Properties

Villas built of weatherboard (clapboard) were the first style of house to be mass-produced in New Zealand. The different style of villa includes the classic *flat-fronted* villa and the *bay villa* (with the addition of a bay window). Villas offer high ceilings, sash windows and craftsmanship. The best examples were made of native timbers especially *kauri* heart wood. The traditional roofing material is iron although when replacing a roof there is a pre-painted steel product that is an acceptable alternative.

The typical villa is single storey with a wide arching central hallway with rooms leading off. The design flaw of the villa becomes apparent in winter. Although the high ceilings look magnificent, their height makes the rest of the house very difficult to heat. Instead of having an inner door or vestibule to provide protection from the outside, the front door opens out to the elements. In the main cities it is becoming increasingly hard to find villas that have not been extensively remodeled inside and 'improved'.

Villas need regular maintenance including painting to keep them looking at their best.

Curtaining a villa can cost a small fortune as it is almost impossible to find ready-made curtains that are long enough. Good heavy duty floor length curtains in winter will help keep out the draughts.

Town Houses. The word Town House means something different in New Zealand than it does elsewhere. A town house is a suburban house, usually built within the past thirty years, on a small site, with a small courtyard garden. Overseas buyers coming to New Zealand for the wide open spaces are often dismayed to find that as many as three town houses can be built one behind the other on one original site. These houses lack privacy and can be overlooked on three sides by the neighbours. There will generally be a shared driveway and only the front town house will have a street frontage.

Town houses have 'low maintenance' gardens (no grass and just a courtyard). For people who travel frequently or who have no time or interest for gardening, they make a good alternative to apartment living.

State Houses. New Zealand pioneered a form of public housing in the 1950s where well-built houses were erected on plots of land big enough for a vegetable garden and with room left over for children to play. These wooden bungalows are now highly sought after either as starter homes or investment properties and when a house is advertised as ex-state it always attracts buyer interest. A renovated ex-state house built in the 1950s or 1960s will require less maintenance than a villa, be warmer in winter as the windows are smaller but will need painting as frequently.

Art Deco. These houses are not just popular with Art Deco fans but with buyers who want a solidly built house that requires less maintenance than a wooden villa. Dating back to the late 1920s and early 1930s there are fine examples of the Art Deco style throughout New Zealand but the best are in Napier. When the town was flattened by the 1931 earthquake, the city chose to rebuild in this style. Built of solid stucco, the only drawback is that the flat roofs can leak if the house is not well maintained.

Californian Bungalows built in the 1920s and 1930s range from grand family homes in the older established suburbs to smaller, more manageable three or four bedroom homes. For those looking for a house with character, the Californian bungalow is a better option than a villa as the ceilings are lower and it will be easier to heat. Like any house made of wood though there is regular maintenance to budget for. But if you are prepared to either put in the work yourself or pay someone to do it for you, these are very agreeable houses to live in. They contain many period features such as hardwood flooring, leadlight windows and finely crafted doors.

Apartments

Only in the past ten to twenty years have New Zealanders begun to embrace apartment living. Up until then most people aspired to their own detached house with a big garden. Some of the most spacious and well-built apartments are in blocks built pre-1990. New Zealand's capital, Wellington has had an apartment market for a number of years because of pressure on space in the central business area and the number of civil servants needing to be housed. The conversion of older buildings into apartment developments has been a feature in the main centres. These older style conversions may lack such amenities as balconies but the fact that they are made of stone or other solid construction does go some way towards alleviating sound proofing issues which are a common problem with the cheaper modern apartments.

At the top end of the apartment market are the apartments built for owner-occupiers who have downsized from the suburban family home. These apartments generally have balconies, good views and are of a reasonable size. In Auckland you could be paying over $750,000, and may not necessarily even own the freehold, for two bedrooms with a view, one to two carparks, a storage locker and if you are lucky, shared access to a gym and a pool. Luxury buildings with a doorman, a marble entrance way and lifts all have to be paid for by the apartment owners. While it is easy to be seduced by luxury living the hefty annual service and maintenance charges (called the body corporate fees) can be as much as $12,500 per annum on a property selling for $700,000. If you have a sizeable mortgage to pay off just think how much better off you would be if you opted instead for an apartment with cheaper maintenance charges and used the balance to make lump sum payments to reduce your mortgage.

In 2005 Auckland City Council was forced to stipulate minimum apartment sizes as the tiny units being built for the foreign student market were so small that many of them could barely fit a bed in. Studio units now have to be at least 35 square metres, one bedroom apartments 45 square metres, two bedrooms 70 square metres and three bedroom units 90 square metres.

Retirement Villages

There are 300 retirement villages in New Zealand, concentrated mainly in the North Island and around 25,000 people live in them. The demand for luxury retirement complexes so far is small, yet it is only a matter of time before New Zealand has more resort-style villages on a par with the sort of five star complexes currently available to retirees in Spain. At present the luxury end of the market, bar one or two exceptions is concentrated on the smarter suburbs in the cities, rather than at the beach. For the well-heeled, being in the same community, near family and friends is perhaps more important than relocating to the seaside.

But given that the first wave of baby boomers are fast approaching the time when they have to think ahead to such matters, the retirement industry is waking up to the fact that you cannot just maroon a retirement resort in a new subdivision, nowhere near anything and expect that to appeal to the generation that, according to a recent article in the *New Zealand Listener*, 'gave us jogging, MBAs, rock music, cholesterol, latte, divorce, silicon chips and counselling'. The next generation of retirement resorts are going to have to put rather more emphasis on well-being, rather than health and provide more of the activities that baby-boomers enjoy – whether that is golf courses, sea views, yoga, pilates or spa treatments.

Retirement Homes and Further Advice

Consumers Institute of New Zealand: www.consumer.org.nz. Search for 'retirement villages' and you will find a very useful checklist when looking at prospective retirement villages.

Eldernet: www.eldernet.co.nz. A useful database of retirement villages, rest homes and home services.

Metlife Care: ☎0800 801 301; www.metlifecare.co.nz. Currently the largest retirement home provider in New Zealand, the company have over 12 retirement complexes, six of which are in Auckland, two in the Bay of Plenty, one in Richmond near Nelson, one on the Kapiti Coast and two further complexes in Palmerston North and Masterton.

Ocean Shore Village: ☎07 575 7120; www.primecare.co.nz. Ocean Shore in Mount Maunganui is but one of four residential developments already open in Auckland and the Bay of Plenty.

The Cascades: ☎07-839 4001; www.thecascades.co.nz. Retirement resort beside Hamilton Lake, Hamilton, Waikato. Independent living, assisted living plus a nursing home.

The Avenues: ☎07 571 0400; e-mail theavenues@xtra.co.nz. Residential resort in Tauranga developed by the same company responsible for The Cascades.

Vision Senior Living: ☎09 9122; e-mail info@visionseniorliving.co.nz. The company has three resorts, in Auckland, Hamilton and the Bay of Plenty with one under development in the Bay of Islands.

The retirement village developments listed below offer the kind of facilities discerning retirees have come to expect such as swimming pools, restaurants, a nearby shopping centre, 24-hour security, medical care on site, a choice of serviced apartments, home cleaning services, room-service food, a restaurant and a laundry service. These facilities cost around $400 per month on top of the purchase price of the leasehold apartment. Developments also organise cultural and sporting activities for their residents.

Self-Build

Buying a plot of land in order to build your ideal home is more than just a dream in New Zealand. There are regulations and procedures that need to be followed but these should be relatively straightforward for an experienced project manager.

Steps to Take Before Buying a Plot of Land

○ The plot (or section as it is called in New Zealand) should be north facing and ideally should capture the sun for most of the day, particularly in winter. The ratio of build to plot is determined by local planning authorities and you should therefore check this with the authorities.

○ Get a lawyer, an architect and a specialist drainage engineer to check over the plot before you buy and obtain price ranges for the area in which you are interested.

○ You should also run checks on the general status of the land:

  ○ Ensure that the section is flat and has no 'fill' in it, ie. that the section is original, natural ground. If it does have fill on the section you will have to construct wooden piles, which adds to the cost.

  ○ Check that the site has good drainage and that you know where the water table is and what else is around it – houses, trees and any other developments.

  ○ How costly will it be to install services such as sewerage, a telephone, electricity, or a water supply?

  ○ Are the ground and resources suitable should you want to put in a swimming pool or tennis court?

○ Consult the district plan at the local council offices. This should tell you the areas that have already been given over to development. The district plan will also tell you at a glance whether the piece of land you are interested in developing has major restrictions imposed on the size or height of proposed building projects.

> ○ Check the details of the other sections around the one that you are interested in. Are they set for further development? Is the view of the sea from your planned home liable to be blocked in the future?
>
> ○ Ensure that you know exactly where your property ends and the neighbours' begins. Ensure the boundaries are marked up on the plans and pegged. After purchase, plan to build a fence around your land so that there is no ambiguity.

To get a plan for your house you will need to get in touch with a firm of builders or an architect. A builder will be able to provide you with details of the type of houses that can be built for you and together you can work out any variations you may want, interior designs etc.

Keep in mind that things rarely go exactly to plan, and that you might want changes made to the original designs. Add in at least 10-30% contingency on top of the original estimate.

Builders. With planning permission granted you can now look for a builder to take on the contract to build your house. Get three estimates. Having decided upon a builder get your lawyer to look over the contract and make sure that any changes and amendments that arise over the course of the building work (there may be quite a few) are added to the contract and signed by both parties. This will avoid any problems when it comes to the reappraisal of the initial estimate and the final demand for payment.

Tips for the Building Process

○ Unless you are familiar with the way houses are built in New Zealand the money spent on paying a project manager who does, may not only save you money in the long run but give you peace of mind as well.

○ When deciding on the specification for the house bear in mind the resale value and do not over capitalize for the area. Granite kitchens and tiled bathrooms are far more important than a $75,000 swimming pool which will not only need a heat pump (which costs money to run) if you are going to use it all year but regular cleaning and maintenance.

○ Your contract with your builder will stipulate what percentage of the fee you can hold back as a final payment should unforseen problems arise.

○ Once all the permissions and consents have been obtained and the drainage works completed you would be amazed how quickly houses are put up in New Zealand – three to four months is not uncommon.

House and Land Packages

Steps to Take Before Buying a House and Land Package

- Ask to see what other developments the developer has built.
- Talk to an owner of one their properties.
- Check that the building company belongs to a registered trade organisation.
- Ask if any of the developer's other properties has been subject to claims regarding weather tightness (see Leaky Building Syndrome below).
- Ask what materials the house is to be built from. Only buy from that developer if the house is to be of solid construction.
- Request a higher level of insulation than is standard for the area and be prepared to pay more if necessary. It will save you money on heating bills in the long term.
- In the top half of the North Island negotiate with the developer to see if a ventilation system can be put in to counteract high levels of humidity and to minimise damp in winter.
- Check that the house comes with a guarantee.

Buying Off-Plan

Before you buy off-plan, ask around to find out if the developer has a good reputation and go and inspect a completed development. Buying off-plan is a risk if all you have to go by are the plans of a property, a model of the development to be built and the interior of a show house.

Many investors have previously bought off-plan and then sold on for a tax-free profit before completion of the project. Nevertheless, this strategy only worked when the market was rising faster than it is at present.

It is very likely that the agent will already have a standard contract. Nevertheless buyers should always have adequate legal checks carried out before signing a contract.

Avoiding Pitfalls

Developers can sometimes cancel contracts and then renegotiate them upwards if there are unforeseen costs and delays on a project. For the purchaser who has been waiting for anything up to a year to move in, the cost increases could mean that the property is no longer within their budget.

Relocated Houses

Buying a piece of land and moving a house onto it was one way many New Zealanders were able to own a little slice of paradise which didn't cost the earth. And it isn't just the humble little bach (basic holiday cottage) that started life elsewhere. Many lovingly restored country landmarks may once have been one of the earliest houses built in Parnell or Remuera, but whose relocation has been so successful that it looks part of the landscape.

Relocated houses are cut in half, moved on to the site and then repiled. The builder will place new wooden supports at regular intervals under the floor, mounted on concrete fittings. One way to tell if a house has been relocated is to check the exterior for original brick chimneys. In the grander houses, these have been rebuilt so successfully that it would be very difficult to tell whether the house had been there for ten years or a hundred.

Houses for removal can be found by checking the Yellow Pages listings for 'house lifting'. Some companies have houses on site that have already been removed and potential buyers can view these and go through them in the same way that you would go shopping for a new sofa or a dining room table. Before you buy a house for removal ensure that you have the plumbing, wiring and general condition checked by a builder. A house which might appear to be cheap could need so much costly work doing to it that it could cost you more than building new.

Buying the right section is as important when moving a relocated house onto a site as it is when building from scratch. Due to increased regulation and compliance costs, moving a relocated house onto a site is not as cost-effective as it once was. You still need to pay to get services from the gate to the house. The moving company will generally pay the compliance cost for transporting the house on a public road but the building and resource consents will have to be paid by the homeowner.

Houses for removal can cost anything from a few thousand dollars to over a hundred thousand. Typical listings include: a 240 square metre bungalow with nine rooms, exposed beams, polished floors and french doors for $120,000 plus GST at 12.5% (Goods and Services Tax), a 130 square metre three bedroom villa for $68,000 plus GST. As well as the contacts listed below, the property section of the regional daily newspaper will list any homes for removal in their classified section.

Homes for Removal	
The House Movers:	☎ 07-357 5770; www.housemovers.co.nz.
Andrews Housemovers:	☎ 09-298 7313; www.andrewshousemovers.co.nz

LEAKY BUILDING SYNDROME

New Zealand's leaky homes crisis surfaced in 1998 when a group of residents in a trendy Auckland neighbourhood noticed that their houses, which were barely 18 month sold, were beginning to rot. When the case finally came to court the cause for the rotting was attributed to a combination of lack of ground clearance and cladding buried in concrete. More serious was the failure to ensure adequate control joints in the stucco plaster, which cracked, allowing water to seep in. Instead of a waterproof membrane behind the plaster there was unsealed and untreated fibreboard. This board acted like a sponge and soaked all the water up. Other reasons for the rotting given in the first test case for the now defunct Weathertight Homes Resolution Service were a failure of the waterproofing on the decks, flat roofing and inadequate flashings.

Monolithic cladding has been a popular product in the building trade for residential construction in recent years. For a developer with an eye on maximising profits it was seen as a cheap product and one that was quick and easy to install. A cladding of sheet material with an applied coating gives the appearance of more expensive solid stucco, concrete or masonry. Referred to colloquially as 'chilly-bin' or 'plastic' houses, these types of dwellings have been most affected by leaky building syndrome.

There is one simple test that the prospective home owner can carry out for themselves on visiting a property built between 1990 and 2002 and that is to knock on an outside wall. If the wall is made of monolithic cladding it will sound hollow. The leaky homes crisis might have become public knowledge in 2002 but New Zealand was not the first country to be affected. Canada and the USA warned of the problems of monolithic cladding and untreated timber back in the mid 1990s. A report on the Canadian crisis was in New Zealand as early as 1998 but Vancouver's leaky condos were attributed to poor construction and the recommendations in the report were virtually ignored in New Zealand.

There were 3000 claims lodged by June 2005 and at least the same number going through the court system. The true extent of the crisis may never be known as between 10,000 – 20,000 homes may be affected and the rot may be hidden. Anecdotal evidence from a study conducted from a small sample group in Auckland suggests that property values have been affected by the stigma attached to leaky building syndrome.

Even if a house has showed no signs of leaks buyers avoid houses built between 1990 and 2002 with: Mediterranean-style monolithic cladding (fibrous plaster or stucco), a flat roof with no eaves, internal balconies, untreated kiln-dried timber and a house situated in an area prone to high winds. Such properties take longer to sell and may be marked down by as much as 10%.

Although the rule *'caveat emptor'* or buyer beware applies as much in New Zealand as it does in Britain, the onus on sellers of Mediterranean -style monolithic-clad homes will be to prove to future buyers that their homes have never leaked. Or that the house has been rebuilt to a much higher standard.

Moisture Detection. Houses can be tested for leaks using a system of probes that measures the moisture content. If you are considering buying a house built between 1990 to 2002 and it fits any of the criteria mentioned previously ensure that your building inspector carries the right equipment to test for leaks.

FEES, CONTRACTS AND CONVEYANCING

Overview
Below is a simple step-by-step guide to property purchase in New Zealand.

Step 1 – Sale and Purchase Agreement. You've found your dream home and want to make an offer. If the property is being sold with a price on it or 'by negotiation', your lawyer should guide you through a standard Sale and Purchase Agreement, discussing possible clauses to put in the contract. These might include: subject to finance, subject to a builder's report, subject to satisfactory local searches – called the LIM (Land Information Memorandum) and a satisfactory Certificate of Title.

Step 2 – Negotiation. You then make a written offer via the agent to the property vendor. This written offer states the date for completion (settlement) as well as the price. Purchasers not familiar with the New Zealand system can come unstuck at this point, not realising that they are signing a legal and binding contract and that there is no 'cooling off period' in New Zealand for the purchase and sale of real estate. In other words only sign if this is really the house you want, as pulling out because you have changed your mind will incur financial penalties. The offer is only accepted when both buyer and seller have signed a contract. The buyer can add clauses to their contract which should be discussed with their lawyer and will be given a short amount of time (five to ten working days) to comply with all the clauses. The buyer then has to put down a non-refundable deposit (usually 10% of the price) for which a receipt is issued. The property is then taken off the market.

Step 3 – Auction or Tender. The main point about buying at auction is that you cannot add in clauses to the contract, so all the pre-auction checks have to be done in advance, including the valuation and the builder's report. If you are the successful bidder, once the hammer falls, you have bought the house unconditionally, and have to write out a cheque for the 10% deposit there and then. Should the house fail to reach the reserve and the sale is negotiated post-auction (even immediately after) clauses/conditions may be added to the contract. If buying through tender (a secret auction where you know neither the reserve nor the other bids) you can include conditions on the contract but be aware that the fewer the conditions the more likely you are to succeed as the successful bidder – providing the price is right.

Step 4 – Pre-Settlement Inspection. Ensure that you have arranged for a pre-settlement inspection with the real estate agent. Should there be any matters arising from the inspection (removal of any of the chattels listed on the Sale and Purchase Agreement), for example, you need to notify your lawyer so that they can take the appropriate action. Arrange with the agent for key collection on settlement day.

Step 5 – Settlement. This is the last step and will give you possession of the property. Check with the lawyer that all the funds are in place and ensure that you have signed the mortgage or transfer documents. Make sure that you are contactable on settlement day as your lawyer will want to telephone you to tell you that as the new owner it is time to collect the keys.

Costs

The good news for anyone buying into the New Zealand market is that there is no stamp duty to pay on purchase, but even without stamp duty the costs of buying can soon mount up. Example costs are given below. Remember to keep money aside for the other miscellaneous costs once you have moved in, such as putting in electrical sockets and plumbing in appliances.

EXAMPLE OF COSTS ON THE PURCHASE OF A $500,000 PROPERTY	
Legal Fees	$1000
LIM Report	$300
Builder's Report	$300
Valuation	$400
Mortgage Cost	$250
Engineer's Report	$400 (for steep sites)
	TOTAL $2160
(Plus GST @ 12.5%)	

Conveyancing

Finding a Lawyer in New Zealand. It is best to find a lawyer through a personal recommendation but failing that, you can obtain a list of lawyers who specialise in residential conveyancing from the *Law Society* (☎04-472 7837; www.nz-lawsoc.org.nz). Another site to try is www.finda.co.nz.

Contracts. Once you have found the right property, you will probably have to act swiftly to ensure that you get it, although you should remember that as the property boom slows down, New Zealand is becoming more of a buyers' market. Never sign anything without having first sought independent legal advice. If for some reason there is such a pressing time limit that you may lose a property that you are interested in unless you sign *now*, then at least try to fax over a copy of the contract to your legal representatives. Contracts are often short, containing the details of the vendor and purchaser, the purchase price, a legal description of the property, the date when the property becomes unconditional (completion and possession date) and the type of payment involved in the sale.

Clauses. Buyers need to be careful about how many clauses they add to a purchase contract, particularly if the property they want to buy is sought after. Sometimes the vendor will accept a lower offer with fewer clauses. If you want to add a number of clauses to your contract, then the best way to secure the deal is to ensure that you can complete all the checks within five working days as opposed to ten. In brief, the clauses that you might want to add include: that the offer is subject to finance if you need a mortgage, that the purchase is subject to valuation, that the purchase is subject to a builder's report, that the purchase is subject to solicitor's approval. This general wording allows the solicitor to carry out the local searches and obtain the Land Information Memorandum (LIM) from the council and ensure that there is nothing untoward with the property.

Purchase contracts for off-plan properties. The developer's agent will have drawn up standard contracts and the stage payments are likely to be designed to suit the developer rather than the purchaser. If you alter any of the specifications of the fixture and fittings this may have cost implications. Ensure that the exterior landscaping is included in the cost of the original purchase price and not added on as an afterthought. Try to withhold 5% of the purchase price for any teething problems once you move, in order that the builders come back and fix whatever needs attention.

Inspections and Surveys

When you initially view a property that you are interested in, give it the amateur eye and check for any signs of subsidence, bowing walls, damp patches or strange smells. A tell-tale sign of damp is when the agent gets the scented candles out at the Open Home. You will want to make sure that all plumbing, electrics, and water heating systems are in good working order, as well as the drainage and water provision. If there is a well on the land ask the vendor if it has been tested recently. Be on the look out for any signs of rising damp. In the top half of the North Island, because of the sub-tropical climate, there is high humidity. Condensation is a side-effect of this humidity especially in winter. Because double-glazing is still rare and not standard, moist warm air can get trapped inside a house particularly on the south eastern side of the house. There are anti-condensation devices available which can be fitted to the house or else you may prefer to use a portable de-humidifier.

While viewing a property, take your time and get the feel of the place – you will usually be able to tell if there are any *major* structural problems. It can come as a surprise to British buyers to find out there is no real equivalent to the structural survey or indeed the structural surveyor. Instead, you will have to make do with a builder's report/inspection carried out by a building inspector. If the site is on a slope, check with the building inspector whether an engineer's report is needed to check soil stability and drainage. If you are buying a property on a mortgage, the lenders may well require a valuation, even if it is only to provide an appraisal of the purchase price.

For new properties, and property that is less than five years old the structure will come with a guarantee. However, during the leaky building crisis a number of builders and developers simply dissolved their companies. You should check with your lawyer as to the status of any guarantee should one of these companies go out of business. Rather than just older properties needing a building inspection, new houses (especially those built between 1990 and 2002 out of monolithic cladding) should be inspected for structural defects and potential leaks

Because of the differences in inspection criteria between the UK and New Zealand systems you should make sure that you know what should be checked and discuss this with the building inspector. Some but not all vendors will sign a contract of sale with a 'subject to builder's report' clause. They can demand that you arrange a building inspection – at your own expense – before they sign anything. Should another interested party come along and sign a contract with the vendor before you have been able to satisfy yourself as to the soundness of the property, you will have lost out on the chance to buy.

Finding a Building Inspector

BRANZ is a building research consultancy that offers pre-purchase inspections either by going to their website (www.branz.co.nz) or calling ☎ 04 237 1170.

Checks That Should Be Made On A Property Before Completion

Resale Properties

○ Are fittings and/or furniture included in the purchase price?
○ Are there any planning restrictions pertaining to the property and/or location which will affect your plans should you wish to build on or alter the property?

- ○ Are there restrictions on the uses of the property?
- ○ Boundaries, access, and public right of way bylaws should be clearly defined and understood.
- ○ Check with the council to see whether there are going to be future developments that may affect the value/view of the property at a later date.
- ○ Check the property is free of any debts or charges; that all utility and rates bills, have been paid up to date.
- ○ Has there been a completion of a builder's report to your satisfaction?
- ○ Has there been any alteration done to the property that has not been registered with the authorities?
- ○ Is there adequate water, drainage, electricity and telecommunication provision?
- ○ Check that the vendor is the legal registered owner of the property.

Additional checks that should be made on off-plan and new build property

- ○ A full breakdown of the materials, fixtures and fittings used in the building of the property.
- ○ Be clear what you are paying for. What are the finishings? Will the surrounding land be landscaped? What will the property look like (have you seen a show home to gauge this)?
- ○ Make sure that the developers or builders are the legal owners of the land and that they have obtained the necessary planning permissions to build.
- ○ Make sure that the payment schedule and completion date are clear.
- ○ Protect yourself against the possibility of the developer going bankrupt before completing the property.

SWIMMING POOLS

As well as enhancing the look and value of your property, having a pool is a convenient way of entertaining friends and family. If you are purchasing a property with an existing pool, this should be inspected carefully by a building inspector as a pool with cracks or other signs of poor maintenance will be an expensive liability rather than an asset.

When the sun is not directly overhead, the pool temperature may be cool enough to consider installing heating and certainly if you want to swim in early summer or into the autumn. The cost of heating a pool is an additional cost over and above regular pool maintenance.

By law all domestic swimming pools and spa pools (even those with a lockable cover) must be fenced off as every year around five New Zealand children drown in domestic pools. Pool fencing has to comply with two sets of legislation - one the Fencing of Swimming Pools Act and the New Zealand Building Code. Further information can be found on the Department of Building and Housing's website at www.dbh.govt.nz.

In addition to the rules governing fencing the design and construction of any pool you install has to be approved through a Building Consent and a Resource Consent.

In the better-off suburbs, considerable thought goes into integrating the design of the outside space with the style of the house and whether you choose an 'infinity' pool over a Balinese themed one will depend not just on looks alone but on the depth of your pocket. Pools though are the one area where it is very easy to over-capitalise and you are unlikely to recover the costs of a recently-installed pool, should you need to sell up.

THE RENTAL SCENE

For those hunting around for property to buy and who intend to live in New Zealand permanently it is always a good idea to initially rent for a while just in case you find that the reality of New Zealand life doesn't quite meet up to your expectations. Renting property means a less permanent commitment and will allow you time to make up your mind about where you want to live, to see if you like the area, the climate and the amenities and decide what kind of property will suit your needs.

Finding Rented Accommodation

The best way to start looking for rental accommodation in New Zealand is by reading the classified sections of local newspapers or visiting local real estate agents. If you want to rent in Auckland, Wellington or Christchurch then you could find information online, but because rental property has a high turnover, website information might be out of date or it might be that the agent does not bother to list online. Larger agencies will fax or e-mail you a rental list but in small provincial towns the list may consist of two or three properties. National real estate agency chains like Harcourts, LJ Hooker and Ray White list rental properties on their websites. Trade Me also lists rental properties for all price brackets. Wednesdays and Sundays are the most popular days for real estate agents to advertise their rental properties in the main daily regional newspapers.

Renting short-term in selected areas around the country gives prospective buyers an opportunity to try out a lifestyle before they buy into it. Many buyers coming to New Zealand hope to live differently from the way they did back home but only by turning the dream into a reality will you ever find out if you are suited to it. And if, for any reason it does not suit you or your family's needs, you can move on at the end of the tenancy, holding your head high and ready for the next challenge, without the worry and expense of having to sell up. What's more, instead of spending the weekend on maintenance or renovation, renting someone else's house leaves you time to explore your new surroundings and community. And when the time comes to make that all-important decision to buy, you will have narrowed down your choices.

Tenancy Agreements

Periodic Tenancy. A periodic tenancy has no fixed date for the end of the tenancy and is suitable for tenants and landlords who want to rent for a short term. A tenant must give 21 days notice in writing and a landlord must give 90 days notice. This kind of tenancy would be most suitable for house hunters or anyone needing somewhere to live on a temporary basis while they wait for the completion (settlement) date on their new house.

Fixed Term Tenancy. Apart from those landlords looking to sell a property or those letting their main home while away for a few months, landlords renting out unfurnished property prefer to let for a fixed term of six months or more. The legal minimum for a fixed term is a month but landlords renting unfurnished properties argue that it's not worth letting a property for less than six months because of the wear and tear on the house caused by the frequent moving of furniture in and out of the house. A fixed-term tenancy can only be ended on the date specified in the lease, unless by mutual consent, or by a ruling from the Tenancy Tribunal.

Renting a property is a relatively easy and risk-free business in New Zealand.

Renting is regulated by a hands-on government agency that mediates between tenant and landlord in a number of ways:

If a deposit or bond against damages is requested by the landlord, any payment must be lodged with the Tenancy Services Centre within three weeks. Landlords cannot gain a financial advantage by investing and then pocketing the interest from what is the tenant's money, nor can they claim that the tenant caused damage to a property and then withhold a large chunk of the deposit for repairs.

Tenancy Services acts as a low cost mediator in case of disputes between landlord and tenant. In addition to the mediation service there is a general help-line, general tenancy information, copies of the Residential Tenancies Act and information on the Tenancy Tribunal – the final arbitrator for disputes between landlord and tenant.

Summary of a Tenancy Agreement

o The care and maintenance of a garden can sometimes cause problems as landlords (or their agents) like to make it the tenant's responsibility to ensure that the grass is cut regularly. If a garden is extensively planted then the tenant cannot reasonably be expected to take care of it.

o Tenants must allow the landlord to enter the premises and consent must not be unreasonably withheld although they do not have to allow this if less than 24 hours notice has been given.

o Tenants are required to notify the landlord when repairs are needed. They are not permitted to withhold rent if they cannot get repairs done. In that event they should seek advice from Tenancy Services on ☎0800 83 62 62.

o Tenants are not permitted to change the locks without the landlord's permission.

o In the case of a periodic tenancy a tenant must give 21 days written notice that they are to vacate the premises.

o Tenants are required to leave the property in the same condition that they found it. It should be clean and tidy and all the rubbish must be removed. If the carpets were professionally cleaned before the start of the tenancy then the same must be done before you hand back the property.

o A landlord cannot ask the tenant to pay more than two weeks rent in advance nor can they ask for more than four weeks rent as a bond against damages.

○ A landlord can only demand key money if the Tenancy Tribunal has agreed and this will only be allowed in special circumstances, for example, where the landlord supplies a lawnmower with the property and asks for a small sum of money as deposit.

○ A landlord must lodge the bond paid to them with the Tenancy Services Centre within 23 working days.

○ A landlord cannot enter the premises without either giving notice or the tenant's consent.

○ A landlord must give the tenant 24 hours notice for repairs and 48 hours notice for an inspection.

○ As soon as any problems arise with a tenancy the landlord and tenant should try to negotiate between themselves to sort out any issues. If the two parties fail to reach agreement then contact Tenancy Services.

> If you find a rental property through an estate agent it is the tenant rather than the landlord that pays the agent's letting fee which is one week's rent plus GST at 12.5%. If a property manager shows you a house or apartment no letting fee is payable. Only a registered agent with the words MREINZ after their name is entitled to charge a letting fee. It is clearly stated in the Residential Tenancies Act 1986 that only registered agents acting in an official capacity (that is, letting a client's house not their own) can charge a fee.

> **Electrical/Gas Safety Checks.** There is no legal requirement in New Zealand for either electrical or gas appliance safety checks although there is provision in the Residential Tenancies Act that landlords have a duty to comply with health and safety standards. It is the landlord's responsibility to ensure that for safety reasons a chimney is clean before the start of the tenancy.

UTILITIES

Organising service connections to properties in towns and cities is simply a matter of proving your identity and that you can pay for the services required. The utility providers ask for standard information from applicants, including personal details as well as those that relate to the house. For renters this will include the name of your landlord and letting agent. New customers needing a landline connection are required to provide a copy of photo ID such as a passport.

In rural areas it is another matter. Not only is it very expensive to get connected to mains electricity and telephone services, there are other factors you may not have considered. For instance, in an isolated rural area there may be no mains sewer or water supply. You will have to pay to maintain these services yourself – services that most city dwellers, who pay for them out of their rates, take for granted.

Electricity

Since deregulation in 1999 the private sector has generated around 40% of the country's electricity. As well as opening up electricity generation to the private sector, deregulation has allowed electricity consumers to switch supplier. There are now around ten electricity retail companies, three of which, Meridian, Genesis and Mighty River Power are state-owned.

New Zealand consumers until recently enjoyed some of the cheapest electricity prices in the world. In 2004 householders were paying 15 NZ cents per Kilowatt-hour compared with the UK equivalent of 25 cents. In 2006 electricity went up by at least 5% across the board. You can find out which electricity company offers the best deal in your area by logging on to the Powerswitch website: www.consumer.org.nz/powerswitch. Run by the Consumers Organisation it provides a good comparison of electricity prices. Where there is a monopoly supplier in a region the site offers advice on how to save money even if you cannot switch.

Meters are supposed to be read at least three times a year although consumers are obliged to pay an estimated bill if the meter has not been read. Ring in with your own meter reading if the company allows this. You can pay your bill through an automatic payment, by internet or telephone banking, with a credit card, by cheque, through pre-payment or in person at any New Zealand Post Shop. A discount incentive scheme may be available if you pay by direct debit.

The domestic electricity supply in New Zealand is 230v or 240v AC, 50Hz. Plugs on electrical appliances are three-pin (not the same as the UK one). UK appliances should perform quite adequately, if a little more slowly, using an adaptor while US appliances will need an adaptor plus a 220-110v transformer. Light bulbs are usually of the continental screw-in type in newer homes but bayonet fittings are more common in older houses.

Heating

Central heating does not really exist in New Zealand the way that it does in the UK because of the mistaken belief that it does not get cold enough in winter to warrant it. New Zealand homes are colder and damper than those in other countries. Very few houses have a system that can be pre-set and when you arrive home after a day out, the house may still be cold. The more expensive type of portable oil-filled electric radiators do operate on timer switches but these will still not give complete coverage of the whole house the way that fixed radiators do.

There are a number of steps that homeowners can take to make their homes warmer. These include putting in ceiling insulation as well as under floor insulation. Wooden houses tend to be raised off the ground and providing there is a big enough crawl space under the house to allow access it is not too difficult to put in this insulation. Alternatively buy a new house and insist on both underfloor heating and a heat pump unit which is an energy efficient way to heat a house. Why solar heating is not used more often in New Zealand is another mystery. Installing a solar hot water system will cost between $3,500 and $8,500 and will halve your energy bills, saving you money in the long term. Fortunately winter in New Zealand is relatively short and it is only cold for four months of the year unless you live in the deep south of the South Island.

A de-humidifier is essential in winter in many parts of the North Island, particularly in rooms that do not get much sun. Many homeowners have one running permanently in the coldest part of the house (usually the south east corner). Make sure the de-humidifier you buy is one with a decent sized water container as it is a chore to have to empty it more than once a day. An alternative to a de-humidifier is to install a ventilation system in the loft space which either uses a heat exchanger or a forced air system. These cost anything upwards of $2750 depending on the size of the property.

Gas

Mains gas is only available in the North Island. Anyone living in the South Island requiring a gas supply will have to use bottled liquid petroleum gas (LPG). The price of mains gas works out favourably in comparison with electricity but the price of bottled gas and delivery charges will vary according to where you live.

There is no statutory requirement for regular gas safety checks to be carried out, but all gas appliances, especially un-flued portable gas heaters should be checked for wear and tear on a regular basis. The fumes that an un-flued gas appliance gives off may affect sufferers of respiratory problems so always ensure when using any gas appliance, that the room is well ventilated.

Gas bottles sold mainly for cooking, barbecues, portable gas fires and patio heaters come in sizes of 4kg and 9kg. The 9kg bottle costs from $46.00 and bottles can be filled at service stations for around $22. Bottled gas can be used for heating, hot water and cooking but this needs to be organised with a supplier. The cost varies from region to region. The gas bottles connect to the outside of the house and a registered gas technician will need to install this.

Long been used as a way of heating a remote rural bach, portable LPG room heaters (with the gas cylinder integral to the appliance) have been banned from sale in Australia based on their previous poor safety record. New Zealand has yet to follow suit. The *Energy Safety Service*, a division of the Ministry of Consumer Affairs at *www.ess.govt.nz/safety*, has a list of safety tips for their use, which are to carry out regular leak tests and to ventilate the room. They advise that an LPG service agent should service the appliance once a year. How realistic this advice is remains to be seen especially when many baches are in isolated areas and the likelihood of finding a service agent locally could be difficult.

Water

Only those on tank supplies should spend their money buying bottled water as mains water in New Zealand is of good quality. Although there are pet theories that roof or tank water is better for you, a recent university study has proven otherwise. Thirty percent of the samples taken contained enough bacteria to make the average person ill. Unless you buy a house with a new water tank or have a new one installed (which will cost anything between $3000 to $4500) you should have the water quality tested by a Ministry of Health approved laboratory. Do not take the vendor's assurances that their roof water is safe to drink, just because no-one in that household has been taken ill. An immunity can build up to unsafe drinking water. Householders are advised to regularly inspect both the tank and gutters for holes and to regularly clean them out. The water should be tested regularly.

Housing Finance

CHAPTER SUMMARY

○ Retaining your UK property, if you can afford to, gives you a safety net should your new life in New Zealand not go as well as expected.
○ Whether or not you decide upon a UK or a New Zealand mortgage will depend on whether you are buying a second home or are emigrating.
○ Interest rates are higher in New Zealand than they are in the UK.
○ There is currently no Capital Gains Tax on New Zealand property.
○ You can save thousands of pounds by using the services of a currency dealer to pay for your property, rather than using a high street bank.

AFFORDING THE MOVE

Deciding What To Do With Your UK Property

Before departing for New Zealand, deciding what you are going to do with your UK home is a vitally important consideration. The decision will vary depending on individual financial situations. The majority of people sell their UK home which should provide them with the money to not only buy a property in New Zealand but leave enough additional funds to live on during their retirement. Those who can afford it may want to hang on to their UK property as security against things going wrong in New Zealand and as a source of income. The pros and cons of these two solutions are discussed below.

Retaining a Home in the UK. Property in the UK is generally a good investment and a second property can be rented out, thus giving you rental income as well as capital growth if property prices increase if and when you do sell the property. If you still have a home in the UK then you can spend part of your retirement back in Britain, visiting friends and family.

Renting out a UK property could help you pay the mortgage on the new house in New Zealand. Whilst rental income received may be subject to income tax, renting out a house means that the property is occupied and therefore less likely to be burgled plus your insurance premium will be lower. If you do decide to rent the property out, you will not be able to go backwards and forwards between the two countries and stay in your UK house when you want but at least you will have additional income. Try to ensure that the tenancy agreement includes a clause that that will allow you to regain possession of the property fairly quickly, should you ever decide to return to the UK.

Selling Up. Selling up completely has the enormous advantage of releasing a large amount of capital that can then be put towards finding the perfect home in New Zealand. As property tends to be cheaper in New Zealand, you should have a lump sum left over which can either be reinvested or used to supplement your retirement income once you get there. There are a number of factors to be considered with selling up. The recent slowdown in the UK property market has meant that it may take you longer to sell your UK property than you expected. If your UK property is the main source of funding, you should delay committing to buy in New Zealand until you have exchanged contracts in the UK. It will still be possible to rent out the UK property whilst you are waiting for a buyer and this will allow you to rent in New Zealand and give you time to find the right property.

Selling the UK base precludes the possibility of rushing home, should life in New Zealand not go as well as you had expected. It may also cause problems in the long term. If at any point in the future you are forced to return home (and circumstances, often beyond our control can be the reason) then it may be very difficult to get back on the property ladder. The amount that you raise from selling your New Zealand property is unlikely to fund the purchase of a similar sized property in the UK.

MORTGAGES

Buying a second home in New Zealand could see you taking out a second mortgage on your UK property as a convenient way of financing the purchase. The amount you will be able to borrow depends on your fulfilling the bank's usual lending criteria and the amount of equity you have available in your house. This would then allow you to buy with cash in New Zealand.

Using your UK property as security allows you to borrow the full amount of the cost of your New Zealand property providing you have sufficient income and equity in the UK house. A re-mortgage could allow you to pay for a more expensive new house than a New Zealand mortgage lender is willing to offer.

If you are going to take out a second mortgage with your existing mortgage lender then a second charge would be taken by the mortgage company. Note that some lending institutions charge a higher rate for a loan to cover a second property. You should ensure that if a loan is arranged in the UK then all of the details of this are included in the New Zealand property contract deeds. The typical costs of re-mortgaging a property are around £650 (solicitors fee of £250, legal disbursements of £150, and a valuation fee of around £250), but some fees may be paid by the lender.

The advantage of a UK mortgage is that the interest rate will be much lower as New Zealand currently has some of the highest bank interest rates in the OECD. However, you will be subject to exchange rate moves when you first bring your money over and when and if you ever had to sell your New Zealand property.

The alternative is to take out a mortgage in New Zealand.

Types of New Zealand Mortgages

New Zealand mortgage lenders generally offer fixed or variable interest rate mortgages, mixed interest rate mortgages and fixed repayment instalment mortgages. However, borrowing money in New Zealand is more expensive than it is in the UK. Although the signs are that interest rates have peaked and that in late 2006 they should fall slightly, it is unlikely they are going to fall to the levels currently available in the UK and Europe. To check the best interest rates on offer for borrowers and savers go to www.interest.co.nz. In January 2006 their cheapest advertised floating mortgage rate was 8.7% with the Southern Cross Building Society, closely followed by Kiwibank at 9%. Note that Kiwibank is not available through intermediaries. The Heretaunga Building Society and Wizard were offering the lowest rates on two year fixed mortgages at 7.75%.

In New Zealand the method used to assess your mortgage is also a little different from that in the UK. You will have to put all your UK and, if you have any, your New Zealand earnings and income forward, and get references from your UK bank. Any other borrowing you have will also be assessed especially credit card or store cards. Make sure you get rid of any cards that you no longer need as banks regard the credit limit as a debt (even if you pay off the balance in full every month).

Repayment mortgages are the most commonly held mortgage as endowment mortgages do not exist. However, the Home Loan, Savings and Transaction account is becoming more popular as it offers a safety net, which ensures that the loan is paid off within the time that the borrower specifies. The best way to use such an account is to have any income credited into the account. It also allows borrowers to redraw any additional amounts they have paid in over and above the repayment schedule.

Revolving credit is supposed to give the borrower greater financial freedom but is only really suitable for those who are careful not to exploit their credit facility.

Those purchasing a country property or a restoration property should be aware that the banks may not consider such a property to be suitable security for a mortgage, and even if they do, they may offer a far lower maximum amount to be borrowed.

Remember that if you take out a New Zealand mortgage you will need to have the currency available in your New Zealand bank account to meet the monthly mortgage repayments. Mortgage lenders deciding how much to advance a potential buyer, both in the UK and in New Zealand, will not take into consideration any possible income derived from renting out the property. However, in truth it may be possible to offset the cost of the mortgage against the income received from renting out a property and so reducing tax demands. And in effect the rental value on a property should repay the mortgage if problems occur.

Equity Release/Reverse Mortgages

The market for equity release schemes and reverse mortgages is small but growing. These types of equity release products are not as extensive as they are in the UK. Equity release or reverse mortgages are designed to allow homeowners that are 'asset rich and cash poor' to stay in their own home without having to worry about where they will get the money to carry out expensive repairs. At the moment there are two basic types – one where you can take a lump sum and the second that provides you with regular monthly income.

However, before you consider such a scheme, make sure that you have worked through the other options first. These include: trading down to a smaller property, sub-dividing your existing land, or moving to a cheaper area or taking in a lodger. Check with your local council to see if they offer a form of equity release scheme to defer your rates payments as some councils do. The problem with allowing a finance company to take a stake in your home, when you have probably already spent many years paying off a mortgage, is that this is a very expensive way to borrow money because of the effect of compound interest. Even if you do not have immediate family, you might prefer to leave your estate to a favourite charity, rather than see it all go to an anonymous finance company.

PROPERTY TAXES

One of the great advantages of buying residential property in New Zealand is that there are no property taxes to pay on top of the purchase price.

The only 'tax' imposed on residential property is not really a tax at all but local authority rates which pays for essential services such as rubbish collection, street cleaning, upkeep of public areas, as well as the running of municipal services such as libraries and public swimming pools. Rates are calculated on the location and local house prices as well as size of the individual property. In recent years rates have risen sharply in the more affluent parts of the country and the *Letters to the Editor* pages of the newspapers often contain complaints about rates rises particularly from those on fixed incomes. Some councils include water rates in the one rates bill but others, such as Auckland City charge for water separately. Auckland is a special case as it not only imposes local rates but a separate organisation called the Auckland Regional Council imposes a separate local authority tax for the upkeep of regional parks.

Goods and Services Tax (GST) at 12.5% is payable on the purchase of business premises and commercial property whether that is a farm, horticultural business or short-let accommodation. If you are planning to turn a business premises into a residential one seek advice from your accountant as the rules surrounding GST in this instance are quite complex.

TRANSFERRING MONEY

Once you have found the perfect New Zealand property you will need to transfer pounds and convert them to New Zealand dollars to pay for it in local currency. The New Zealand dollar is a volatile currency – so much so that five years ago some lucky migrants were getting as much as $3.30 to the pound. Those days are long gone and since then it has been high against all major currencies over the past few years although the signs are that the dollar is starting to weaken. This is good news for those with pounds to transfer.

You can also transfer money directly from your bank in the UK by SWIFT electronic bank transfer. This can take several days and you may not necessarily know what exchange rate you are getting until the money arrives in your bank in New Zealand. You can remit large sums by opening a foreign currency account with a New Zealand bank, keeping the bulk of the funds in pounds while waiting for the best rate of exchange.

There are alternatives to using your bank, in the form of specialist foreign exchange providers such as Currencies Direct (www.currenciesdirect.com; ☎0845 389 0906). They can help in a number of ways, depending on your circumstances, timing and currency requirements. As an alternative to the bank, they offer more competitive exchange rates, no commission and lower transfer fees. They also give you the possibility of 'forward buying' – agreeing on the rate that you will pay at a fixed date in the future; or buying with a limit order, which involves waiting until your specified rate is reached. For those who prefer to know exactly how much money they have available for their property purchase, forward buying is the best solution, since you no longer have to worry about the movement of the pound against the New Zealand dollar working to your detriment. Payments can be made in one lump sum or on a regular basis.

INSURANCE

When taking out a loan for a house through a bank or mortgage broker they will be keen to sell you buildings, contents as well as car insurance at the same time. This is how many brokers and bank officers earn their bonuses and while it can be convenient to take out insurance at the same time that you buy your house, take time to read the small print. Don't assume that you will get the same benefits as you would expect in the UK as many policies only provide a basic cover, excluding wear and tear and not allowing new for old replacements.

Some considerations that need to be taken into account while looking for an insurance policy on your new property include:

○ Is your property covered by insurance in the event of your letting the property to someone who accidentally causes a fire, flood or damage?
○ Is the property covered for insurance purposes even if it remains empty for part of the year?
○ Does the insurance policy allow for new-for-old replacements or are there deductions for wear-and-tear?

The Insurance Council of New Zealand (☎04-472 5230; www.icnz.org.nz) provides a list of insurance companies that are members.

Part three

A New Life
in New Zealand

Adapting to Your New Life
Quality of Life
Personal Finance
Healthcare
Crime, Security & the Police

Adapting to Your New Life

CHAPTER SUMMARY

O **Shopping.** In most areas of New Zealand the shopping mall has replaced the department store.

O With fewer fashion chain stores and more individual shops you are less likely to bump into ten other people all wearing the same outfit.

O Eating out or going out for coffee or brunch is an important aspect of social life in New Zealand.

O **Motoring.** The driving standards are generally lower than they are in the UK and using a hand held mobile phone while driving is still legal.

O You can drive on your UK licence for up to a year before taking a written test.

O The New Zealand equivalent of the MOT is the WOF. All cars over 6 years old must pass an WOF every 6 months.

SHOPPING

At the same time as cars became the favourite mode of transport, out-of-town malls sprung up in the suburbs. As shoppers deserted the city centre, the once smart department stores failed to attract enough customers and one by one they were forced to close. Wellington, which has always managed to retain a decent public transport system has been the exception. Kirkcaldies and Staines is the closest you'll get to a Selfridges or John Lewis. 'Kirks' is in the heart of the downtown area of New Zealand's best walking city. The once grand Queen Street in Auckland lost its glamour the day Milne & Choyce was forced to close. The remaining department stores in comparison seem like provincial Britain's were 30 years ago.

Markets. There is no tradition of city centre markets and although Auckland has three outstanding food markets, you'll need a car to reach them. The excellent fish market is the closest to the downtown area. The West Auckland market is the place for South East Asian vegetables including *gai lan* and *pak choy*. Otara in South Auckland has a food market specialising in Pacific Island produce as well as a general market selling bric-a-brac, *tapa* cloth, and straw baskets. In the rest of the country, the markets are smaller scale, without the variety of Pacific or Chinese vegetables on offer.

Farmers Markets. Farmers markets are the place to find organic and locally produced cheeses, bread and fruits and vegetables. Some of the specialities on offer include locally produced olive oil and avocado oil.

Handicrafts, Knitwear, Glassware and Pottery

Luxury items such as throws, bedspreads, gloves and socks made of merino wool and 'pest' (possum) fur are locally produced. Merino wool has been fashioned into high quality fashionable outdoor clothing. Icebreaker is the stylish outdoor clothing brand using finely woven Merino wool and Untouched World is a luxury brand producing super soft Merino products.

The best places to buy genuine New Zealand made products made out of high quality material such as jade are in museum shops such as the Auckland Museum at the Waitangi Treaty grounds or at Te Papa in Wellington. Good quality pottery and hand-blown glass should be bought from specialist outlets, which are often found in the smarter parts of town.

Auction Sites

New Zealanders are keen bargain hunters and where in the past people might have fossicked around in bric-a-brac markets or at car boot sales, now they do this on-line. The auction site *Trade Me* (www.trademe.co.nz) is New Zealand's most popular website and sells everything, (new and used) from cars and houses to just about anything that you can think of.

Fashion

In contrast to the bland shopping mall experience of the UK, the majority of shops are small individually owned businesses. Although there are national chains that sell reasonably priced clothes, the designer end of the local fashion industry produces many one-offs. If you shop at Zambesi and Trelise Cooper (catering to a more grown-up clientele than Karen Walker and Kate Sylvester) you are unlikely to see ten other people walking around wearing the same outfit. The Australian labels Country Road, Cue and Veronika Main are chain stores in the main centres selling smart and fashionable clothes for grown-ups.

Necessities

Consumer Durables: prices go up and down according to the strength of the New Zealand dollar. Refrigerators, washing machines, electronic and electrical equipment and cameras tend to be slightly more expensive in New Zealand than they are in the UK. Only the more expensive brands of British televisions work in New Zealand so it is probably better to buy locally.

Furniture is more expensive in New Zealand than in the UK as there is not the range available. New Zealand's population is too small for an Ikea. Freedom Furniture sells fashionable homewares and is similar to Habitat.

Home Comforts

All large towns have modern, self-service supermarkets which, as well as stocking usual supermarket items, also carry other goods such as tableware and toiletries. Supermarket hours vary. In the bigger cities they may open as early as 7.30am and close as late as 10.00pm. In small towns expect opening hours to be a standard 9 to 5 day. Any supermarket that offers 24 hour shopping will be more expensive than the others. Supermarkets in retail parks do not sell petrol like their British counterparts.

There are a few specialist shops catering for British expats dotted around the country but the price of the imported brands may encourage you to find local equivalents. You could try shopping on-line through websites such as www.britbuys.com; www.expatshopping.com and www.expatdirect.co.uk.

Shop opening hours

General shopping hours are Monday to Friday from 9am to 5pm. On Saturdays and Sundays main centre shops are open from 10am to 4pm. The only public holidays that shops close are Christmas Day, Good Friday and until 1.00pm on Anzac Day. Out of town malls tend to be open for longer.

FOOD AND DRINK

New Zealanders have adventurous tastes and the country has borrowed heavily from the food traditions of many of the immigrants who made the country their home. The tradition of baking cakes and biscuits comes from the Scots and English, yet the emphasis towards a healthier style of eating and cooking came from migrants from Asia who arrived during the 1980s. There is no regional or even national cuisine, but for people who love to cook, New Zealand offers some very high quality fresh produce.

The meat, especially the beef and lamb, is superb. New Zealanders take for granted that their animals are fed a natural diet of grass, rather than reared indoors on grain. Fish and seafood lovers can buy freshly caught, delicately flavoured fish and a number of different varieties of seafood. Kaikoura in the South Island is the place for *crayfish* (a small lobster) and Bluff, is where the best oysters come from. While the fish species caught in New Zealand waters may have unfamiliar-sounding names, for firm white fish try *snapper, hapuka, tarakihi* and *blue cod. Pipis*, a clam-like shellfish are delicious served with spaghetti to create a local version of the Italian *spaghetti al vongole* and fresh *green-lipped* mussels taste nothing like the tough, frozen sort found in British supermarkets. The best place to try them are the Belgian beer chains in the main centres where that winning combination of mussels and chips is served. *Whitebait* (a tiny sweet-tasting fish) are usually served in a light pancake batter called a fritter.

Eating Out and Entertaining

New Zealanders are very informal and although eating out is a part of social life, this is just as likely to be for coffee and cake as it is for lunch or dinner. Coffee drinking is taken very seriously. Whether you want a latte, (milky coffee), a flat white, (less milk) a cappuchino (frothed milk) or a long-black, meeting for coffee is a regular ritual. On weekends, people meet for an informal brunch. Portions in restaurants and cafes are large.

Meals are eaten at roughly the same times as the UK although New Zealanders tend to eat dinner earlier in the evening at around seven or seven thirty. Entertaining is informal in New Zealand and often takes the form of an invitation to a barbecue. In provincial towns expect this to start as early as 6pm. Tipping is optional in New Zealand and people usually tip as a result of great service.

Drink

New Zealand is known for stand-out sauvignon blancs but the exciting developments taking place are with the much more fickle and labour-intensive pinot noir grapes. The new wine hope of the future, according to Bob Campbell of *Cuisine*, is along the Waitaki River in Canterbury and pinot noir is still the favourite grape to plant. What's all the excitement about? Canterbury is sunnier during the crucial summer fruit ripening months and so has the edge on its Central Otago neighbour. In all there are 14 wine regions spread across both islands. Hawke's Bay is the premier area for wine and food tourism.

Boutique breweries have sprung up in the hop-growing regions in the South Island. Look out for brands such as Speights, Macs, and Monteith, all of which offer a range of pilsners, white beer, ales, lager and seasonal specials. 42 Below is making an impact with locally produced vodka and gin.

MEDIA

New Zealand Television

There are six free-to-air terrestrial channels, two of which are run by the state broadcaster. Television New Zealand operates TVONE, a mainstream channel and TV2, aimed at a youth audience. Their biggest competitor is TV3 owned by the Canadian broadcaster Can West which also owns the youth-oriented music channel C4 and a number of radio stations. The revamped Prime Television was recently sold to Sky TV. Maori Television broadcasts in both English and the Maori language, *te reo*.

Television New Zealand (TVNZ) is an odd mix of public and private. On the one hand it has a charter yet with no licence fee it has to seek a substantial proportion of its revenue from advertising. As a result heavy weight documentaries are rarely broadcast and seldom in prime time. There are two more advertising slots per hour at peak times than there are in the UK. You cannot watch a film or sports coverage uninterrupted. A 90 minute film will take two hours to broadcast.

TV ONE offers a selection of imported reality series as well as series drama from the USA and the UK. *Coronation Street* addicts need not fret as it is one of New Zealand's most popular programmes, broadcast three times a week and not too far behind the UK. Locally produced television is mainly current affairs, news and a limited amount of local soap opera and series dramas.

Satellite Television

Satellite television is the only way to guarantee access to live sports coverage. Dedicated night owls can cheer on their favourite English Premier League football team or keep up with the play at Wimbledon. While BBC World and CNN provide coverage of international news, Sky News UK broadcasts the evening and morning news bulletins live. Viewers in New Zealand can watch the news, sports results, weather and even the traffic report and may know where it is raining or which junction to avoid on the M6, before many Britons have even got up.

Sky offers a range of different packages which are bundled together. The most expensive package is the movie channels and sports. UK TV runs mainly older comedy classics as well as period dramas and has proved very popular with nostalgic expats, as well as locals.

Radio

The public broadcaster is Radio New Zealand, which operates two radio stations that are advertiser free. National Radio has much in common with the BBC's Radio 4 and *Morning Report* from 7-9am week days is the definitive news and current affairs programme. Concert FM is the classical music station. For frequencies go to www.radionz.co.nz. By the end of 2006 all but the remotest regions should be able to receive these stations on FM, which is also available on the Sky Digital network.

The commercial radio station Newstalk ZB is a talkback station but the downside to Newstalk, or any of the other commercial radio stations is the repetitive and mindless advertising. Sports fans are well catered for with Radio Sport.

It is also possible to get the BBC World Service on short wave, although the frequency can change. To check the frequency visit http://www.bbc.co.uk/worldservice/schedules/frequencies/index.shtml.

New technology has meant that the BBC can now offer far more than the World Service to overseas listeners with a broadband connection. While drama and comedy is now streamed over the internet allowing listeners the opportunity to listen to that week's episodes of *The Archers*; radio-on-demand is the new development. This is a system whereby programmes can be downloaded via the internet and then recorded onto an MP3 player for playback at a later time. Only talk programmes were available during the podcast trials in 2005 as there are still rights issues to be negotiated for the use of drama and comedy. Go to www.bbc.co.uk for more information.

Newspapers

There is no national daily broadsheet newspaper in New Zealand although *The New Zealand Herald* (circulation 200,000) tries to lay claim to that title. Previously known as the Auckland Herald it is really just a regional paper. *The Dominion Post* is Wellington's daily, with a circulation of 95,000. The other city newspaper with a sizeable circulation of 90,000 is Christchurch's *Press*. The *Sunday Star-Times* is the only national Sunday paper. Although there are syndicated stories that may have appeared previously in British newspapers the quality of local journalism, with one or two exceptions, is lacklustre. New Zealand has no real equivalent of British tabloid newspapers with their cheeky headlines and celebrity gossip.

Keeping up with News from Home

British newspapers and the *International Herald Tribune* are available at specialist news retailers in the three main centres but if you live elsewhere you will have to take out a subscription. A *Sunday Times* with all the supplements can cost $27 while an *Independent on Sunday* could be $17. If you cannot afford to buy a broadsheet every week find an expat friend or two to share the cost. Many of the bigger city supermarkets stock both *The Guardian Weekly* and *The Weekly Telegraph*. If you want to subscribe the rates for *The Guardian Weekly* for New Zealand are currently $147 for six months ($261 for a year) available from *The Guardian Weekly* (164 Deansgate, Manchester M3 3GG; ☎0870-066 0510; e-mail gwsubs@guardian.co.uk). *The Weekly Telegraph* is a similar digest of news culled from *The Daily Telegraph*. A year's subscription currently costs £88. The Telegraph also has a section of its website devoted entirely to people living abroad: www.expat.telegraph.co.uk (it is also possible to subscribe to the Weekly Telegraph here).

These days many expats keep up with the news via the internet. The BBC and all of the major UK newspapers allow access to news stories that are updated day and night via their websites.

Magazines

The magazine market is thriving in New Zealand, catering for specialist interest as well as general interest. Celebrity gossip is found in the rather shallow *New Idea* and the *Woman's Weekly* titles of Australia and New Zealand. *Cuisine, New Zealand Home and Garden,* and *North and South* are some of the higher quality publications to look out for. Whether you are interested in fishing, gardening or yoga, there will be a special interest magazine catering for you. *Listener* is the weekly listings publication.

Bookshops and Libraries

New Zealanders are avid readers, which is surprising considering books are relatively expensive. The major book chains are Dymocks and Whitcoulls supplemented by a great many independent book retailers. Auckland has a branch of the international book chain Borders. It may be cheaper to source books via the internet and have them delivered.

CARS AND MOTORING

Driving Safety and Standards

The standard of driving is generally lower compared to the UK, with New Zealanders generally having a rather immature approach to driving. Despite the signs urging drivers to merge 'like a zip', there will always be the inconsiderate idiot trying to muscle their way in front. On the urban motorway network each lane is treated as a separate entity, therefore few drivers bother keeping left. Slow drivers can hog the outside lane, holding up all the traffic, exacerbating urban congestion. Impatient drivers will overtake on the inside lane and weave in and out of the traffic. Tailgating and an aversion to indicators is another factor of driving on New Zealand roads. Stop signs are treated like Give Way signs and Give Way generally means go if you can sneak in.

Negotiating narrow and twisty roads can be a challenge for international drivers used to the motorway system in the UK. There is in fact no long distance motorway network. Auckland has a limited motorway system that only extends as far south as Mercer and up to the North Shore. State Highway One, the main road between Wellington and Auckland would be considered an A road in the UK. Mainly single carriageway with passing places, the further south you travel, the more the road detours through town centres. This adds to the journey time. Roads are not as smooth as they are in the UK and can at times be very uneven so take extreme care when overtaking.

New Zealanders drive on the left hand side of the road.

Traffic Management

Around schools drivers will be ticketed if caught going more than 6kph or so over the speed limit while in other urban areas drivers will be fined if going over more than 10kph. Police make good use of speed traps. As drink driving is a contributory factor in a great many road accidents, a rigorous system of random breath testing is enforced. 0.8mm of alcohol per mm of blood is the legal limit for anyone over the age of 20.

Main Differences in Driving Rules

○ The minimum driving age in New Zealand is 15.

○ Drivers and all passengers are required by law to wear seat belts at all times.

○ The speed limits are 100km/h on the open road and 50km/h through towns.

○ Using a mobile phone while driving is still not illegal although if you cause an accident while doing so you can be prosecuted for dangerous driving.

○ Drivers turning left must give way to oncoming traffic turning right. This is known as the Right Hand Rule and causes more potential problems with international visitors than any other. Confusion arises in built up areas when there are two lanes and there is another driver in the outside lane going straight on. While the car turning right must wait the car turning left will often take the opportunity to turn.

○ Drivers can be fined for not carrying their driving licence while driving.

Driving Licences

Overseas drivers can drive for a year on their current licence before they have to pass a driving theory test and an eye test to obtain a New Zealand licence. Sample question and answer sheets can be purchased prior to the test. Anyone who has passed the demanding British driving test should sail through. Licences have to be renewed according to your age and the type of licence held. Drivers over 75 must renew their licence and at 80 they must renew their licence as well as pass an Older Driver Practical Test.

Buying a Car in New Zealand

The new and used car market is dominated by imports from Japan. Cars are reasonably priced, unless you want a European one, which will not only cost more than the same make and model in the UK but you will also pay more for spare parts. Two websites to check the most up-to-date prices are: www.autotrader.co.nz; and www.carport.co.nz for direct European car imports.

> The New Zealand equivalent of the UK MOT is known as the WOF (*Warrant of Fitness*) and all cars less than six years old must pass the test every 12 months. All other vehicles require a WOF every 6 months.

Insurance

New Zealand must be one of the few OECD countries where there is no compulsory third party insurance. Instead, there is a no-fault accident compensation system called ACC. You may end up with less money through ACC than you would if the case went to court but claims tend to be settled quite quickly, allowing the injured party to get on with their life.

VOTING IN NEW ZEALAND

The criteria for voter enrolment are: you are a New Zealand citizen and have been in New Zealand in the past three years or that you are a permanent resident who has been in the country in the past 12 months.

> **New Zealand Post Limited Electoral Enrolment Office :** Level 2, Mainzeal Building, 181 Vivian Street, Wellington; Freepost 2 ENROL, PO Box 180, Wellington ☎04 801-0700; email; enrol@elections.org.nz; www.elections.org.nz.

Retaining Your Right to Vote in UK National and European Elections

A British citizen living abroad can apply to become an overseas voter in UK parliamentary and European elections if their name appears on the UK electoral register within the previous 15 years. For more information contact www. aboutmyvote.co.uk or for Northern Ireland www.electoralofficeni.gov.uk.

RELIGION

New Zealand is a secular and liberal society and while individuals are free to worship with any faith they choose, religion plays very little part in public life. Reflecting the historical ties with the British Crown, New Zealand is officially Anglican/Protestant. Although 50% of the population regard themselves as nominally Christian, the number of people actively participating in the major Christian religions is in decline. The Anglican church claims around 600,000 affiliates while the Catholic faith 486,000. The third largest denomination is Presbyterian at 417,000. The mainstream Christian religions have been losing out to the Pentecostal religious movement and the Mormon church. Non-Christian religions still account for no more than 2% of the population.

Quality of Life

CHAPTER SUMMARY

○ You will assimilate much more quickly with the locals as you won't need to learn a new language to communicate.

○ The local Citizens Advice Bureau is a good place to find out about clubs and special interest groups.

○ Senior concessions apply for those over 65 on ferries, buses and coach travel.

○ There are a number of conservation projects that require volunteers.

○ New Zealand has 11 national public holidays. Activities at local level range from a jazz festival on an island in the Hauraki Gulf to a vintage air show in Wanaka.

WHERE TO GET INFORMATION

Retiree Sheila Gavin gives advice on where to find out about clubs and groups to join: *'I went to see the Citizens Advice Bureau in Queenstown who were incredibly helpful. I found out about walking groups and Scottish country dancing'.* If there is no Citizens Advice Bureau where you live then try the local *I-SITE* visitor information office. There are over 90 I-SITES located throughout New Zealand, offering a tourist information service.

The library is also an excellent source of information on community events – whether you want to join a book club, obtain listings of classical concerts or to find out where you can learn to salsa. National Radio broadcasts an excellent arts magazine programme, *Arts on Sunday* which highlights upcoming cultural events. The Living Channel, on the Sky Network, lists local activities such as craft fairs and exhibitions. Newspapers are a good source of information for events as is the internet. Arts Calendar at www.artscalendfar.co.nz is a very useful site to bookmark.

A useful organisation concerned with all aspects of quality of life for the over 50s is the lobby group: Grey Power (www.greypower.co.nz). Membership of Grey Power also entitles you to various discounts.

MAKING NEW FRIENDS

You will integrate so much more quickly into the new culture as your friends are more likely to be New Zealanders than they are fellow Brits. The best piece of advice on relocation that anyone coming to New Zealand can heed comes from Mike Cole who runs BritsNZ (www.britsnz.co.nz), a company that assists British people to make the move to New Zealand:

> *You have to make every effort to get out into the community and never pass up any opportunity or invitation to listen and learn. Never say 'we didn't do it like that at home.' That will not endear you to anyone. We have found that Kiwis respond very positively to people who make an effort whereas if you hold back they will not come forward.*

SENIOR CONCESSIONS

There are concessions applicable to seniors over 65 in New Zealand which can contribute to your quality of life, including public transport and visits to cultural and arts events. If you have a seniors card issued overseas, some but not all organisations will recognise these and offer you a concession where there is one.

- **Local Buses, Trains and Ferries.** Reduced travel is available on local buses, trains and ferries from 65 years of age.
- **Intercity Coach Services.** Intercity Coachlines and Newmans Coachlines with their network of national coach services offer Golden Age fares where persons over the age of 60 receive a 20% discount off standard fares (some services excepted).
- **Trains.** Long distance train travel in New Zealand is strictly for tourists rather than for travellers or commuters. You would be better off doing what everyone else does which is to either fly, drive or take the bus to your destination.
- **Visits to Museums and Galleries.** Museums and galleries all operate different policies but permanent collections and certain exhibitions offer free entry to everyone. When exhibitions do charge an entrance fee always ask for the seniors' concession.

SPORTS

The key to a well-balanced fitness routine as we age is to combine aerobic activity with core training. Pilates, Yoga and Tai Chi are three ways to increase core strength and these disciplines are practised by men as well as women. Health benefits include joint mobility and may even help to keep balance problems at bay in later life. Private Pilates sessions using specialised machines can assist those with knee and hip joint problems and many long distance runners regard this as an essential part of their training routine.

Most towns have a selection of sports clubs, details of which can be obtained through the local telephone directory, council or library. Otherwise contact the national organisations; the main ones are given below.

Air Sports – Hang Gliding and Paragliding – New Zealand Hang Gliding and Paragliding Association; www.nzhgpa.org.nz.

Alpine and Cross-country Skiing – For ski reports and weather conditions two good websites are www.nzski.com and www.snow.co.nz. Skiing clubs offer cheaper skiing than commercial fields although lift passes at the commercial resorts are reasonably priced from $35 to $75 per day. The ski season runs from June to October although Mt Hutt, near Christchurch is open for longer. Ruapehu is the main resort in the North Island while in the South Island the main resort for skiing is Queenstown. Waiorau near Wanaka is the only commercial resort for Nordic (cross-country skiing.)

Climbing – New Zealand Alpine Club, PO Box 786, Christchurch;. ☎03 377 7595 www.alpineclub.org.nz.

Cycling – Cycling Advocates Network, P.O. Box 6491, Auckland; ☎04 972 2556; www.can.org.nz. Cyclists are required by law to wear a helmet.

Dance – www.feelinggreat.co.nz is the dance site for Wellington City Council as dancing classes operate at local rather than national level. In the Wellington region alone you can try something different like salsa (which is fantastic for loosening the hip joints), ceroc or even tango and samba.

Golf – New Zealand Golf Association, PO Box 11842, Wellington. www.golf.co.nz. It costs, on average just $30 for a round of golf although if you want luxury this can cost up to $200. The New Zealand Golf Guide lists all the major golf courses on their website, www.golfguide.co.nz.

Horse Riding – Equestrian Sports New Zealand , Level 4, 3-9 Church Street, Wellington; ☎04 499 8974; www.nzequestrian.org.nz; A website listing upcoming equestrian events for spectators as well as participants.

For information on trekking try www.tourism.net.nz and follow the link to horse trekking.

Kayaking and Canoeing – Kiwi Association of Sea Kayakers, P.O. Boc 23, Runanga, West Coast, 7845; www.kask.co.nz: or for details on river kayaking try New Zealand Recreational Canoeing Association, P.O. Box 284, Wellington; nzrca@rivers.org.nz; www.rivers.org.nz. Sea kayaking is suitable for all levels of fitness and a way of taking in some beautiful scenery and getting fit at the same time.

Pétanque – Petanque New Zealand www.petanque.net.nz is an Auckland based organisation which lists the Auckland parks where petanque can be played. Most towns and cities have council-run petanque facilities.

Running/Walking – YMCA ☎04 802 5524; www.ymca.org.nz. Running and walking clubs are a great way to keep motivated. In the Auckland area contact www.nzymca.com. Hiking (tramping) is hugely popular and any local tourist office will give you details of the tracks in your area.

Sailing – Yachting New Zealand, P.O. Box 33 789, Takapuna, Auckland; ☎09 488 9325; www.yachtingnz.org.nz. As well as information on where to learn to sail, this is the site for information on crewing in local sailing competitions.

Scuba Diving – New Zealand Underwater Association, ☎09 623 3252; www.divenewzealand.com. The Poor Knights Islands, The Bay of Islands, the Hauraki Gulf and Great Barrier Island as well as the Marlborough Sounds in the South Island are all excellent diving spots.

Swimming – Swimming New Zealand, P.O. Box 11 115, Wellington; ☎04 801 9450; www.swimmingnz.org.nz; Your local council will have details of the pool nearest you.

Tai-Chi-Chuan – Tai Chi is popular in New Zealand particularly for older people. ACC publishes the location of classes at www.acc.co.nz.

Tennis – Tennis New Zealand, P.O. Box 18308, Glen Innes, Auckland; ☎09 528 5428; www.tennisnz.com. This website includes a player handbook. Tennis is a popular year round sport in the northern half of the North Island and especially in the Auckland region.

Windsurfing – Windsurfing New Zealand, P.O. Box 66 029, Beach Haven, Auckland.

Yoga and Pilates – Yoga Organisation New Zealand, PO Box 8036, New Plymouth; www.yoga.org.nz. Also has information on Pilates on this site. Stick to Pilates studios where the staff have done an accredited Pilates course. Yoga teachers also need to have attended accredited courses.

LEISURE INTERESTS

Below are some of the more popular leisure interests and contacts in New Zealand.

Bird Watching: Royal Forest and Bird Protection Society of New Zealand, 172 Taranaki Street, P.O. Box 631, Wellington, New Zealand; ☎04 385 7374;www.forestandbird.org.nz. A link on this site details viewing sites for bird watching including the world's only mainland breeding colony of Royal Albatross.

DIY: If DIY is your passion there are great many DIY shops. Mitre 10, Hammer Hardware and Bunnings should have everything you need.

Fishing: Fishing is the most popular recreational activity in the country. www.fishing.net.nz is a website listing fishing sites and includes a link to the government site www.fish.govt.nz. which regulates the catches of recreational anglers.

Pet Adoption and Puppy Walking. Adopting a pet, particularly a dog, is one proven way of increasing well-being. Not only will your new pal get you out walking more often but dog ownership is an excellent way to meet the neighbours. Puppy walking is another option for dog lovers who cannot commit to owning a dog long-term. Puppies selected for training as working dogs have to be socialised before they start their training. And a puppy walker and their charge get VIP treatment wherever they go – whether that is in the queue for a domestic flight or at the cinema. Walkers have to be prepared to give their new friend back after a year.

Reading. Although books are more expensive than in the UK, New Zealanders are avid readers. In the main centres public libraries are even open on Sundays.
    Joining a book group is a great way to share the pleasure of reading. Many libraries run book groups if you would prefer to join one already established.

Ballet, Concerts and Theatre. Music and theatre are important aspects of New Zealand cultural life. Details of local events will be advertised in the newspaper and your local library. Free concerts are often given in churches.

TAKING COURSES

New Zealand's seniors now have the chance to study all manner of different courses from the art history of Venice to the vulcanology of Vesuvius. There are university level academic courses, courses just for interest, or practical courses. They can be based locally, at academic institutions in towns and cities, or a combination of distance learning and class contact. You can even undertake virtual study these days thanks to the internet.

The international organisation University of the Third Age is a good starting point as well as the Massey University Extra Mural Programme if you want to study at tertiary level. If you live in a city with a university then contact their continuing education department. The academic year starts in March and runs until November. Some useful contacts and sources of information are listed below:

Course Providers

U3A Online: www3.griffith.edu.au. Griffith University in Australia calls itself a virtual university of the third age and lists all the U3A locations throughout New Zealand. There is no national contact for the University of the Third Age in New Zealand.

Massey University Extra Mural Programme: ☎0800 627 739; www.extramural. massey.ac.nz

Department of Continuing Education at the University of Auckland: ☎0800 864 266; www.cce.auckland.ac.nz.

University of Canterbury Continuing Education: www.uco.canterbury.ac.nz. Non-degree arts courses for lifelong learning.

Victoria University of Wellington Department of Continuing Education: ☎04 463 6556; www.vuw.ac.nz/conted.

GARDENING

If you adore gardens and gardening, New Zealand is the perfect place to indulge your passion. In the upper part of the North Island and in Nelson and Golden Bay you are only limited by your imagination in what you can grow. One of the country's most beautiful gardens to visit is Pukeiti in New Plymouth. At the foot of Mount Taranaki, this garden has to have one of the world's most stunning backdrops in which to see rhododendrons and azaleas, incorporated into a native bush setting.

You don't need much room to create a kitchen garden – even tomatoes can be grown in a pot. If you do have some space, imagine the satisfaction of being able to pick your own produce or donate the surplus to a neighbour. Growing your own produce will help you connect with the 'upside down' seasons in your new homeland. Whether you want a grapefruit for breakfast, or lemons for the evening gin and tonics, all you will have to do is walk across the back lawn to get them. In the sub-tropical kitchen garden, how about growing figs, limes or avocados? About the only downside to gardening in New Zealand, apart from the abundance of plant pests is that it is a year-round activity in the warmer parts of the country. While Northern Hemisphere gardeners get a chance in the winter to pack away the gardening gloves and retreat to the sofa with next year's seed catalogues, in New Zealand you will still be mowing the lawn and weeding.

TRAVELLING AND TOURISM IN NEW ZEALAND

Packed within the two main islands is a diversity of landscape that is generally only found in entire continents; with lakes, mountains, volcanoes, sub-tropical beaches and rainforest. Because many of the best sights in New Zealand are in wilderness areas, one of the best ways to experience them is to stay amongst the scenery in a motor home.

Camping and Caravanning

Camping facilities vary from low cost and from one to four stars, the latter having mod cons and many activities laid on.

Motor home hire in peak season (November – March) is as much as $300 per day for a four-berth cabin but you can reduce your costs by half at other times of the year. Alternatively you can even buy a second-hand van from one of the hire companies.

New Zealand accommodation providers are not as pet friendly as those in the UK and Europe and sites that accept animals will be indicated by a 'pets by arrangement' symbol. Dogs owners may have to produce up to date vaccination certificates and ensure that their pets are not allowed to run free around the site. On Department of Conservation land and in parts of Northland in the Bay of Island where kiwis roam, dogs are not permitted. Because there is no tradition of common land or public rights of way across farmland in New Zealand, private property is just that, and farmers take a dim view of unauthorised parking or camping on their land.

Where to Get Travel and Holiday Info

There is something of a revolution going on in the travel business with an increasing demand reported for more challenging holidays. '50 is the new 40', according to market researchers and tourism agencies in New Zealand are beginning to respond as seniors look for more adventurous ways to spend their leisure time including mountaineering, deep-sea fishing, trekking, and scuba diving holidays (among other things) as couples, singles or in groups.

Details of travel and tourism in the regions can be obtained from I-SITE visitor information offices found in towns and cities across the country.

Eco-Tourism

One new venture recently set up by Hands Up Holidays (☎0800 426 3787; www.handsupholidays.com) combines a holiday with community development work. Tourists would spend around two thirds of their time on holiday and one third working with a local community in overseas destinations on jobs such as teaching English and environmental work.

Air

Grey Power members are offered cheaper fares than normal on domestic flights operated by Origin Pacific Airways Ltd on certain week days but the amount of discount depends on the destination. Air New Zealand and Qantas with their no frills domestic service offer budget fares to all passengers. Many companies as well as the Bank of New Zealand offer a loyalty air miles scheme called Fly Buys. Domestic and international airlines which offer discounts are listed below. Otherwise look out for off-season deals.

Airlines

Air New Zealand: www.airnz.co.nz; 0800 737 000. National and international carrier working with a network of regional affiliates throughout the country.

Fly Buys : www.flybuys.co.nz; 0800 359 2897. Details the companies that participate in the air miles scheme.

Freedom Air: www.freedomair.com;1800 122 000. A budget airline flying between Australia and New Zealand.

Origin Pacific Airways Ltd: www.originpacific.co.nz. 0800 302 302 Links regional domestic destinations using smaller aircraft than the two main carriers. The Silver Wings programme offers discounts to Grey Power members on Tuesdays, Wednesdays and Thursdays.

Pacific Blue: 0800 67 0000 www.flypacificblue.com and *Polynesian Blue;* www.poly nesianblue.com. Part of the Virgin empire, offering cheaper flights from regional airports in Australia and New Zealand to Pacific Island destinations.

Qantas: www.qantas.co.nz; 0800 808 767. Qantas competes with Air New Zealand on the profitable main centre routes but does not have the same country-wide coverage as the national airline.

Ferries to Great Barrier Island and Stewart Island

If you tire of mainland New Zealand then the rugged and beautiful islands of Great Barrier in the Hauraki Gulf and Stewart Island at the tip of the South Island are accessible by ferry. The carriers to Great Barrier Island are Subritzky (☎09 373 4036; www.subritzky.co.nz) and Sealink (☎0800 732 546; www. sealink.co.nz). Ferries depart from Auckland. Journey times from six hours. The passenger ferry that links Bluff in the South Island to Stewart Island is Foveaux Express (☎03 212 7660; www.foveauxexpress.co.nz).

INTERNATIONAL TRAVEL FROM NEW ZEALAND

During the Southern Hemisphere winter you may want to travel back to the UK, to take advantage of a second summer or to soak up the sun in Australia's year round tropical holiday destination, Northern Queensland or in any one of the Pacific Island destinations. Love Paris but can't face the 24 hour plane ride? How about croissants, café au lait and warm tropical sands in the French overseas department of New Caledonia or Tahiti – a mere three hours away. You can of course book all manner of holidays and travel through the internet these days and while a seat on an aircraft is no different whether you buy it from a travel agent or online, sometimes 'net only' hotel accommodation may not be the bargain it seems. A travel agent who has been to a particular hotel or resort can advise you on where in the complex it would be best to stay or what age group the hotel caters for.

Bargain Travel

Senior concessions and off-season deals are not the only bargain travel opportunities that New Zealand has on offer. A few weeks before departure dates, agents and air travel companies put unsold flights and holidays on the market at discounted prices through discount websites. If you are prepared to take a punt on the holiday, without knowing much about the resort before you get there, last minute hotel and accommodation deals can be good value.

Travel and Hotel Websites	
www.houseoftravel.co.nz	Compares airlines for the cheapest deals on flights and hotels.
www.wotif.com	Last minute accommodation deals.
www.zuji.co.nz	Deals on hotels and flights.

PUBLIC HOLIDAYS, EVENTS AND LOCAL FESTIVALS

New Zealand has 11 national public holidays and unlike the UK, the holidays that commemorate something, such as ANZAC Day and Waitangi Day are taken on the day that they fall on. If this happens to be on a weekend, there is no official day off in lieu to compensate.

PUBLIC HOLIDAYS	
1 January	New Year's Day
6 February	Waitangi Day
Good Friday	as UK
Easter Sunday	as UK
Easter Monday	as UK
25 April	ANZAC Day
1st Monday in June	Queen's Birthday
4th Monday in October	Labour Day
25 December	Christmas Day
26 December	Boxing Day

In addition to the national holidays each region celebrates an Anniversary Day. Most of the North Island except for Taranaki and Hawke's Bay celebrates theirs in late January while in much of the South Island it is in December.

Festivals

Many of the events listed below attract both national and international tourists. The following is just a selection of some of the more interesting events on offer. The phone numbers are sometimes only in use during the month before the event.

EVENTS AND FESTIVALS IN NEW ZEALAND

Month	Festival	Telephone	Website
January	Open Tennis Championships. Auckland.	☎09 307 5000 (Ticketek booking)	www.aucklandtennis.co.nz www.premier.ticketek.co.nz www.heinekenopen.co.nz
	Auckland Anniversary Day Regatta.	☎0800 734 2882	www.regatta.org.nz
February	Harvest Hawke's Bay Wine and food festival	☎0800 44 29 46	www.harvesthawkesbay.com
	International Arts Festival Wellington (biennial event)	☎04 473 0149	www.nzfestival.co.nz
	Art Deco Weekend Napier	☎06 835 1191	www.artdeconapier.com
March	Pasifika Festival	☎09 379 2020	www.aucklandcity.govt.nz
	Waiheke Island Jazz Festival.	See website For contact details.	www.waihekejazz.co.nz
	Wildfoods Festival, Hokitika	☎03 756 9049	www.wildfoods.co.nz
April	Warbirds over Wanaka, International airshow.	☎03 443 8619	www.warbirdsoverwanaka.com
	Balloons Over Waikato, Hamilton.	☎07 839 6677	www.balloonsoverwaikato.co.nz
July	New Zealand International Film Festival.	☎04 385 0162	www.enzedff.co.nz

September	World of Wearable Art (WOW) Wellington.	☎ 03 548 9299	www.worldofwearableart.com
November	Toast Martinborough Wine, Food and Music Festival	☎ 06 306 9183	www.toastmartinborough.co.nz
	Ellerslie Flower Show, Auckland	☎ 09 579 6260	www.ellerslieflowershow.co.nz
	Coromandel Pohutakawa Festival.	☎ 07 867 9832	www.thamesinfo.co.nz

KEEPING IN TOUCH

Communications

For the cheapest new way to communicate, which doesn't tie you to a landline and costs the same whether you call next door or next country, you will need a broadband internet connection and the latest innovation VoIP (Voice over internet protocol). There is supposed to be 90% broadband coverage of the populated areas throughout New Zealand although some cynics might suggest that it is not as extensive as the telecommunications companies claim.

Telephoning Using Landlines

Telecom is a state controlled monopoly and is the only company that can install your phone although calls can be made at cheaper rates by signing up with a company that on-sells airtime. Rural customers now have to pay the actual cost of phone installation for a new line, which can be hugely expensive in the more remote areas. Telecom's main competitor is TelstraClear but until the telecommunications market is de-regulated Telecom will continue to make the most of its monopoly.

Mobile Phones

If the landline telephone market is virtually a monopoly then the mobile phone market is a duopoly with Telecom and Vodafone, the two big players. Mobile phones can be purchased from other retailers selling electronics as well as directly from Telecom and Vodafone. You can try to have the SIM card in your phone replaced with a New Zealand one, so you can carry on using the same phone unless your UK phone is 'SIM-locked', i.e. the card cannot be changed. There is as yet no number portability so users cannot retain their old numbers when switching networks. The regulator has given Telecom and Vodafone until April 2007 to address this.

Internet and E-mail

Telecom's monopoly has had a negative effect on the take up of broadband in New Zealand as it is seen as very slow by international standards and expensive. ADSL (broadband) is available in some of the more densely populated areas; remote country areas present more difficulties, although you could try installing a dish on your house. As this book went to press the Government ordered Telecom to unbundle its local loop to competitors. From 2007 faster, cheaper broadband really will be a possibility.

Calling via the Internet

VoIP (or Voice over the Internet Protocol) is a development that strikes fear within traditional telecommunications companies. In 2005 over one third of all New Zealand's broadband subscribers were using the VoIP system, Skype. Offered as a free download over the internet any computer with a low-cost telephone headset can be used as a telephone, calling others with the Skype software. Skype Out allows those with Skype to call standard phones and cell phones via a pre-paid account. The drawbacks are that users cannot receive calls from landlines or mobile phones and are unable to dial the emergency services. And some analysts say that although Skype rates are very competitive they are in some instances beaten by the easy to use low-cost calling cards, available from local shops.

Having Friends and Family to Stay

While it is a bonus to have space for visitors, there are alternatives to buying a bigger house than you need. Your guests and family can stay in a local bed and breakfast or if you are in the country and have room you could always build a guest chalet which could be let out in the future. If you are not far from an airport the chances are that you will get more visitors, or more frequent visits than if you are in a remote country location. It may be a good idea to tactfully advise visitors on the necessity of hiring a car – as otherwise you will be in danger of becoming the local taxi service.

WORKING, VOLUNTEERING AND STARTING A BUSINESS

Finding a Part-time Job or Voluntary Work

From all the studies and research on positive ageing, one of the keys to a successful life in the Third Age is being connected to the world around you. And one of the best ways to do this is to go back to work part-time in a job that you enjoy. In September 2005 New Zealand had the developed world's lowest unemployment rate at 3.4%. Some companies make it their policy to recruit older workers who, they say have a much steadier attitude to work than their younger colleagues. As well as trying the usual channels such as local newspapers for work, see the two specialist agencies below that actively recruit older workers.

A voluntary organisation such as the Citizens Advice Bureau are always looking for volunteers as it is becoming increasingly difficult in the fast-paced 21st century to find people willing to donate their time. Citizens Advice are reputed to offer some of the best training available in the voluntary sector. But if you came to New Zealand to get away from being stuck indoors in an office, you could volunteer for an interesting outdoor conservation project instead.

Useful Contacts

Grey Skills: www.greyskills.com; You only have to be 40 to qualify to join Grey Skills but this organisation, with offices in both Auckland and Christchurch is a network of experienced and mature tradespeople.

Silver Works: www.silverworks.co.nz; A specialist human resource agency for the 50 plus group, based in Auckland, their website lists jobs such as call centre staff, sales representatives, accounts workers and a building supervisor on a construction site.

Citizens Advice Bureaux: www.cab.org.nz; This website will tell you everything you need to know about becoming a CAB volunteer.

Conservation Volunteers: www.conservationvolunteers.org.nz; Voluntary conservation work can really make a difference in helping to enhance and restore New Zealand's wild places. Restore footpaths, help build bridges, eradicate plant pests and plant trees.

Department of Conservation: www.doc.govt.nz/Community; Volunteers work on bird counts, assist at whale strandings and plant trees. You may be allocated to a project according to your interests and experience. The site has a volunteer registration form.

Gaby Heinrich who lives in St Heliers is living testament to the benefits of volunteering: *'I've volunteered all my life- for the Red Cross and Meals on Wheels. There's a new hospice shop up the road and I'll probably work there for 4-5 hours a week.'*

Starting a Small Business

Sub-dividing Land. Because the available building material was wood, rather than stone, a New Zealand outbuilding is more likely to be left to rot than renovated. However, there is still the opportunity to make money from your property if the house you bought is on a piece of land that can be sub- divided.

Sub-dividing a section is a way for people on fixed incomes to free up some capital. You can either sub-divide the land and then sell off one part of it or you could pay to build a second house yourself and then sell it. Should you wish to investigate sub-division your first step is to contact your local council.

Even if the main home is in the centre of the land, it can be moved a few metres by a house lifting company in order that a second house can be built in front of it or behind it. Although this might sound incredible from the British perspective, house lifting is an established industry in Australia and New Zealand. One house lifting company brags that they are so careful that you don't even need to pack away the crystal glasses.

Running a B & B. Offering bed and breakfast is one way to supplement your income although property owners who live in popular tourist or lifestyle destinations do this not just to make money but as a way of meeting people. You can either open your home to bed and breakfast guests, build self-catering chalets or buy an established business. Even if your guests are self-catering, hosting is still a labour-intensive job as there is the laundry change and cleaning to attend to as well as taking the bookings.

To be listed in a guidebook such as *The Bed and Breakfast Book*, would-be hosts should first read the schedule of standards listed at the back of the publication. These include compliance information on safety, including the requirement to provide fire and smoke alarms. Dining and guest rooms as well as communal areas and the kitchen all have to be kept spotless. But the hard work does have its rewards, one of which is repeat custom.

If you are considering offering bed and breakfast you should check with your local council first to ensure that your property complies with the local by-laws. These include having the right insurance and compliance with pool fencing requirements, if you have one. How much you can charge will depend entirely on which market you are catering for and where your house is situated. Prices start at around $50 per head. Should you not wish to go to the expense of upgrading in order to comply with council regulations an alternative to bed and breakfast for those that live in cities is to offer home-stay accommodation to foreign students. B & B is offered by a mixture of overseas residents, empty nesters as well as the active retired. If you specialise in a particular cuisine or cook with organic produce you should include this in your advertising.

Whichever option you choose be sure to consult your accountant or local tax office first as all income has to be declared to the Inland Revenue Department. Make sure that you have considered all the possibilities for tax deductions including interest on any loans that you have taken out. Given that New Zealand is a nation of small business owners, there is a great deal of good (free) advice offered to anyone running a business no matter how small. The Business Information Zone, www.biz.org.nz is a government initiative, which addresses the fundamentals of starting your own business as well as buying an established one. Whether you are intending to become a sole trader or set up as a limited liability company such issues as tax, ACC (Accident Compensation Corporation), employing staff, as well as health and safety are covered.

Personal Finance

CHAPTER SUMMARY

○ **Financial Advisors.** Ensure that your financial advisor belongs to one of the three organisations listed below.

○ **Banking.** It is a good idea to maintain a bank account in the UK.

   ○ It is not advisable to overdraw your New Zealand bank account without prior arrangement.

○ **Pensions.** You can choose a payment option that minimises commission charges.

   ○ Seek advice on whether to continue paying National Insurance contributions in the UK, should you move before you retire.

○ **Taxation.** Tax residence is determined on whether or not you have a permanent residence in New Zealand or if you spend 183 days or more a year there.

   ○ There is no personal allowance and you are liable to pay tax on every cent earned.

   ○ Neither death duties nor inheritance tax are payable in New Zealand.

FINANCIAL ADVICE

Anyone considering retiring to New Zealand should first consult with a tax and financial adviser.

The financial services industry does not have quite the same regulatory framework as in the UK. The Retirement Commission recommends that your advisor be a member of either the Institute of Chartered Accountants, New Zealand Stock Exchange or the Financial Planners and Insurance Advisors Association. For cross-border advice a larger firm is more likely to have the expertise to advise you on both New Zealand and UK financial matters.

Financial Advisers

PRISM Xpat Cross Border Finance and International Pension Transfers: www. prismxpat.com; ☎0845 4004.

Financial Planners and Insurance Advisors Association: ☎04 499 8062; www. fpia.org.nz.

Institute of Chartered Accountants: ☎04 473 6303; www.nzica.com.

Retirement Commission: www.sorted.org.nz.

BANKING

Off-shore interests own most of the so-called New Zealand banks – even if the image conveyed by the local high street bank is that of the friendly local branch, willing to lend a sympathetic ear when a customer comes in looking for a loan. The Commonwealth Bank of Australia owns ASB, the ANZ now owns the National Bank and the BNZ is owned by the National Bank of Australia. Kiwibank and the TSB are the only two left that are New Zealand owned.

ATMs

ATMs (automated teller machines) are all over New Zealand and you can generally use any ATM to draw money from your account, whether that is from your UK account or your New Zealand one. Using your own bank's network of ATMs is the cheapest option. ATMs in New Zealand will usually only allow you to check your balance and make cash withdrawals.

New Zealand banks charge the usual fees – whether for processing cheques, using an ATM belonging to another bank or running your accounts. Transaction charges can be reduced by maintaining a minimum balance in your account. Overdrawing your account without an authorised overdraft facility will incur hefty fees. A swipe card (EFTPOS) and pin number is the method of payment preferred by retailers as there is no cheque guarantee card system for personal cheques.

Internet and Telephone Banking. Most banks offer account holders internet and telephone banking facilities. With a username and password, most banking transactions can be carried out online. There are also a number of internet/telephone only banks operating in New Zealand, such as *BankDirect* (☎0800 500 400; www.bankdirect.co.nz) and *Superbank* (☎0508 226 546; www.superbank.co.nz).

Banking Procedures

Bank statements are available by e-mail or via the post. All the usual services, such as standing orders, direct debit overdrafts and loans are available from New Zealand banks.

Even if you are relocating permanently, keeping a bank account open at home allows you to use it for visits to family and friends. It will also allow you to transfer money (from a pension or income accrued from property rentals or business) between accounts if you wish.

Opening a New Zealand Bank Account from the UK

The ASB, through the Commonwealth Bank of Australia which has an office in London, allows those moving to New Zealand (or Australia) to open accounts before they leave. But whether you open an account through an overseas office or via a high street bank's website, whilst the banks are happy to take your money, you are not permitted to withdraw any until you get to New Zealand and have presented your passport in person to be verified by a bank official. High street banks restrict non-residents to a limited range of accounts. Check the banking websites for more details. The National Bank states on its website that customers need to be resident for more than six months to open an account.

Trusts

Setting up a family trust can ensure that a family asset does not become classified as relationship property in the unfortunate case of separation or divorce. The advantage is that even though the trust owns the assets, you still have control over them, provided this is written up in the deeds. For example, if your house is sold to the trust, you will still most likely live in it, even though you do not own it. The trust tax rate is 33% and the advantages of setting up a trust applies particularly to top rate taxpayers who are taxed at 39 cents for every dollar they earn over $60,000. There are tax advantages in giving away the assets that the trust owes you. Individuals are allowed to gift up to $27,000 per year, while for couples the allowance is $54,000.

Offshore Banking

If you have £10,000 or more to invest and depending on where you are tax resident, you should consult a financial advisor as to whether an offshore savings account might be the best place to invest your money. You should first investigate a tax-saving option like cash ISAs (Individual Savings Account), which the high street banks and building societies all offer in Britain. As well as that, because New Zealand offers higher interest rates for savers than the UK, your advisor might find a better rate of return for your investments elsewhere.

Offshore Trusts

One option for the investor moving to New Zealand is offshore trusts. Shares, bonds, funds, bank deposits etc. can all become free from New Zealand income tax by putting them into trust. Trusts, though are complicated, cost money to set up and while useful for those with substantial investments wishing to minimise their tax liability, are not suitable for everyone. You will need specialist advice on how to set up such a trust.

Useful Contacts

Bank of Scotland International (Jersey) Ltd: ☎01534-613500; www.bankofscotland-international.com.

Bank of Scotland International (Isle of Man) Ltd: ☎01534-613500; www.bankofscotland-international.com.

Bradford and Bingley International Ltd: ☎01624-695000; www.bbi.co.im.

Ex-Pat Tax Consultants Ltd: ☎0191-230 3141; www.expattax.co.uk.

Lloyds TSB – Isle of Man Offshore Centre: ☎08705-301641; www.lloydstsb-offshore.com.

UK PENSIONS AND BENEFITS

Receiving Your UK State Pension in New Zealand

To have your UK pension paid directly into a New Zealand account you should contact the pension service in the UK (www.thepensionservice.gov.uk; ☎0845-6060265) and request details of Overseas Direct Payment in local currency. In New Zealand, like other Commonwealth countries, the UK State Pension is frozen at the level it reached on your arrival and you will no longer be eligible for increases or Christmas bonuses. Further help and advice is available from the International Pension Service (☎0191-218 7777).

UK Government (Public Sector and Civil Service) pensions are normally paid into UK accounts only after basic rate income tax has been deducted.

The tax paid cannot be reclaimed even if you are non-resident. This does form part of the UK's Taxation Treaty with New Zealand and you should declare this income in your New Zealand tax return as taxed income, noting the amount of tax you have paid.

Private UK company pensions are paid per the rules of the individual company which could mean that your private pension may only be paid into a UK account. To access the money you will need to set up a standing order from your UK account to your New Zealand account.

To minimise the number of commission charges and exchange rate fluctuations when receiving a pension from abroad, it may be more prudent to have the money transferred quarterly rather than monthly. Alternatively a currency dealer, such as Currencies Direct (☎020-7813 0332; www.currenciesdirect.com) will allow you to make an annual arrangement that fixes the exchange rate for a year, insuring you against currency fluctuations.

Those who move to New Zealand before reaching retirement age, but do not intend to work, may wish to continue paying national insurance contributions in the UK in order to qualify for a British state pension when they reach 65. This is important especially in the early years of your relocation in case, for whatever reason, you have to return or want to retire to a third country. Seek advice on this issue from the Inland Revenue National Insurance Contributions Office (☎0845 302 1479; www.hmrc.gov.uk/nic/).

Those planning to start receiving their pension in New Zealand should request a Retirement Pension Forecast, which will tell you the amount of state pension you have already earned, and the amount you can expect to receive at state pension age. This should help you to plan exactly how far your pension will go in New Zealand. To receive a forecast, complete form BR19, available from any Jobcentre Plus or online at www.thepensionservice.gov.uk/resourcecentre/br19/home.asp, and return it to HM Revenue and Customs.

Exportable UK Benefits

On top of your UK pension, once you have received New Zealand residence, you are still entitled to some UK benefits such as any Bereavement Allowance (payable for up to one year), and Widowed Parent's Allowance. However, there are a number of benefits that you can no longer receive once living abroad. These include Disability Living Allowance, Income Support, Pension Credit, Attendance Allowance, and Carer's Allowance. Some pensioners therefore find their income substantially reduced upon moving to New Zealand.

Further information is available in three leaflets; *'Going Abroad and Social Security Benefits'* (GL29), available from your local social security office, the DWP's leaflet SA 29 and leaflet SA8, *Social Security Agreement Between the UK and New Zealand*. A useful source of advice and information on any of the above issues is the International Pension Centre (see address below).

Useful Address

International Pension Centre: DWP, Tyneview Park, Benton, Newcastle-upon-Tyne NE98 1BA; ☎0191-218 7777; fax 0191-218 3836; www.dwp.gov.uk.

Private Pensions

You may want to continue contributing to a UK personal pension after you leave the UK. Tax relief on contributions will cease after you have utilised any unused tax allowances left behind. Thereafter, you can still contribute but without the additional tax relief credit. Alternatively, those who retire to New Zealand early may consider transferring their pension benefits to New Zealand. You should seek advice on your individual circumstances as to whether or not it is more prudent to leave the pension frozen in the UK. **At any rate, since April 6, 2006 new UK regulations came into force which means that the New Zealand scheme you choose to transfer your pension into must be a 'recognised overseas pension scheme' or else you may have to pay a penalty of up to 55 per cent on transfer.** There is also a fee for transfer services based on the value of the transfer.

The best pension (superannuation) savings regimes in New Zealand are work-place schemes where the employer and the employee contributes. There is currently a low take up of private superannuation because there is no tax incentive. Unlike the UK system where contributions come from pre-tax income, in New Zealand it is post-tax. After taking into consideration the 2-3% of fees and expenses that the superannuation companies charge, returns are only marginally better than bank deposits. It is little wonder then that New Zealanders have one of the OECD's poorest long-term savings records – preferring instead to take care of their retirement themselves by buying a second property.

Useful Contacts

Pensions Advisory Service (OPAS): ☎0845 601 2923; www.opas.org.uk.
Britannia Financial Services Ltd : ☎ 09 414 4215; www.ukpensionstonz.com.

PERSONAL TAXATION

It is generally considered that New Zealand has high taxes, but international comparisons prove otherwise. Although you don't have to earn all that much to be put into the top tax bracket, at least high income earners pay no more than 39 cents in every dollar. And there appear to be fewer of the 'stealth' taxes than in the UK. There is no stamp duty payable on property purchase, no capital gains tax on property and no death duties. The Goods and Services Tax (GST) is less than VAT at 12.5% and there is no National Insurance payable either.

However, unlike the UK, there is no tax-free personal allowance and you are taxed on every dollar you earn, even if you are on a low income. Residents are liable to pay New Zealand tax on their worldwide income, whether that is from a pension, private investments, dividends, or interest. All those eligible to pay tax in New Zealand are allocated an IRD number. You can apply for an IRD number in person at any Inland Revenue department office or download the form over the internet and print it out. As documented proof of your identity, a certified copy of your birth certificate or passport has to be provided with the application form it cannot be emailed but must be sent to your local IRD office.

Most taxes are based on self-assessment whereby the individual is responsible for reporting and calculating any taxes due. Depending on how complicated your affairs are you should be able to complete the self-assessment forms yourself or else pay an accountant to do this for you. Finding one versed in the tax laws of both the UK and New Zealand may mean paying more and engaging the services of an international accountancy firm with offices in both countries, rather than using the cheapest local accountant.

Taxation Status

The New Zealand tax authorities work on both a residence-based system of taxation and whether or not you have a permanent place of residence in New Zealand (regardless of whether or not you have one elsewhere). Anyone spending 183 days or more in New Zealand during the New Zealand tax year (ending 31 March) is deemed to be a resident and will be liable to pay New Zealand tax. For further information contact the New Zealand Inland Revenue Department, ☎0800 227 774, (from overseas ☎64 4 801 9973), www.ird.govt.nz.

Double Taxation Agreement

New Zealand has reciprocal tax agreements with the UK. The theory is that this avoids someone being taxed twice on their income from rental property, pensions, gifts, inheritance, etc. However, it still means that anyone who is tax resident in New Zealand is going to end up paying more personal income tax than they would in the UK because in New Zealand you are taxed on all your world-wide income and there is no tax free personal allowance.

Income Tax

Residents are taxed on all sources of worldwide income, both earned and unearned at a rate which varies between 19.5 cents to 39 cents in every dollar. In most cases, UK state and private pensions received in New Zealand by a tax resident will be subject to New Zealand income tax.

Tax Returns. Those whose financial situation is relatively uncomplicated can fill out their own tax return.

Calculation of Overseas Income. Anyone who receives income overseas has to calculate the value of this income in New Zealand dollars. The IRD issues currency conversion tables, which enables you to calculate the exchange rate on the day you received your income.

o The New Zealand tax year runs from 1 April to March 31. Returns should be made between July and February. Late filing of a tax return leads to a surcharge on the tax due.
o To file your tax return you should have all the documents to hand, including an end-of-year bank statement, which will show any interest you have been paid. You will also need any paperwork detailing major assets you own, as well as details of any shares, stocks, investments, insurance policies or bonds. You will also want to declare any tax paid in another country.
o You need to state your IRD number when dealing with the tax agency.

Proposed New Tax Rules on Overseas Investments Affecting Offshore Investors

The New Zealand government is proposing to do away with the exemption from capital gains tax in equities and funds in all foreign countries except

Australia. The proposals include paying capital gains tax on 85 per cent of the rise in the fund or share price over the previous 12 months – whether or not these have been sold. If these shares were bought in an overseas market, each year five percent of the gain will be taxed and the rest rolled over until the investment is sold when you will pay capital gains tax on the remainder of any gain. You will not be able to claim any loss against income tax, it has to be rolled forward. Individuals are exempt if the original purchase price was less than $50,000 or $100,000 for a couple. Family and other trusts get no such exemption. The new rules are due to come in to force on 1 April 2007.

WILLS AND INHERITANCE

Making a Will

After purchasing a property in New Zealand, you will want to ensure that your will is up to date and that you leave your New Zealand property assets to your nominated heirs. It makes sense to make a will with your solicitor at the time of the property purchase. It may be best to have two wills – one regarding your UK assets and the other which is solely for those in New Zealand.

For those with straight forward financial affairs, a free will writing service is available online via the New Zealand government-owned Crown entity, the Public Trust. Providing you make the Public Trust your executor, the service is free and can be updated at any time.

Having made the will it should ideally be kept in a safe place along with bank accounts and insurance policies. Another copy should be held by the executor of your estate, or by your lawyer. If at any point you decide to change your will then it is possible to revoke provisions made in a will.

Bereavement

In the unfortunate event that a relative, partner or close friend should die while in New Zealand there are a few essential formalities which will need to be dealt with. Under normal circumstances a doctor will issue a Medical Certificate of Cause of Death and the body can be released for burial, cremation or repatriation. Where there is doubt about the cause of death, the doctor is required to report this to the coroner.

You will need to use the services of a funeral director if you wish to hold the funeral in the home country as there are certain procedures that have to be attended to including the preservation of the body and the transportation. Otherwise funerals can be arranged by the family or friends of the deceased or by the person before he or she dies.

All deaths must be registered with the Registrar of Births, Deaths and Marriages in the Department of Internal Affairs. Either the funeral director sends the paperwork or the person in charge of the funeral must do so within three days of burial or cremation.

You may need a number of copies of the death certificate as many authorities may require one. British citizens will need to notify the British consular office in your location, Department of Work and Pensions in Newcastle, Paymaster General, Inland Revenue, probate office, banks, insurance companies etc. It is also a good idea to keep a copy for your own records.

Executing the Will

The executor of the will must apply for probate (for which a fee is payable) through the High Court. This is usually arranged through a lawyer. Probate is an order showing that the will has been proved and that the executor has the authority to deal with the estate.

If there are problems in locating a copy of the will you could ask a local lawyer to instruct a legal firm in the country of origin to make enquiries or you could also try using the International Index for Last Wills and Testaments on the internet at www.willsindex.com. This only works of course if the will has been registered on the index. There are neither death duties nor inheritance tax payable in New Zealand.

Healthcare

CHAPTER SUMMARY

- The New Zealand system of public healthcare is not as comprehensive as the NHS.
- The government operates a no fault Accident Compensation scheme but visitors should still take out a comprehensive travel insurance policy.
- Pensioners should bear in mind that once they have become resident in New Zealand, they are no longer entitled to free NHS treatment in the UK.
- All dental practices in New Zealand are private.
- **Hospitals.** Waiting lists for elective surgery in public hospitals is a fact of life in New Zealand.
- There is a safety net for looking after the elderly – whether that is in their own home or in a public facility.
- Home care is provided by a combination of registered charities, private facilities and social services.

THE NEW ZEALAND HEALTH SERVICE

There is nothing wrong with the standard of healthcare available in New Zealand – it is just that it is not as heavily subsidised as the NHS or the public health services in Northern Europe. New Zealand, like other OECD countries with ageing populations, is trying to grapple with how to publicly fund its health services in the future.

There are the usual waiting lists for elective surgery – whether for hip replacements or cataracts and although it is not essential to take out private healthcare insurance, many people these days believe that their quality of life is reduced while they wait in line to be treated in a public hospital.

You have to pay to visit a GP and for prescriptions and although reductions are available to holders of a Community Services Card (a means-tested benefit for those on a low income), pensioners still have to pay for basic day-to-day healthcare. Dental treatment and visits to opticians are not covered either.

You may choose your own general practitioner, provided that the GP has room for you. Your medical records can be sent to your new doctor once you are registered with one. It is also a good idea to find out the generic name for any prescribed medication that you are taking, as this can vary from country to country.

Pensioners should bear in mind that once they have become resident in New Zealand they are no longer entitled to free NHS treatment in the UK.

However, those with a holiday home in New Zealand may spend up to six months a year there and still be eligible for NHS treatment.

Reciprocal Medical Arrangements

Reciprocal medical arrangements exist between the UK and New Zealand. UK nationals who are in New Zealand on short-term visits are eligible for immediately necessary healthcare under the same terms as New Zealand residents and citizens by showing their UK passport. Existing medical conditions can be treated if it is needed to stop the condition getting any worse. You will still have to pay for prescription medicine and treatment at a doctor's surgery. This arrangement may well be helpful for those going on a home-searching trip to New Zealand or those who already have holiday homes there.

No Fault Government Assisted Accident Insurance

If you are injured in an accident you cannot sue anyone for damages but the government runs a no-faults claim system administered through the Accident Compensation Corporation (ACC). ACC provides free treatment for both residents and non-residents involved in accidents, whether a motor vehicle accident or an accident in the home. Designed to avoid expensive and drawn out litigation, the ACC system guarantees those on low incomes access to the justice and compensation often denied them in countries where such claims have to be pursued through the courts. However, the amount of money awarded through ACC is modest, although claims are processed relatively quickly. ACC can be contacted on ☎0800 101 996, www.acc.co.nz.

Visitors should not rely on ACC to fund them and should always take out a comprehensive travel insurance policy. The case of the British couple, who were hit by a drunk driver in 2002, causing permanent injury highlights this need. According to a report in the New Zealand Herald, Tony and Jenny Legge, who live in Wales, were offered just £4200 when Mr Legge estimated that the crash had cost him £400,000 in lost earnings.

Registering with the Health Service

It is essential that all British nationals intending to move to New Zealand register their change of address with the Overseas Division (Medical Benefits) of the Department for Work and Pensions Benefits Agency before leaving the UK. Once in New Zealand it is advisable to register with a local GP as soon as possible.

Other Medical Services

Dental Care. All dental practices in New Zealand are private and the standard of dentistry is generally high. The price of dental treatment is slightly lower than in the UK, although it is worth shopping around before registering as fees can vary.

Opticians. Make sure you bring a copy of your prescription with you when you move to give to your new optician.

Pharmacies. Pharmacists are well trained and can recommend some treatments over the counter. Pharmacies operate in a similar way to the UK with standard shop opening hours (8.30am – 5.30 or 6.00pm) and a rotation system for nights and public holidays. Not all product ranges are available in New Zealand and certain asthma and cold remedies that are used in the manufacture of illicit drugs, may be kept out the back. Supermarkets stock a limited range of pharmaceutical products.

Emergencies

Ambulance and Medical Emergency: ☎111
National Poisons Centre (24hr helpline): ☎0800 764 766
All ambulances are equipped with emergency equipment and drivers and staff are trained to provide first-aid. All public hospitals provide 24-hour casualty and emergency treatment and there are also 24 hour private medical centres,

LOCAL HEALTH ISSUES

There are very few health concerns that are specific to New Zealand apart from over-exposure to too much of the good life – including the sun. The large hole in the ozone layer over New Zealand can reduce burn times to as little as ten minutes even in spring and autumn. Unfortunately this has led to one of the highest rates of skin cancer in the world. Golfers, sailors and water sports enthusiasts especially should use a high factor sun block, wear good quality sun glasses and a hat.

New Zealand, thankfully, is rabies free and diseases transmitted by insects are not a concern. Nevertheless insects and bugs that can cause irritation are discussed in the box below.

Creepy Crawlies

Even an outdoor paradise like New Zealand has a few annoying insects but thankfully, with no snakes or scorpions and only two very rare poisonous spiders, you can rest easy as you walk through the wilderness.

Mosquitoes: Your best defence against mosquitoes is to ensure that you cover up with long trousers and a long shirt at dusk, when mosquitoes like to feed. Some of the most enduring insects on the planet, mosquitoes can even lie dormant when there is no stagnant water around for them to breed in. Mosquitoes have a very localised habitat and only need an inch or so of water to breed in so ensure that you keep bird baths, water features and even plant saucers emptied. Disinfectant down drains will also help. Always use repellent.

Sand flies: Sand flies are more annoying even than mosquitoes as they are so small you cannot see them or hear them approaching. The West Coast of the South Island is the sand fly capital of New Zealand.

Spiders. There are two poisonous spiders in New Zealand, both of which are rare. The native *Katipo* is found only in coastal areas. It is a tiny black creature with a red mark on it. If you suffer from allergic reactions then the bite could be fatal but antivenin, available from hospitals, works up to three days after the bite. The other one to watch out for is the introduced *White-tailed Spider*. Their bites can cause ulcers and you should seek medical help.

PRIVATE MEDICAL INSURANCE

Private health insurance does not to give you a better standard of treatment or surgery but what it does do is take away the additional anxiety of having to wait for treatment. You have to pay for treatment and then claim it back from your insurance company.

Southern Cross Healthcare, ☎0800 800 181; www.southerncross.co.nz) is the largest private healthcare provider in New Zealand. The problem with most private health insurance policies are that they will not insure against pre-existing medical conditions and rates not only increase annually in line with inflation but with increasing age. *Activa Health* have launched a 'bank card' system where you put in a minimum of $25 per month. This is targeted at families who do not have insurance and are focused on wellness. You can use the card at the gym, GP or pharmacy.

Useful Contacts – Private Medical Insurance

New Zealand

Sovereign: ☎0800 500 103; www.sovereign.co.nz.

Unimed: ☎0800 600 666; www.unimed.co.nz.

United Kingdom

AXA PPP Healthcare: ☎01892-612080; www.axappphealthcare.co.uk.

British United Provident Association (BUPA): ☎0800-001010; www.bupa.co.uk.

Exeter Friendly Society: ☎01392-353535; www.exeterfriendly.co.uk.

Expacare Insurance Services: ☎01344-381650; www.expacare.net.

Goodhealth: ☎020-7423 4300: www.goodhealthworldwide.com.

Healthcare International: ☎020-7665 1627; www.healthcareinternational.com.

Taurus Insurance Services Ltd.: ☎+350 52776; www.tarusinsuranceservices.com.

RETURNING TO THE UK FOR TREATMENT

Under the current Department of Health regulations **anyone who spends more than three consecutive months living outside the UK, with the intention of permanently living abroad, is no longer entitled to free NHS hospital treatment in England**, except in the case of an emergency. This includes people in receipt of UK state retirement pensions.

Those who are not permanently resident in New Zealand (i.e. spend less than six months a year there and have not applied for residence) and spend more than six months a year in the UK may still receive NHS treatment free of charge.

Returning to the UK permanently. The moment that you take up permanent residence in the UK, you are once again entitled to the full range of free NHS treatment.

CARE IN THE HOME AND RESIDENTIAL CARE

There is an infrastructure in place in New Zealand for the care of the elderly, although provision of social care does vary from one local authority to another.

Retirement Homes

The majority of New Zealand retirement homes are privately run and like the UK, retirement homes range from sheltered accommodation, through to nursing homes with 24-hour care. Subsidised help from the government is available in some instances for those who qualify. Contact the Department of Work and Income (WINZ) for the latest information on rest home subsidies. If a family home has been in a family trust for a number of years (see the *Personal Finance* section above), the householder cannot be forced to sell it to pay for ongoing retirement home fees.

> **Help and Advice in Finding a Retirement Home**
> **Age Concern – New Zealand:** ☎04 801 9338, www.ageconcern.org.nz.
> **Residential Care New Zealand Inc.:** ☎04 499 4156, www.residentialcare.co.nz.
> **WINZ – Rest Home Subsidy Information:** ☎0800 999 199, www.winz.govt.nz.

Care in the Home and Home Support

Home care and home support is provided by a variety of different sources including Age Concern, religious organisations, private homecare companies as well as social services. Help with cooking, cleaning, shopping, delivered meals-on-wheels and gardening are all available. Subsidies are available for those on low incomes and from ACC (the subsidised no-faults accident insurance scheme). Mobility aids such as stair and bath lifts, mobility scooters, wheelchairs etc can be purchased from a number of sources including the company listed below. Ministry of Health funding may be available to help with this. For eligibility see the disability funding website below.

> **Contacts for Care in the Home**
> **Age Concern – New Zealand:** ☎04 801 9338; www.ageconcern.org.nz.
> **Ministry of Health Disability Funding:** ☎04 496 2000; www.disabilityfunding.co.nz.
> **Mobility Warehouse:** ☎09 827 6699; www.mobilitywarehouse.biz/nz.
> **Presbyterian Support (Central area):** ☎0800 100 277; www.pss.org.nz.

MENTAL HEALTH

Problems with mental well-being can affect anyone during the course of their lives. However, not everyone who retires from the workforce does so willingly and many feelings of isolation and loneliness can be alleviated by being needed. If there was ever the time to be thankful that you have moved to a country where you can speak the language, it is during life-changing events such as bereavement or a marriage break-up.

Tackling Social Isolation and Loneliness

Below are some suggestions for expanding your social network and adding to the range of activities in your life:

Develop a new interest. The activities discussed in the *Quality of Life* section are just a taste of what is available in New Zealand.

Part-time work. The camaraderie of being around work colleagues can do wonders for morale.

Volunteer work. The voluntary sector is always looking for people to help out and it can be an immensely rewarding activity.

Depression. New Zealanders are not wildly demonstrative and outgoing and for many older people, the thought of pouring out their problems to a stranger, even though they might be a trained counsellor, is simply not all that appealing. Instead, they would rather seek help from a GP they know and trust and get an anti-depressant prescription.

Thankfully, attitudes have changed and there are mental health professionals that your GP can refer you to although these are services you will need to pay for.

Alcohol and Drug Dependency. Unfortunately New Zealand does have a similar binge-drinking problem to the UK, although this tends to be more visible over the Christmas and New Year holidays. Because a car is such a necessity in New Zealand it is very important that you seek help before you are pulled over in a random breath test and found to be over the limit.

Bereavement Support. In special circumstances the Department of Work and Income can provide funeral grants for those who are having difficulty meeting the cost of a funeral for an immediate family member or if the person had no family. If the person died as a result of an accident, ACC will pay a grant towards funeral expenses. Banks will release funds to meet funeral expenses from the deceased's bank account if the executor signs a statutory declaration.

There are a number of groups and organisations offering counselling and support to the families and friends of a person who has died. These include the Samaritans, church support groups and Women and Grief Homecare. Contact your local Citizens Advice bureau for further information.

Help and Support

Alcoholics Anonymous (NZ): ☎0800 229 6757; www.alcoholics-anonymous.org.nz.

Alcoholic & Drug Helpline: ☎0800 787 797.

Relate: ☎0800 735 283; www.relate.org.nz.

Samaritans: ☎0800 726 666; www.samaritans.org.nz.

Women and Grief Homecare: www.womenandgrief.co.nz.

Crime, Security and the Police

CHAPTER SUMMARY

○ One of the greatest joys about life in New Zealand cities is the freedom to walk around without having to be on your guard.

○ Camper vans and cars parked at scenic spots can be easy pickings for thieves if valuables are left in them.

○ Good quality locks on doors and windows and other common sense precautions are the first step to make life for thieves more difficult.

One of the greatest joys about life in New Zealand is the freedom to walk around, without having to be constantly on your guard, the way that many city dwellers in European countries are obliged to. There is a level of innocence about the country that was underscored when for the first time, in 2006, an overseas criminal gang (this time the media are blaming a Russian gang with Canadian connections) came to New Zealand and 'skimmed' a few ATMs in the Auckland region.

Bike gangs control the manufacture and supply of certain drugs but they keep to themselves. Occasionally a territorial dispute will turn nasty and lead to revenge killings but generally the public are not involved. These gangs operate mainly in the larger population centres. Unfortunately a few overseas students from South East Asia have fallen prey to blackmail and extortion from within their own community, particularly those in trouble over gambling debts.

It is safe to walk around city centres at night, although not in bad neighbourhoods on the urban fringe. Car jackings and violent crimes are rare enough to make headline news, rather than being so commonplace that they are quietly tucked away in the middle of the paper. Robbery from parked cars, which is on the increase, is largely preventable, as the police point out, by the public being more vigilant about removing valuables from their vehicles.

Numbers and Types of Recorded Crimes

In 2004/2005, a total of 396,018 offences were recorded. Just over half were for dishonesty, which includes burglary and theft as well as fraud. Property damage and property abuse, including arms offences and trespass, as well as the more minor crime of littering was the second highest category at 59,965 recorded crimes.

Drug and anti-social offences came in third accounting for 51,230 offences. This includes drugs, gambling and vagrancy offences. In certain parts of the North Island, including Counties Manukau, Northland, Waikato and Bay of Plenty; robbery, often linked in with a rise in drug crimes also increased.

There were 45 murders throughout the country out of a total of 45,941 violent crimes, which includes homicide, assault and robbery. And many of these violent offences were inflicted on children and young people by family members. Immigration and racial offences and other administrative crimes were next at 11,982 and the smallest numbers of recorded crimes at 3187 were sexual offences including sex attacks and indecent behaviour.

While car crimes are less common in suburban neighbourhoods where houses come equipped with at least some form of off-street parking, in some of the poorer regions, what might seem like an average car may prove too tempting to someone less fortunate, particularly if anything has been left inside it.

New Zealand is officially one of the world's least corrupt countries and in local and central government there is a level of transparency that is matched only by Scandinavia. Bribes, kickbacks and corruption in officialdom occur very rarely, probably because with a population of just over four million it is too easy to get found out.

Avoiding Car Thieves and Petty Crimes

By taking common-sense precautions such as these listed below, you can minimise your risk to petty crime:

○ Whilst travelling in New Zealand you should keep your passport, credit cards, travel documents and money separately. And you should ensure that you have a good insurance policy.

○ When dining out never leave a bag unattended on a neighbouring chair.

○ Never leave valuables in your car or campervan, especially when visiting isolated scenic spots and driving a hire car. Campervans are vulnerable to theft as they are so visible and generally only driven by tourists.

○ Lock your vehicle when paying at petrol stations.

○ Make sure your car is fitted with an alarm and/or steering lock.

Reporting a Crime

Police resources in New Zealand are over-stretched, particularly in urban areas. Although you should report petty crime such as bag snatching for insurance purposes, such incidents, unfortunately are given low priority. Car accidents must by law be reported to the police if someone is injured or killed. Otherwise the police leave minor traffic accidents to the insurance companies to sort out.

Police Telephone Numbers
EMERGENCY NUMBER ☎111
Drivers' Hotline ☎*555 (from a mobile)

SECURITY

As soon as you move in, get in contact with a household security company who can advise you on how best to make your house as unattractive to burglars as possible. Sometimes expensive security devices can lull the homeowner into a false sense of security, particularly if they have forgotten about the basics such as good quality mortice locks on external doors and lockable windows. If you live on your own on the ground floor you might want to consider security grills but thankfully New Zealand has yet to reach the stage where prison-style iron bars on windows are necessary.

As burglar alarms can be triggered by the wind or even a spider getting into the system, you should pay for this to be monitored by a 24-hour security company. Another good deterrent are external security lights that detect movement – although they cannot tell the difference between a possum and a burglar.

Join the local neighbourhood watch organisation and get to know your neighbours so that they can watch your property for you and collect your post when you are away. For longer absences, consider employing a house sitter.

SCAMS

New Zealand is not without its shady characters and dodgy dealers but these tend to be of the white collar variety, who, in an unregulated financial services market offer the unsuspecting investor financial returns that are too good to be true.

Internet Scams. The best way to avoid these is to have good anti-virus software which blocks unsolicited e-mails asking for bank account details.

Skimming from ATMs. The first such case occurred in 2006 in Auckland and was traced to a visiting Russian couple who were based in Canada.

Investment Scams. If you have any suspicions whatsoever about a company, then you should contact the Securities Commission – (☎04 472 9830; www. sec-com.govt.nz) before parting with any money at all.

Appendices

Appendix 1: Returning Home

CHAPTER SUMMARY

O Retiring abroad is not cheap, and many of those who return home do so because they had not fully planned their finances before leaving and have spent far too much on their property or renovations.

O The pull of family ties, especially when there are problems at home or grandchildren come onto the scene can be immense. This is another reason for people returning home.

O When you return to the UK contact HM Revenue and Customs and request form P86, which allows you to re-enter the UK tax system after time spent abroad.

O Pensioners who have returned to the UK through financial hardship may be able to claim UK benefits such as Pension Credit aimed at pensioners on low incomes.

O If you return to the UK with the intention of taking up permanent residence again, you will be entitled to receive free NHS hospital treatment from the moment you return.

O **Selling your Australian property.** The Home Open is a standard property marketing tool in Australia and involves opening the property to all-comers at a specified, advertised time, usually for an hour or two every weekend.

O **Selling your New Zealand Property.** Agents' commission and marketing costs are expensive in New Zealand, but one alternative is to market the property through a website like Trade me.

REASONS TO RETURN

For some people, life in Australia or New Zealand simply does not work out. Some find that they are beset by unforeseeable problems and others simply find that life abroad does not match up to their expectations. For some, living in Australia or New Zealand was just a phase of their retirement, and having got it out of their system, they are ready to try new things.

Older people tend to return because of a change in personal circumstances, such as the onset of ill health. Not only can this cause financial strain, but it can also make people pine for the familiarity and the people that they have left behind. Some other common reasons for return are discussed below.

False Expectations. Many people rush into retirement abroad, without having fully considered all of the implications. Having enjoyed a memorable holiday in Australia or New Zealand, with wonderful weather, food and scenery, they suddenly decide that they would like to live like that permanently. Sadly it is fairly difficult to live the holiday lifestyle on a permanent basis.

Others convince themselves that moving abroad will be a universal panacea for all of the worries and problems that they faced at home. If your expectations of the new life are too high, then you cannot fail to be disappointed. Once the honeymoon period is over and the adaptation period sets in, many find that the vision does not match up to the reality and they start to romanticise the things they miss about the UK.

Lack of Preparation. Before moving to Australia or New Zealand you should fully research what the day-to-day reality of retiring abroad will entail. Without sufficient preparation, the practicalities of your new life could come as something of a shock.

Family Ties. Although technological advances such as e-mails, text messages, and internet telephone calls have made the world an even smaller place, many still find that they miss their loved ones terribly. The pull of family ties, especially when there are problems at home can be immense and not everybody can cope with the long distance commute every time there is a family crisis.

Social and Cultural Isolation. Whether they miss the unique sense of humour or the rituals of a Sunday lunchtime pint, some people simply cannot adapt to their new life. The sense of loss for the old life is felt most keenly during a crisis, especially if there is no one to turn to for emotional support in the new country.

Financial Pressures. Retiring abroad is not cheap: property purchase, renovations, transporting personal effects, buying a car, health insurance mean that the initial stages of retirement can be very costly. Many expats get caught up in the excitement of their new life and fail to make sufficient financial provisions. It is essential to have planned your finances extremely carefully and to have an emergency budget to cover any unexpected crises that may arise.

TAX, SOCIAL SECURITY AND HEALTHCARE

Whatever your reasons for moving back to the UK, there will be practical and financial implications. Before you return to the UK you should go through all of your financial affairs including bank accounts, pension schemes and other income and consider the effect the return to the UK will have on your financial situation.

Tax Considerations

It pays to be very careful regarding your taxation position when returning to the UK. It is just possible, for example, that you may be forced to pay tax arrears for the time that you were out of the country. This can happen if you return within three years of your departure from the UK, and in the eyes of HM Revenue & Customs (the new name of the Inland Revenue, which merged with HM Customs in 2005), you have only had provisional non-residential status. Check with a financial adviser before returning home to ensure that you are not liable for any unexpected taxes.

You should also ensure that your taxation affairs abroad are in order before you leave. It may be wise to appoint a fiscal representative who will assume responsibility for any final payments that are due.

When you arrive back in the UK you should request HM Revenue and Customs/Inland Revenue form P86 or download it from their website (www.hmrc.gov.uk). After you have completed the tax form you should return it to the local tax office (consult HMRC if you do not know which this is).

Pensions and Social Security

It is sensible to contact the Department for Work and Pensions (www.dwp.gov.uk) well in advance of your arrival back in the UK in order to switch payment of your pension to a UK bank account. Follow up any telephone calls to the DWP with written confirmation.

Pensioners on low incomes and with limited savings may qualify for income-related state financial assistance on their return to the UK. Benefits include Pension Credit (towards weekly income) and Housing Benefit (help towards rent). You can enquire about these from the DWP on your return. They are not usually payable outside the UK.

Useful Contacts for Pensioners	
Benefit Enquiries	☎0800-88 22 00
Age Concern	www.ageconcern.org.uk
Pension Assessment	☎0845-3000 168
Pension Credits	☎0800-99 1234
NHS Direct	☎0845-4647 (www.nhsdirect.nhs.uk)
Winter Fuel Payments	☎0845-915 15 15
	(www.thepensionservice.gov.uk/winterfuel)

Healthcare

Ill health can be one of the main reasons for people having to return home. Worsening health combined with financial pressures can make it difficult for retirees to cope in a foreign environment. There is also the fact that as the health of one partner worsens, the other one often finds the strain easier to handle by returning to a place where there is a family support network. As health worsens, there may also be a wish to see the UK again.

Those who are resident in Australia or New Zealand cannot return to the UK simply to receive treatment. However, if you return to the UK with the intention of taking up permanent residence again, you will be entitled to receive free NHS hospital treatment from the moment you return. According to the Department of Health, you should expect to be asked to prove your intention to remain in the UK permanently. You may need to furnish the hospital with evidence, such as documents showing the sale of property overseas.

Once resident again in the UK you should register with your nearest GP or health centre and you will be issued with a new medical card. If you can remember your old NHS number, this process is much quicker.

Healthcare Useful Contacts	
Care Homes	www.nursing-home-directory.co.uk (by areas)
Retirement Homes	www.bettercaring.co.uk
NHS Direct	☎0845-4647 (www.nhsdirect.nhs.uk)

SELLING YOUR AUSTRALIAN PROPERTY

Most people sell their property through a local real estate agent. The agent is responsible for advertising your property and for negotiating the best possible price. Normally, your home will be advertised in the local press and the larger statewide newspapers generally publish a property section at the weekend (often on Saturday). In addition, most agents will have extensive photo displays in their office window. The distribution of detailed description sheets giving measurements of each room, location of power points and other features is not an Australian practice, although top-of-the-range homes are often marketed through glossy, descriptive brochures. Private inspections or 'Home Open' are arranged by the agent. The Home Open is a standard property marketing tool in Australia and involves opening the property to all-comers at a specified, advertised time, usually for an hour or two every weekend. During this time the agent is in attendance and the owners are absent. Prospective purchasers, who are most likely to have seen the property advertised in that morning's paper, are free to walk around the house and garden and examine its suitability in privacy.

If you are selling your home, which has been your main residence, you are exempt from capital gains tax (CGT). CGT only applies when you sell a second property, such as a holiday house, hobby farm or rental property.

SELLING YOUR NEW ZEALAND PROPERTY

New Zealanders can, on average, expect to stay in one property for seven years. However long you thought you were going to stay, life may have got in the way and you could find that you need to sell up. Selling through an estate agent is not cheap, as expat Helen Davies points out:

> The cost of all the advertising and the commission is huge. It cost £250 to sell the old house in the UK – compared with $30,000 here.

Although most New Zealanders grumble about the high costs of marketing and commission, the majority of houses are sold through an agent. Agent commission is paid solely by the seller. For a $600,000 house you will be paying an agent commission of around $24,000. On top of that you would be expected to pay around $3500 for marketing, a total of $27,5000. For that you get a sign outside your house and colour photographs, colour advertising in the property press and on real estate websites.

Not everyone can afford the high cost of selling through an agent and many sellers are turning to the popular internet site, Trade Me. The listing costs less than $100 and home sellers can display up to 20 photographs on the site. You could retain an agent to conduct Open Homes and negotiate with buyers while saving on the marketing costs.

ARRIVAL BACK IN THE UK

Moving back to familiar shores should be fairly simple. However, moving anywhere can be fairly traumatic, especially if you have been forced into the move and feel that you may miss the sunshine and relaxed lifestyle of previous years. It will certainly feel unsettling for the first few months as you re-adapt to the life you once knew so well. Below is a list of tasks that will help to ease the transition:

- Visit your financial adviser in order to keep up-to-date with your changing tax liabilities.
- Contact HMRC for a P86 form, or download it from their website, in order to reinstate yourself into the UK tax system.
- Keep proper financial records from the time you arrive back in the UK. These will be essential for your self-assessment tax form.
- Open a UK bank account (if you haven't kept one open) so that you have access to funds for daily expenses, without paying unnecessary charges.
- Review all of your insurance policies.
- Alter your will to reflect the fact that you are back in the UK.
- Contact the Department for Work and Pensions (if you have not done so in advance) to ensure that your pension payments are not interrupted and are sent to the correct place.
- Register with your local GP so that you are able to use the NHS free of charge.

Appendix 2:
Case Histories

AUSTRALIA

BRIAN HAVARD

Brian has been living in Australia for 16 years. He is no stranger to foreign cultures. After school he spent a five-year stint in the RAF from January 1944 as a radar mechanic. When he demobbed, he became an export merchant for 17 years, travelling throughout Europe and the Americas and after that sold computers in Eastern Europe in its extreme Communist days. In the meantime his wife, who was born in Berlin, had become an Industrial Market Researcher travelling Europe and North Africa, the Philippines, Indonesia and every major city (except Darwin) in Australia. Before retirement, both were working for the American forces in Germany.

When their daughter got married and moved to Australia, they decided to follow them out there. Now they are happily enjoying their retirement in Stirling, an attractive township in the beautiful Adelaide Hills.

What factors led to you making the decision to retire?
We had both experienced health problems during our time in Stuttgart and were able to retire on health grounds some nine months early.

Why did you decide to move to Australia?
Our daughter's American husband, fluent in every computer language but having no French or Dutch, wanted to live in an English speaking country, but not the USA or England; Canada was too cold, New Zealand too remote, South Africa too political (with which rationale my wife and I agreed). He made a reconnaissance of Australia for employment possibilities and lifestyle, reported favourably, and the proposal was made for us to join them in due course.

Do you have any regrets about leaving the UK?
Not really. I miss my family and the beautiful countryside, but dislike how the cities have developed, especially London. There is simply too much congestion, overcrowding, frenetic traffic and air pollution.

What about red tape – any problems?
We emigrated in 1990 under the 'Family' scheme; red tape was minimal. It will be much more difficult now, since only skilled people in specified categories are wanted.

Have you bought a property here or do you rent? Why?
We bought because fortunately we could afford it. Many people find that their job commits them to Sydney, Melbourne (and increasingly Brisbane) where house prices are sky high. Renting might be a better solution in these places.

Do you find the quality of life to be superior to the UK?
I find it difficult to say, not having lived in the UK for almost 25 years, but I certainly enjoy the space and, in our hills, the beautiful air. I also love living among the vineyards and driving almost empty roads. We have a small but comfortable home with efficient reverse cycle air conditioning and a pretty garden. We have family and friends around us and many interests to pursue – is there more to life?

Do you feel part of an Australian or British community?
With our mongrel provenance – Anglo-German, American, Dutch, Belgian, and now Australian, with our son (who settled in Perth WA) now working in South Africa and the Congo, and with family and friends in the UK, USA, France and Germany, I suggest we are justified in regarding ourselves as internationalist.

What leisure pursuits do you enjoy here?
We have made many memorable car journeys here. One of the most memorable was a 17,000 km journey over 10 weeks. We drove through Alice Springs to Darwin, then through the magical Kimberley to Broome, all down the West Coast to Perth, then the South Coast and back home via the Nullarbor Plain.

What advice would you give to people thinking about retiring to Australia?

For those who have worked sufficiently long in Britain to qualify for at least a part pension (11 years for men, 10 for women), start by demanding a meeting with your MP and get his commitment to support repeal of the pensions' regulations which perpetuate the gross injustice (the British pension is frozen at the level it was when you left the UK).

You should also do the calculations carefully on how to fund your desired lifestyle; remember that you now have to have been resident for ten years before you can even apply for the Australian means-tested pension for which one in three UK pensioners – my wife and I among them - do not qualify. Foolishly when young we listened to exhortations to save in order to fund our retirement, forgoing many of life's little luxuries. Sadly the little nest-egg we managed to create is just sufficient to deny us an Australian pension – and at the same time our UK pension is frozen.

Do you intend to return to the UK ever? If no, under what circumstances would you change your mind?

I cannot conceive of any circumstances which would induce us to return – not even taking revenge for the stupidity which denies uprating my pension. I cannot speak for those who would retire here for reasons other than to be near the family. Watching our grandchildren mature into young adults is a pearl without price.

MIKE AND MARY OSBORNE

Mike and Mary have been in Australia since February 2000. In the UK, Mike worked for Volvo Penta, in the sale of marine and industrial engines. Mary worked part time as a secretary at the local church.

What factors led to you making the decision to retire (early)?

General dissatisfaction with the lifestyle in the UK. My company had a major change in 1998 and at one time it looked as if many of us would be moved or made redundant. We were asset rich but cash poor.

Much of what we liked about our birthplace seemed to be at risk and it seemed that we had to have a 'plan' rather than be pawns in someone else's game. Also, we knew or worked with folk who died or got ill early- strokes or heart attacks, just when they were due to start enjoying life a bit more.

Do you think that the concept of retirement has changed?

To some extent yes. 60 no longer seems to be very old. Perhaps I am just saying that because I'll be 60 this year. However, when we look back, we looked on people at 40 as old: they dressed as if they were going to funerals and didn't enjoy sporting activities. Nowadays, many older folk dress younger and are active in sports or other pastimes. I think most of us expect more.

How do Australians treat retirement? Is there a different attitude to getting older from the UK?

Possibly similar to UK but many are much more adventurous. It is not uncommon for pensioners here to take long trips of months and sometimes years. The lifestyle is aided by the climate and the spaces available. Outdoor life is the norm, as opposed to folk in the UK huddled over a fire and worried about the power bills.

Why did you decide to move to Australia?

We came here on holiday on the way to New Zealand in 1990. My brother-in-law was a '£10 Pom', back in 1963, living in Adelaide. We loved the country and the people, so kept coming back. He moved from Adelaide to the Yorke Peninsula town of Ardrossan in 1992 and we thought it was quiet at first, but grew to like it.

We made friends here on holiday. The big advantages of Australia are that people speak the same language, have similar values and are easy going. Also there is a general acceptance of us Brits- just roll with the jokes!

Do you have any regrets about leaving the UK?

Many would say that they wished they had done it earlier. When we left, my mother was still alive at 92. We had held off as long as we felt we could, but in the end, I had to think of my wife.

What about red tape – any problems?

Aussies love paperwork but are generally pretty helpful about it. Just get it right and don't try to be smart. Getting the 410 retirement visas was lengthy as is the renewal. but if you are honest and friendly, they usually help you.

Have you bought a property here or do you rent? Why?

We built a house before we got here and subsequently a second new home in 2005. We rent the first one out. There are restrictions on people with 410 visas that make it better to build new or off-plan. That way, you can do what you like with the property, as if you buy a used home, you are not supposed to rent it out.

How were you able to finance the move?

We scrimped and saved in the last few years we were in UK, aided by a small residue after our mortgage was paid off in 1998. This allowed us to buy the land for $17,000 and then the house cost us about $90,000. It was hard, but we did it without a lot of borrowing. Our UK residence was worth about £250,000 when we first got our visas in 1998 but it had doubled in value by 2001 when we sold up.

Did it take long to acclimatise, make friends and settle in?

We have made a conscious effort to get stuck in, shake hands and meet people. We could have sat in our house and just mixed with a few friends and relatives but we now know more people here than our relatives. When we bought the land, we made a point of writing to our neighbours, saying who we were and asking if they had any specific views on what we should build.

How do you spend your time here? Do you do any voluntary work, part time job, run a business?

The visas are meant to restrict the work carried out by folk like us. There is a limit of 20 hours per week. Until recently this seemed to have meant paid work, but the latest info sheet makes mention of voluntary and community work. This is somewhat alarming as I am now a Volunteer Ambulance Officer with SA Ambulance. I also do three hours every Tuesday morning, plus other times when required, for a project called Tidy Towns. I was also asked to create a town newsletter in late 2002 and this has been going well. It is a bi-monthly publication of about 16 pages, distributed to 600 homes. My wife has joined St John Ambulance. So we are fairly active.

What leisure pursuits do you enjoy here? Are they things that you could not do so easily in the UK?

We have a collection of old cars – three Alvis and one MG. I have been secretary of the local car club for three years. Costs are lower and the roads more enjoyable for older vehicles. We play golf on an 18-hole course for just $170 per annum – try that in the UK. We've both also taken up bowls which is a good way of meeting locals and going to outlying towns. We hope to be able to use our caravan and travel a little shortly.

Has your new life in Australia met your expectations?
Certainly! We have to pinch ourselves to believe we really live here.

JANE KNIGHT

Jane was a Chartered Physiotherapist managing Marks & Spencer Head Office's Physiotherapy Department and a private practitioner treating patients in their central London homes. She has now been in Australia for four and a half years.

What factors led to you making the decision to retire?
Mainly it was the demise of Marks and Spencer as UK number one retailer. My peer group was going for voluntary redundancies and I said that I would be interested if there was brown envelope on offer. I could see the writing on the wall and knew that things would never be the same. I was fortunate to get out at the right time having spent 11 very happy years there.

How do Australians treat retirement? Is there a different attitude to getting older from the UK?
As in the UK, there is a growing trend to retire early. People are realising that life is not a dress rehearsal and there are a lot of things they want to do with their lives. Many take up voluntary work, travel around Australia in their campervans or travel overseas spending the kids inheritance (SKI). They spend more time with their grandchildren acting in a 'caring' capacity so that both parents can go out to work.

Why did you decide to move to Australia?
My tennis club, which had been the hub of my social life was closing down for two years. I knew that whenever it reopened it wouldn't be the same and I have been proved right. My first grandchild was in Australia and I wanted to enjoy her and see her grow up. At the age of 58 I felt my life was going nowhere. I was on my own having been divorced for 15 years. Work and tennis had come to an unexpected end so I needed to close the door and to move on. As a result I undertook a monumental change.

What about red tape – any problems?

As a temporary resident, having to wait to get Foreign Investment Review Board permission to buy a property in a sellers market was a problem. Luckily I was recommended a conveyancing lawyer who got through the red tape on my behalf. I found it incredible that having been granted the Visa and brought out the requisite amount of cash you couldn't just go and buy a place!

But I found a house within week of being here and in the end was able to buy it. I bought it through Private Sale and luckily did not have to go through the angst of buying at auction, which is prevalent in this state. I had thoroughly sussed out the area prior to buying for all the amenities I would need.

Where in Australia do you live and why?

Melbourne/Bayside. It's close to my daughter, close to the beach, close to golf courses, has easy access to the city by both road and train for cultural entertainment and good medical facilities and hospitals.

What do you like best about your new life in Australia? Do you find the quality of life to be superior to the UK?

The main advantage is that a lot of my new life is spent outdoors. People are very welcoming. I think the cost of living is probably comparable but the quality and choice is better. Yes, it is superior in that, if I had stayed I would still be working in Private Practice, my needs would be entirely different and I would be travelling along the same path, whereas this new life is exciting and challenging.

Did it take long to acclimatise, make friends and settle in?

No. I knew four people when I came, but six months later I was able to invite 60 people to my house warming!

How do you spend your time here? Do you do any voluntary work, part time job, run a business etc.?

I am not registered to practise as a Physiotherapist here as it would mean taking three lots of exams and being supervised. Something I really didn't need at my age. However, I was determined that I was going to use my people skills in another capacity.

Initially, my visa did not allow me to work so I found some Voluntary work. Now that my Visa allows me to work 20 hours a week I have been

"Hostessing" for a major property developer, meeting and greeting prospective clients interested in their apartments. I also have been "hostessing" for a market research firm.

I am currently not working, preferring this year to work on a more casual basis rather than a regular basis and am exploring a role in Relocations.

What leisure pursuits do you enjoy here? Are they things that you could not do so easily in the UK?

Golf, cycling, walking, concerts, opera, theatre, travel. Although I could do all these in the UK, they are cheaper and the weather is usually more conducive to outdoor activities.

There is so much to see in this country and I am trying to go to different areas each year as it really is the land of contrasts. I look out for the special travel deals with the airlines. I would recommend anyone to experience the Outback for its harshness, vastness and incredible colour and scenery. I have just completed a seven day drive back to Melbourne from Noosa (Queensland) with a friend of mine and got to see some of the East coast by road rather than by air. I would like to do more of this in the future.

What advice would you give to people thinking about retiring to Australia?

Try it first on holiday for a three-month period to see if you really like the country and the people. I had been coming here on holiday to see my daughters for 10 years prior to my big move and always said that if the opportunity ever arose for me to live somewhere else this would be the place!

If you have medical problems then you would probably be better off staying in the UK with the good old NHS picking up the bill. Treatment here is expensive and in spite of private health insurance there are gaps to pay and I know of stressed out people who have gone back. They cannot afford to stay on and pay medical bills for ongoing treatment.

Do you intend to return to the UK ever? If no, under what circumstances would you change your mind?

I only go back each year to see my children if they haven't been out here in the meantime. Obviously then I catch up with friends as well. I shall never return to the UK to live. My home is here.

STUART ROBERTSON-FOX

Stuart was a professional airline pilot prior to retiring to Australia and spent the previous 10 years in Singapore. He has been in Australia for four and a half years.

Why did you decide to move to Australia?
I love the country and the people, plus there is an excellent climate, lots of space, a sound economy, a reasonably low cost of living, especially compared to the UK, and we feel safe here! The Australians have a very good attitude towards retirement. They retire as soon as they are able to do so – often as young as 55. Leisure time and sports rate very highly to Australians.

Where in Australia do you live and why?
Drouin, Gippsland, Victoria. It's a beautiful rural area and a centre of dairy farming so the countryside is pastoral, roads are uncluttered, everyone is so friendly and the views are both beautiful and restful.

Did it take long to acclimatise, make friends and settle in?
No, Australians are as nosey as anywhere else and making friends is easy!

How do you spend your time here? Do you do any voluntary work, part time job, run a business etc.?
My wife is very active in the sewing group who meet every week and go away twice a year for a sewing holiday and she is a visitor at a local hostel for the elderly. I shoot target rifle and spend a lot of time on the computer. I am also a member of the Lion's club. We both also belong to sports clubs, so we are very busy.

What advice would you give to people thinking about retiring to Australia?
If they can they should but find out as much as they can about the cost of living, medical issues, driving licences and so on, just to ease the transition. The sub-class 410 visa doesn't exist anymore so newcomers will either have to have the majority of their family already here or be able to put up a $500,000 bond as well as satisfying other financial requirements and will possibly have to settle in a rural area rather than a town.

Do you intend to return to the UK ever?
Certainly not in the foreseeable future and certainly not permanently. I can't imagine any circumstances that would make me change my mind so I think I would only leave if I was thrown out!

NEW ZEALAND

SHEILA GAVIN

Born in Britain, Sheila Gavin, who is in her late 60s, first came to New Zealand in her 20s but returned to live in Aberdeenshire in 1988. Like so many people that have spent time in New Zealand, Sheila found that she couldn't get the country out of her system. Unable to settle in Scotland, this former nurse has been living in the picturesque town of Arrowtown, in Central Otago since October 2005.

On the morning we caught up with her, Sheila was reading a copy of *Wilderness* magazine, already planning which long distance walk she was going to tackle next. 'It's a beautiful sunny day and the mountains are all around me.' Sheila only got back from walking the Milford track in early April. She did this independently with three friends, where they self-catered and carried their own packs on this three day walk.

What was it about Arrowtown that made you choose it as a place to live?
I came over in January 2005 to find somewhere to live. I looked in Auckland, Napier, the Kapiti Coast and Nelson but couldn't settle on anywhere. They all seemed quite big. Even Nelson is a city and I didn't think I'd find a niche for myself there. I had no intention of living this far south, even though my son lives here. One of the reasons for choosing to move back to New Zealand was that I had family here but that wasn't the only reason – I have left a daughter behind in the UK.

Was it easy to find a property?
I fell in love with this little house in January 2005. I put a deposit on it, went back to Aberdeenshire and sold my house there, which my friends there thought was madness. Then I returned to New Zealand.

What facilities are there locally?

There's a lovely cinema and they're opening up another small cinema. Tai Chi is coming soon and I've put my name down for that. I've joined the Spinners and Weavers Club which is a new activity for me – I got chatting to someone in the supermarket about that.

What advice would you give about making new friends?

Just get out and about and meet people. I accept every invitation that comes my way. You have to make the effort. For example, I went to a historical society meeting because I heard it was there and met new people through that.

How did you go about joining groups and clubs?

I went to see the Citizens Advice Bureau in Queenstown who were incredibly helpful. I found out about walking groups and Scottish country dancing. I walk twice a week, once with a group and again with friends. I play golf twice a week. Scottish country dancing is an hour's drive from me and I probably won't start that until spring because of the ice on the roads at night.

How did you manage to become accepted into the local community so quickly?

A week after I moved I had a 'get to know your neighbours' invitation. There's new housing in this area and the person that organised it had moved into the area recently and found it difficult to meet people. Now this barbecue is going to be an annual event.

So which long distance walk are you going to tackle next?

Either the Hollyford or the Routeburn Track in November and the Milford track next February but this time as family are coming we'll do it the catered way (where meals are cooked for you and someone else carries your pack).

What is your advice to anyone thinking of retiring to New Zealand?

I feel it's the best move I've ever made and I'm trying to persuade a friend from Scotland who came out here recently that he should do the same.

DOUGLAS JARVIS

Douglas Jarvis made such a success of his business back in the UK that he was able to retire at 40. Now in his mid fifties, Douglas has lived in New Zealand for just over 15 years and runs the Jarvis Family Farmstay & Equestrian Centre in Pakaraka, a country area in the Bay of Islands. Wife Fredi still works as a teacher. The Jarvis family emigrated from Northamptonshire where they ran a very busy and successful country inn. Compared with the open-all-hours hospitality trade, Douglas says that his New Zealand business is a part-time job.

Negotiating the immigration system is probably one of the biggest challenges for anyone emigrating to New Zealand. How did you manage it?
Between us, because Fredi is a teacher, we were eligible under the points system as well as under the business migrant category because of my background in tourism and being able to bring in the money from the business in the UK, so I wasn't going to be a burden on the system.

What was it that attracted you to New Zealand in the first place?
My family have a long association with New Zealand dating back to my great-grandfather who pioneered the first refrigerated cargo system from New Zealand back in the 1880s. With all the family tales of Australia and New Zealand I came and hitchhiked around in the 1970s, ending up working in a hotel in the Bay of Islands where coincidentally my daughter is working now.

What did you do when you arrived in New Zealand?
When we got here we had no idea what we were going to do or where we were going to live. We landed in Auckland, stayed with friends and were booked to go to the South Island, but on the spur of the moment I said, let's go up to the Bay of Islands. The first shock was all the new motels that had sprung up in Paihia. While we were there, we saw this property advertised in an estate agent's window. When we asked about it, it was under offer to another British family. We went off in a campervan to see our friends in the South Island and came back to find out that the deal had fallen through. Within three months the place was ours.

What about the cost of living?
Housing is cheaper (in NZ). You can buy more with a ten dollar note in New Zealand than you can with a ten pound note (back in the UK).

How did you find the experience of making new friends?
Having been a host before, it was fairly straightforward plus we made friends through the pony club.

Is there anything you'd have done differently which could be useful advice to others making the same move?
My advice is to rent first and not rush into things. Estate agents are the same everywhere – even in country areas. Agents see you as an easy target if you have sold in the UK. When we came we were used to getting things done quickly and if we'd slowed down a bit we could have saved ourselves a bit of money but the first thing we did was go and buy the horses and ponies for the equestrian centre. We had promised our children (aged 12 and 14 at the time) that we'd buy land as back in the UK we only had the stables.

How have you found the health service in New Zealand?
ACC (Accident Compensation) is wonderful as it's available to everyone.

Has New Zealand lived up to your expectations?
Thoroughly. There's bureaucracy but you get that anywhere you go.

GABY HEINRICH

Gaby and her late husband Guy were originally from Germany. Gaby has lived in the UK, New Zealand, Australia but since 1992 St Heliers in Auckland has been home. Gaby found that although Queensland sounded like an idyllic place for retirement, with its sunny climate, the heat didn't suit her active lifestyle and she decided she preferred New Zealand.

You and Guy originally retired to Queensland's Gold Coast. What was it that made you want to leave?
I knew Guy's health was getting worse and I didn't think I could cope there on my own. Plus I found it very hard to get any sort of response from the locals – I like to chat to people, as you know. The area we lived in was inland and it was so hot in summer there that I had to go walking long before sunrise.

What's the secret to a happy and healthy retirement?
Not to sit around all day. Ageing is a question of mind over matter. I clean my own house, mow my own lawn, walk for at least two hours every day and go

to the gym for an hour three to four times a week – using the exercise bike, rowing machine and all the other equipment.

How old are you Gaby?
82 and I'm still driving.

Where in New Zealand would you recommend for visitors?
I've been all over – right up north to the very top (Cape Reinga) – that's beautiful and so are Milford Sound and Mount Cook.

Apart from the exercise, how do you keep busy?
I read biographies, go to the library, museums and galleries. I've volunteered all my life – for the Red Cross and Meals on Wheels. There's a new hospice shop up the road and I'll probably work there for 4-5 hours a week. I went up to the local retirement home to help out but it was a bit depressing as they all just sat there – and most of them are younger than me.

What made you choose St Heliers?
We were staying in a motel nearby for months as my husband couldn't decide where he wanted to live. One day he just went and bought this apartment without telling me. And so here I am.

How do you keep in touch with family and friends overseas?
I don't use the internet that's for sure – although I've been tempted. I'm scared I'd get addicted and then I wouldn't get out and about. I pick up the telephone instead. Calls are so cheap now – I can call my family in England, Israel and Canada for eight cents a minute.

SUE SEDDON

Sue Seddon, 60, is another of our contributors who defies all the stereotypes of ageing. Sue has been a teacher in Leicester, a councillor in Marple, and raised a family in Christchurch. But Sue always hungered for exciting adventures and loved to travel. This yearning for adventure has endured – despite personal tragedy. Sue has a zest for life which has taken her volunteering in Tonga and partying at the Rio Carnival in a long silver wig. On a campervan trip around Australia Sue ended up in Exmouth on the coast of Western Australia and stopped long enough to set up a business. In 1999 while she was in

Rarotonga studying for her dive certificate, Cyclone Vance destroyed most of Exmouth including Sue's office.

After battling for a year to try to get the business up and running Sue set off on her travels once again – this time to Cambodia, Laos, India, Tibet and Fiji, Sue then went to catch up with family – now that she had three grandchildren and went to visit her daughter who lives in Nelson.

And this is where we pick up Sue's story.
My daughter brought me to the Bay on a day trip – 'Want somewhere to live, Mother? This place has eccentrics – you should fit in well!'

The Bay is Golden Bay, an idyllic coastal spot at the western end of the Abel Tasman National Park.

For someone who has been to so many places, what is it about Golden Bay that's good enough for you to hang your hat when you are home?
This is a very special area with an interesting mix of people. There are locals – village types then there the hippie types and now the intellectuals who are coming in. It's not a trendy area but it could become one in the future.

Where did you look before you settled on Golden Bay?
I thought about going up to the North Island and living in Gisborne and involving myself in the Maori community or Greymouth on the West Coast. Greymouth was a possibility because it wasn't too far from Nelson and my grandchildren. But it turned out to be too wet. Golden Bay has a very warm climate.

Where did you live when you first arrived?
I stayed in the Telegraph Hotel for six months right in the middle of Takaka, when I arrived. It's an old hotel – the pioneers would have hitched their horses to the railings outside.

How did you involve yourself with the local community?
I wanted to get the feel of the place and walked up and down the high street, went to the library and joined the Wednesday Walkers. There are some wonderful walks around here – bush walks, mountain walks and gold trails. I joined the Golden Bay choir – we're putting on *Carmina Burana* next week.

Tell me about the house that you live in?
I share a wooden house in the bush, eight miles out of Takaka on 50 acres. My

friend who owns it built it from scratch. It's an eco-house – a Pelton water wheel drives the power so that there is constant hot water. I don't want to have my own house.

What is it about New Zealand, of all the countries you've visited, that makes it the place to use as a base for your travels?
The quality of life available at a reasonable price. It's an egalitarian society. I found that Christchurch was different. When I went to join the choir they were very nice but asked me what school I went to! It was only after I'd left I realised what an odd kind of place it was.

Where do you get your energy from?
Since the age of 27 I have been practising Iyengar yoga. I was lucky enough to be taught by Iyengar himself in London and I have an Iyengar teaching certificate. I practise for 20 minutes every day. The walking helps of course. You have to be fit to get on and off buses and so on for the kind of travelling I do.

In June you leave for Crete. What do you plan to do there?
I plan to absorb myself in the pattern of daily life. I get to places and things just evolve.

As Sue said in a talk she gave recently, *'I live life to the full – I push myself always to see as much as I can and to understand the people and places I visit. I always travel hopefully.'*

On the future:
I can imagine myself sitting in a old folks' home, shaking with laughter over some of my exploits while the other old biddies exclaim, 'what's she laughing about, the silly old bag'?!

Complete guides to life abroad from Vacation Work

Live & Work Abroad

Buying a House Abroad

Property Investment

Retiring Abroad

Starting a Business Abroad

Available from good bookshops or direct from the publishers
Vacation Work, 9 Park End Street, Oxford OX1 1HJ
☎01865-241978 ∗ Fax 01865-790885 ∗ www.vacationwork.co.uk